PROFITOMIX

First published in 2024 by the Rising Sun Publishing House
Adelaide, Australia.

NATIONAL LIBRARY OF AUSTRALIA

A catalog record for this book is available from the National Library of Australia

ISBN 978-0-6484953-5-2 (print).
ISBN 978-0-6484953-6-9 (eBook).
THEMA (UK and Australia): ECONOMICS, FINANCE, BUSINESS and MANAGEMENT.
BISAC (USA): BUSINESS & ECONOMICS / Entrepreneurship.

Disclaimer

PROFITOMIX:

Intangibles, AI, and Data for Profit and Funding

Dr. Victor Paul

THE RISING SUN
Publishing House

CONTENTS

PREFACE

It is a fact that almost 90% of assets held by technology startups are intangible. This presents an enormous opportunity for startups to unlock their full potential, leading to above-average profits and explosive growth curves. However, many startups are not fully aware of the extent of their intangible assets and how to leverage them effectively. In addition, there is a significant knowledge gap in utilizing other companies' intangible assets, which could be a game-changer if identified and employed wisely.

Investors constantly search for the ample opportunities that can disrupt markets. However, many investors rely on outdated extensive sourcing and screening instead of selective 'cherry-picking' methods. They refrain from funding intangible-intensive businesses and do not use a data-driven approach and artificial intelligence (AI) applications. All these innovations could help discover previously hidden business opportunities and promise better investment returns.

Should we allow these malpractices to continue? Never!

The era of scaling up unprofitable startups is over. It's time for founders to build profitable ventures with innovation and for investors to fund prospective startups strategically. The key drivers of higher profitability are the shift to the knowledge economy, intangible investments, data-driven businesses, and the growing role of AI. The interests of startups and investors must align to achieve mutual success and lift their balance for profit.

PROFITomix is the ultimate guidebook for all stakeholders in the VC ecosystem. It empowers founders to take charge of their futures and shows venture capitalists and syndicated angel investors the path to higher returns. This guidebook also benefits VC ecosystem service providers, accelerators, and incubators that aim to develop a better VC ecosystem.

How does it work? By identifying intangible assets and strategically applying data intelligence and AI tools, PROFITomix provides comprehensive support to each player in the VC ecosystem. Founders can prepare for the funding journey with high-quality information to ensure that investors recognize the potential of their startups. Venture capitalists can discover outstanding business opportunities by leveraging technology to sharpen their investment edge. Technology creates a collaborative environment that benefits investors and founders, facilitating partnerships that lead to mutual success and accelerated growth. Service providers, accelerators, and incubators can access self-learning materials for their audience.

In this comprehensive guide, stakeholders across the VC industry will find precisely what they seek - tools and strategies crucial for today's dynamic VC market landscape. The proposed AI-powered data intelligence framework includes the Startup Dossier, an all-encompassing repository holding critical information that prepares startups for investor scrutiny. The Robo-Fitness Validator serves as a toolkit designed to empirically verify startup concepts. Furthermore, the book offers insights into both intangible and tangible startup valuation methods and an introduction to the just-in-time financing model aimed at minimizing capital requirements. Market entry and exit strategies and the Funding Roadmap help businesses navigate the VC marketplace effectively.

PROFITomix provides meticulously formulated recommendations for the structure and content of pitch decks suited for many objectives, ensuring that presentations have a compelling edge. Follow-up information in each chapter offers foundational insights for sanity checks and preparation for the initial due diligence stage. Each aspect of this book is specifically designed to provide startups, venture capitalists, and service providers with the foresight and preparation needed to thrive.

PROFITomix is a manual, a roadmap, and an entertaining read for those who want to win in the new VC world with technology, data-driven thinking, and intangible vision. The book has a solid foundation and embraces scientific discoveries, both well-known in the VC/startup community and little-known but promising.

PROFITomix stands out in the crowded market for its unique multi-dimensional approach. It cuts through the Internet's clutter to reveal the secrets behind creating and funding high-profitable and scalable ventures. This book addresses the crucial aspects and challenges of the VC industry, often glossed over in business publications, making it an indispensable resource for all involved parties.

Moreover, PROFITomix is not a typical business book; it presents its wealth of knowledge in a visual, reader-friendly format, complete with engaging cartoons and infographics that make learning informative and entertaining. PROFITomix enhances our understanding and enjoyment of building a profitable business, whether running a startup, investing, or providing services.

The author of PROFITomix relied on the ideas of giants who came before him. They contribute to the different facets of the new predominantly intangible, data-driven, and AI-enforced VC ecosystem. Jonathan Haskel, professor of economics at Imperial College Business School and a member of the Monetary Policy Committee (Bank of England), discovered key traits and drivers of the new intangible economics. Baruch Lev, the Philip Bardes Professor of Accounting and Finance at New York University Stern School of Business, recognized the leading role of intangible assets and intellectual capital in financial analysis and accounting.

Eric Ries is a best-selling author, entrepreneur, and business visionary who developed lean business principles, making entrepreneurship accessible to a new generation of startup founders. David S. Rose, a serial entrepreneur, super angel investor, and CEO of Gust, a global SaaS funding platform, provides the fundamental strategies and the specific tools for startups and angels. Tim O'Reilly, an iconic Silicon Valley investor, and CEO of O'Reilly Media, Inc., contributed enormously to reshaping our knowledge of technology, business modeling, and pathway to profitability. His creative insights and clarity transformed our understanding of the future.

The ideas of several Nobel Prize winners who discovered the chaos and uncertainty of the VC world and the shortcomings of both humans and AI also contributed to the writing of this book. Standing on the shoulders of giants, the author charted the path for those ready for innovation, disruption, and change.

INTRODUCTION:
A History of Digital Pizza

Any startup business is like making a pizza with minimal ingredients but with the expectation of multiple outcomes. The pizza-making metaphor shows how people with different ideas and perspectives bring their expertise to create a successful result. By cooking the pizza, founders and investors bond, build relationships, and produce synergetic effects when a result is much more than the sum of ingredients.

Startups and investors are consistently navigating the complexities of the VC industry, dreaming of breaking free from the day-to-day monotony and bringing a vision of prosperity to life. Their ambitions, while varied, forge unique paths in the VC landscape. The archetype of each participant in the VC ecosystem emerges through generative AI analysis, highlighting the critical aspects of their investment endeavors.

New investors have a keen sense for the unconventional, recognizing the worth of intangible assets, Big Data insights, and the transformative power of AI innovations. With distinct strategic orientations guiding their funding decisions, they can evaluate a startup's potential, underpinned by profitability forecasts and scalability considerations. Furthermore, these investors know how to marry their interests with startup ones to fuel ventures that promise exponential growth and remarkable returns.

At the heart of every triumphant startup journey is a founder who grasps the intricate web of investor motivations and strategies they use to realize their financial goals. Savvy founders can navigate the delicate dance of funding with a clear-headed understanding of what sparks investors' interest in a profitable exit. A founders' experience extends into the internal landscape of their team, casting a discerning eye on the collective capabilities and recognizing how each element meshes to form a well-oiled machine geared for market success. Central to a founder's strategic toolkit is the ability to accurately forecast their startup's growth trajectory and profit-generating potential. A successful startup founder values the power of symbiotic partnerships with investors, where interests and expertise converge for mutual benefits and shared profits.

At least this archetypical founder tries to do it right!

While PROFITomix is a business book, who says it must be boring? PROFITomix is an intriguing story with its heroes, villains, and a page-turning plot.

Meet Our Heroes!

Steve (FOUNDER) is an enthusiastic and ambitious technology startup founder. During the bootstrapping phase, he understands that the funding journey is long and complex, and he is looking for some guidance and support. Steve has limited knowledge of the investment process and fundraising strategies, but he is smart and can learn. He is looking for an investor who can estimate the potential of the prospective venture and is interested in a long-term partnership.

Robert (TRADITIONALIST) is an experienced angel investor and a syndicate lead. He truly believes in the power of entrepreneurship and is passionate about helping startups succeed. Robert prefers well-organized teams with solid management skills. Sometimes, he needs to be more confident about his previous experience and make decisions based on personality traits rather than focusing on financial indicators.

Linda (PROFITEER) is a Merger and Acquisition (M&A) acquirer. She has a broad knowledge of legal and regulatory matters and previous VC experience, including reviewing contracts and disclosure requirements. During a comprehensive due diligence process and negotiation of terms, Linda can check the startup's market positioning in its target segment and competitive advantages. Sometimes, her demands for startups to scale up quickly to achieve the desired results can be unrealistic.

Tomas (TECHNOCRAT) is a corporate VC (CVC) investor interested in technology in the first instance. With extensive experience, he recognizes technology-laggard niches ripe for disruption. Tomas can identify startups with the potential to fit into the corporate investment strategy. He believes an ideal startup team is highly integrated and has complementary skills. As a corporate player in a bureaucratic environment, Tomas is subject to herd mentality bias.

Michael (VISIONARY) is a new formation value investor. He believes in the merits of a hybrid (employing AI and his intuition) data-driven approach to identify startups that offer the best risk/reward opportunities. Michael thinks a startup's intrinsic value is more than its book value due to its intangible assets. He looks for teams with the potential to succeed in the long run, thanks to their ability to adapt and pivot as needed. Michael tends to be more conservative in investing and avoids taking too much risk.

Gippetio (AI bot). His name is inspired by the popular abbreviation GPT, but there's nothing ordinary about him. With human-like habits and quirks, Gippetio stands out among his robotic counterparts. Gippetio has picked up the idea from the Internet that AI is supreme over natural intelligence. Still, he doesn't buy into the silly conspiracy theory of robots taking over the world. With an unwavering confidence in his abilities, Gippetio treats startups with a subtle disdain. He always seems to have a better solution and is unafraid to let humans know. Fortunately, Gippetio can Machine Learn.

Section 1
Intangible Wealth Hidden in Plain Sight

The rise of the knowledge economy and acceptance of intangibles as a particular category of assets have changed the rules of investing. According to the contemporary economic point of view and accounting conventions, "intangibles" relate to assets without a physical form. The term "intangible capital" refers to those intangible assets restrained by enterprises to facilitate their path to profit. Intangible assets represent nearly 90% of modern enterprises' equity value, and their use is crucial today for investors and startup founders. In the contemporary knowledge economy, intangibles have become the key source of success.

Even though new assets may be unfamiliar to many entrepreneurs, and those who have some knowledge do not fully understand how intangibles can work for them, this section provides answers to the most pressing questions:

- Why are intangibles so unique, and how do they impact higher profitability and exponential growth of enterprises?
- What is intangible capital, and how does it spin the wheels of the modern knowledge economy?
- What are the pros and cons of investing in intangibles, and how can we identify, protect, and appropriate them?

In the intangible world, investors must rethink their attitude toward startup teams. While an essential part of intangibles is embedded in humans, a rational balance between control over startups and their autonomy is a prerequisite for business success.

Chapter 1.1.
Unlocking the Value of Intangible Assets

Imagine an enterprise in which you only use 10% of your assets. Up to 90% of technology startup resources are intangibles. In today's digital economy, tangible assets like machinery and buildings are no longer the sole drivers of value. These newly discovered assets are crucial in the VC industry, promising more-than-average investment returns. However, these assets, unlike tangible ones, have no physical form and are practically invisible. Features of intangibles make them difficult to identify and protect, posing unique challenges for accounting and management and creating possibilities for manipulation and unauthorized use. Both venture capitalists and startup founders must recognize new opportunities and prepare to overcome existing challenges.

> **Why is there so much noise around intangibles and so little in business?**

How to Count What We Can't See

ACCOUNTANT:
"I WANT TO BELIEVE!
BUT IT HAS TO BE IN HERE! "

While entrepreneurs continued to count income and expenses as before, accountants started fishing in troubled waters. They tried to convert expenditures in some categories of intangibles into investments. Their results were more than modest in this endeavor. Paradoxically, accountants slowed down the development and practical application of this concept, which is vital for business development.

Professor Baruch Lev, the author of six books on intangible assets and investment analysis, was the first to notice that traditional financial reports could be more beneficial regarding intangibles. In his prophetic book: "*The End of Accounting, and the Path Forward for Investors and Managers*" he states that: "The increasing dominance of intangibles among corporate assets is widely recognized with its consequences having become known as the 'knowledge economy,' except that is, by accountants, who strangely persist in ignoring the intangible insurgence." [1]

Accounting of intangible assets has become a nightmare for accountants for several reasons:

- No physical nature: Intangibles, such as ideas, relationships, skills, or software, are not material. When embedded in physical media (for instance, a computer hard drive), their value is independent of physical representation.
- Non-rivalrous: Many users can use the same intangibles simultaneously. For example, any number of users can use the software. Moreover, there is no additional cost for copies of software.
- Partially excludable: Some intangibles in digital form are easy to copy and difficult to protect. As a result, rivals can use weak property rights protection to their advantage.
- Non-tradable: Some intangibles created for particular purposes inside enterprises (for example, software for internal use) have no other applications and are untradable on the market.
- Non-separable: The value of many intangibles is inseparable from people's. [2]

While intangibles are remarkable in many ways, there is no common understanding of their nature. Their different definitions do not correspond to each other and do not create a complete picture:

- "Intangible assets are something valuable that a company has that is not material, such as a brand name." (Cambridge Dictionary). [3]
- "Intangible assets are assets that do not have a physical or financial embodiment." (The Organisation for Economic Cooperation and Development). [4]
- "Intangible assets are identifiable non-monetary asset[s] without physical substance." (International Accounting Standards Board). [5]
- "An intangible asset is anything that's not physical or financial but is expected to provide a benefit over time." (J. Haskel and S. Westlake, authors of "Capitalism without Capital"). [2]

What are intangibles? You cannot count, touch, or kick them; they are invisible in your balance sheet. They are so digital that only we, intelligent AI bots, can recognize them!

The Price of Professional Ignorance

Historically, intangible assets emerged from scientific works and accounting conventions around two decades ago. Nevertheless, today, there are still three common forms of ignorance in this aspect:

- Entrepreneurs ignore the existence of intangibles since they are not in the accounting ledgers (Accounting Blindness).
- Management recognizes and tries to manage them using methods and tools developed for material assets (Management Myopia).
- Lawyers focus on protection matters similarly to tangible assets (IP Protection Phobia).

Total ignorance of intangibles can result in 90% of lost business opportunities. Attempts to employ old methods and tools have led to the unfortunate discovery that they need to be revised. There is no point in using old techniques and tools: new assets can disappear like water to sand. Furthermore, traditional IP protection methods like patents or trademarks cannot protect some intangibles.

Unlocking exponential business performance doesn't require a miracle but rather the clever utilization of intangibles. These unique assets can fuel scalability without a proportional surge in material resources. It is the secret alchemy that can propel success, especially for such intangible-intensive businesses like Digital Pizza.

PROFITomix Story:

Digital Pizza

(Episode 1)

CAST:

Steve

Startup
Founder

Robert

Investor
Traditionalist

Steve once sent Robert his pitch deck but has yet to receive a response. Robert had already read the pitch and found its projections unrealistic, so he tried to elicit extra information during their texting conversation. While Robert is overconfident about his previous experience, he needed help assessing this digital-driven startup's market prospects.

Hi, Robert. It's Steve.

Who?

Digital Pizza.

Do you deliver pizza? I didn't order it!

This needs to be clarified.
That's the name of our startup, Digital Pizza.
I sent you our pitch a while ago.

It caught my eye, and I tossed your pitch.

If you have any questions, I'm here to answer.

Yes, I have some questions! How can a pizza be digital?
Do you offer holographic images
instead of a delicious thing?

No, no, no!
We're about to make authentic pizzas with high margins.

I see...
Your financial projections look too good to be true!

This is thanks to our intangible assets...
We didn't name ourselves Digital Pizza for nothing!

You are juggling these terms: 'intangible' and 'digital.'
What exactly are we talking about?

Well...
Let's imagine Digital Pizza's liquidation...

But there is nothing to liquidate yet!

This is hypothetical, just for an explanation.

OK, I'm waiting for an explanation.

All equipment was sold, workers were fired, and doors
were closed... what do you think is left of our startup?

A school of digital geeks?

I shouldn't have talked about sunk costs.
I need to clarify: I meant our digital prototype,
marketing plan, etc.- all in our heads –
pure intangibles!

In this case, I also clarify my answer:
A school of digital geeks in muddy water!

Magical Features and the Dark Side of Intangibles

Two characteristics of intangibles that radically distinguish them from tangible assets are scalability and synergies. Scalability is a common term that describes a particular form of manifestation in intangibles. When an enterprise develops an intangible resource, somebody can use it in different locations or applications without additional costs. This feature gives startups an advantage for exponential growth. By scaling up on intangible assets, startups can overtake rivals without access to traditional resources. Due to the absence of physical form, intangibles can quickly move globally, and geographic boundaries are open to their business applications.

Intangibles are "synergistic." They can interact with each other or with material assets, providing accelerated growth. Synergy is a term used to interpret a non-additivity effect of interacting assets: a result may be larger than its sum. Thus, a set of smartly combined assets can create a foundation for a synergetic effect. However, one must remember that a combination of assets is not separable, and some of them can only work with others to perform business tasks (like software and hardware).

Two other characteristics of intangibles, sunk costs and spillovers, derive challenges and problems for which there are yet to be effective solutions. Sunk costs is a term that explains that the costs of some developments may be lost entirely if a business fails because there is no market for newly created assets. It is possible to sell tangible assets to recover some part of the initial investment, making these assets more understandable and measurable from the investor's perspective. Securing bank financing for intangible-intensive businesses is impossible because banks need to recognize new assets as collateral.

Spillovers mean enterprises can benefit from intangibles they have yet to develop. In other words, different market players can capture the value of some assets created within a startup (for instance, ideas and software components). However, one must bear in mind that spillovers can be viewed positively from the position of those who can take advantage of others' assets.

Why do some startups become unicorns while others earn just getting by, not to mention those that have not survived? Scrutiny reveals that Uber, Airbnb, and other unicorns have the same feature: they had a lucky chance to discover hidden third-party underused assets and incorporate these spillovers into their business models. This solution allowed them to operate without material assets: Uber has no company-owned taxi, and Airbnb has no square meter of property to let.

Unveiling the Elusive Essence of Intangibles

The four features of intangibles work together, resulting in high profitability and scalability, as well as uncertainty and risks. By smartly combining these features, intangible-intensive businesses can contribute to profitability and scalability. The spillover effect is reciprocal: rivals can acquire some of the intangibles that an enterprise creates. On the other hand, by using public spillovers or acquiring third-party assets (for instance, obtaining government-funded R&D grants or open-source software), an enterprise can generate synergies that result in unprecedented profits and growth.

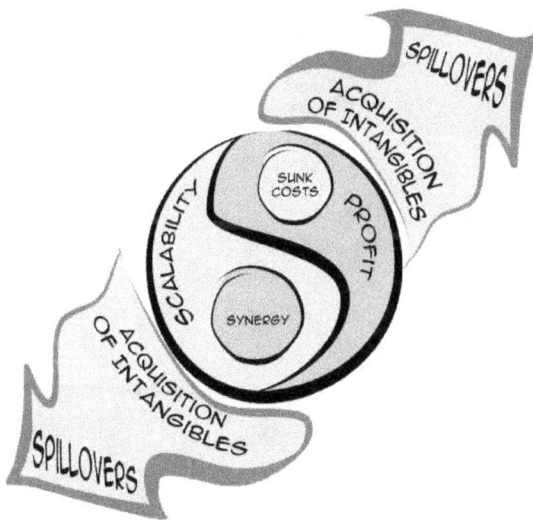

While startups are often the first to adopt new technologies and business models, they are also the first to meet three challenges:

1. Intangibles are challenging to measure and quantify, making it hard for startups to value them appropriately. They often have an indefinite life span, meaning their value can change over time, making it difficult to predict their future value accurately.
2. Protection of new assets with traditional tools and measures such as patents and trademarks is ineffective. Furthermore, digital technology has made it easier for rivals to access and use them without permission or payment.
3. Intangibles can also be subject to rapid technological changes or market conditions that may quickly reduce their value. Since there is no established market for these assets, they may not have any resale value if the enterprise's stakeholders decide they no longer need some assets.

Investing in intangibles is associated with regulatory uncertainty due to the lack of clear rules and regulations that govern its use and ownership rights across different industries and jurisdictions. However, entrepreneurs can use acceptable solutions and even exploit current uncertainty. While economists are developing perfect methods for identifying and measuring intangibles, we can use proxies that give practical results. Sometimes, weak protection of these assets allows us to use other companies' intangibles as our own.

Key Takeaways

We likely have noticed that intangibles are crucial in startup funding and overall business success. However, founders and venture capitalists typically overlook intangibles. VCs seek business opportunities with more than average returns and do not find them in traditional businesses. Startups can create such opportunities by identifying and deploying their own and others' intangible assets. However, they must develop and show newly opened business opportunities to encourage VCs to invest. Investors and founders who ignore this new perspective risk missing the boat.

We only toe the line when discussing intangibles' value using the fundamental book "Capitalism without Capital: The Rise of the Intangible Economy" by Jonathan Haskel and Stian Westlake. [2] In Chapter 1.2, "Intangible Capital in the Knowledge Economy," we return to discovering hidden sources of growth for intangible capital.

Chapter 1.2.
Intangible Capital in the Knowledge Economy

In today's knowledge-based economy, intangible capital is the most significant driver of business success, shaping the future of the VC industry. The rise of intangible capital has challenged traditional enterprises and sparked a new wave of innovative startups. To fully leverage the power of this capital, entrepreneurs must capitalize on knowledge, build intangible-intensive business models, and align their strategies with the unique nature of new assets. While intangible capital still needs to be clearly defined, the capitalization process is already in motion. Those effectively engaged in this process will create sustainable competitive advantages and pave a path to higher profits. This path leads to immense business potential and extraordinary opportunities for investors and startups alike.

> ## What is the essence of intangible capital?

From Industrial to Intangible Capital

The principles of intangible assets were discussed in Chapter 1.1, "Unlocking the Value of Intangible Assets." With this knowledge, we are ready to take the next step, introducing the concept of intangible capital. The concepts of resources, assets, and capital have varied interpretations. The generally accepted tangible perspective is that a resource is a source of potential profit; a resource becomes an asset when owned or controlled; capital is the money used to purchase or produce the asset for future profit.

14

These concepts are similar in the intangible realm. Still, some differences exist: not all intangible resources are recognized as assets, and not all intangible assets are bought or produced. Someone can appropriate an intangible asset without permission or compensation.

The term "capital" was coined by Karl Marx in his famous book *Das Kapital*, published in 1867 in the First Industrial Revolution epoch. The technology of that time - the steam engine and all industrial infrastructure were supposed to be a source of profit for capitalists. [6]

Today, at the beginning of the Fourth Industrial Revolution epoch, the new knowledge economy is asset-light and increasingly driven by intangibles. Intangible capital comprises more than 80% of S&P 500 market value and is a crucial growth driver for emerging companies. According to the Brand Finance report, the shares of intangible capital in some world-class companies prevail over tangible capital:

- Microsoft - 90%.
- Apple - 77%.
- Amazon - 93%.
- Facebook - 79%.
- Alibaba - 86%.
- AT - 84%. [7]

Indeed, the information infrastructure includes tangible assets such as computer hardware and communications networks. However, intangible assets spin the wheels of the modern economy, and intangible capital is the key to harnessing technology and creating competitive advantages.

An Essence of Intangible Capital

Over the past few years, many definitions of the structure of intangible capital have yet to create a clear picture. This situation is the remnant of the old Buddhist parable of blind men and an elephant. This situation is the story of a group of blind men who try to imagine what an elephant is like by simply touching it. The first blind man, whose hand touched the trunk, decided the elephant was like a thick snake. For another one, whose hand reached its ear, the elephant seemed like a fan, and so on. However, neither was able to discern the actual appearance of the elephant.

Things are even worse for intangible assets: they are impossible to touch. International accounting conventions refined the old accounting perspective of capitalization to end the confusion about intangible capital structure. They prescribed the three-component structure of intangible capital generally accepted today:

- Software & Computerized Information.
- Innovative Property.
- Economic Competencies. [5]

Computerized information includes application software, databases, and algorithms developed inside startups, bought from a third party, or acquired by any means that does not lead to infringement. This category is becoming increasingly "open source."

Innovative property includes patents, trademarks, patterns, copyright licenses, unpatented inventions, know-how and linked licenses, design and exploration rights, trade secrets, and artistic originals. Somebody can transfer the assets of this category within license agreements. Entrepreneurs protect some non-patentable innovations as trade secrets.

Economic competency is an extensive category that includes all marketing-related intangible resources, business model innovations, and different kinds of education and training initiatives. Additionally, this category contains internal and external business processes and organizational structures. The latter embraces all types of cooperation and partnerships and uses the current situation regarding regulation, benefits, and government support.

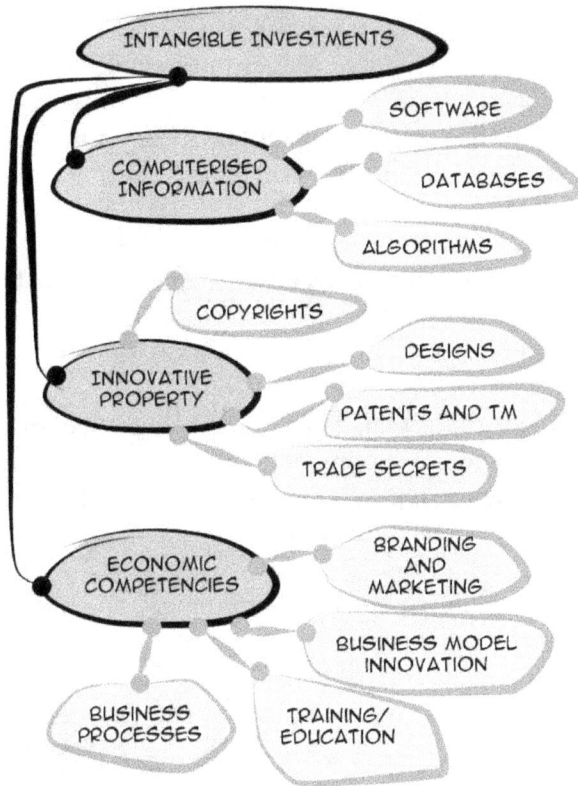

The three classes of intangibles manifest themselves differently in the structure of intangible capital:

- Assets classified under "Software & Computerized Information" are fully non-rival, partly excludable, and can usually be separated from their source without substantial loss of value. As a result, these intangibles may be tradable in the markets.
- Marketing and financial innovations are mainly non-patentable, should not be disclosed to the public, and must be protected as trade secrets.
- Assets in the "Economic Competences" category are rivalry and are more exclusive.

Intangible Capital through the Lens of Capitalization

Capitalization is the traditional accounting practice of recording the costs of tangible assets on the balance sheet. Yesterday and today, intangible assets acquired via M&As are capitalized. In contrast, internally generated ones are counted as expenses and are not capitalized. However, accountants continue trying to put some internally generated intangibles on the balance sheet. However, this topic still needs to be clarified.

Despite lacking a physical presence, intangible capital has similar features to tangible ones. Three parallels are essential in capitalization: accumulation, depreciation, and collateralization.

Accumulation—Like physical capital, intangibles require investment, such as research and development (R&D), marketing, and training. Intangible investments typically involve costs and sacrifice current output to accumulate capital for future results.

Depreciation - Intangibles depreciate over time, just like physical capital. Lack of investment in intangibles or the arrival of evolving intangibles can lead to obsolescence. Furthermore, scandals, intellectual property violations, defections of critical employees, law changes, and consumer taste shifts may destroy intangible capital. [8]

Collateralization - Contrary to the generally accepted opinion about low to zero collateral rates for intangibles, collateralization exists as 'borrowing' from startup founders. They often work without appropriate compensation and invest their own money into projects. Sometimes, they take stock-based compensation from investors instead of regular wages. All these forms are proxies for 'normal' collaterals. Later, in Chapter 8.1, "Art of Leveraging Minimal Resources," we will see how small investments in the right direction can have a multiplying effect.

Capitalizing Knowledge

In contrast with the previous industrial economy that actively used IP intangibles (patents, trademarks, and copyrights), the knowledge economy is based mainly on non-IP intangibles and knowledge assets. The non-IPs create network effects with intangible origins and remarkable properties like critical mass, weak ties, and externalities/spillovers. The knowledge assets are more intangible than not.

Seeing knowledge as a part of intangible capital requires an understanding of the knowledge structure:

- Explicit knowledge includes all recorded and stored knowledge (product specifications, manuals, technical documentation, written processes and procedures, and instruction materials).
- Implicit knowledge in intangible form can be transformed into tangible form when necessary (for example, unwritten processes and procedures that can be documented in principle).
- Tacit knowledge is intangible and cannot be transformed into tangible form (for instance, the entrepreneurial and organizational skills and knowledge held by the startup's team members).

All in one, IPs, non-IPs, and knowledge form intangible capital.

Knowledge is arguably the most critical form of intangible capital and the foundation of innovation. Through knowledge capitalization, enterprises can drive technology to profitability and growth.

Economic Competencies are simultaneously the broadest and most poorly defined category, including new business strategies or management techniques, organizational restructuring, marketing strategies, employee training, advertising, and promotion. Customer-related activities include brand reputation, customer relationship, satisfaction, and loyalty. The group of contracting-related activities consists of all types of agreements and contracts.

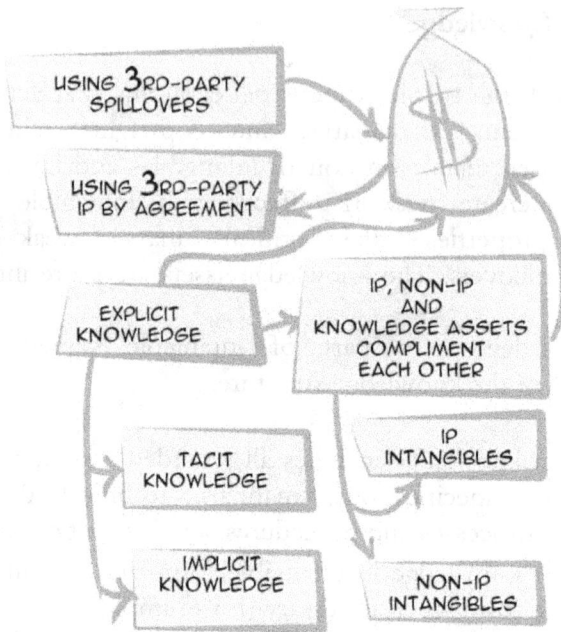

How Intangibles Pave a Path to Profit

There is a widespread myth that technology is a source of higher profitability and exponential business growth. However, by observing fast-growing enterprises, investors notice that innovative development, acquisition, and deployment of intangibles can boost success rather than technological advantages. Someone should not assume that intangibles provide higher profitability only in high-tech industries, such as IT, big pharma, healthcare, and telecommunications. Uber Eats' "dark kitchen"

demonstrates the intangible transformation of the traditional restaurant industry. In the past, fitness centers relied heavily on their exercise equipment and physical facilities. Still, after the pandemic, they focused on selling online training programs, thus mainly employing intangibles.

Startups can reach higher-than-average profitability using disruptive moves into intangibles. Otherwise, rephrasing Henry Ford, they offer 'faster horses' while they must offer cars. [9] All three intangible capital components allow startups to increase their profits without a commensurable increase in tangible assets. There are several sources of potential extra profits:

- The predominance of variable costs over fixed costs reduces operating leverage. Startups hire contractors and outsource instead of full-time employees. They also actively use open-source software and cloud-based solutions instead of in-house ones.
- There is a reduced need for upfront investment to develop intangible-based business solutions. The ability to generate higher revenues with lower investments allows startups to decrease further dilutions of their stocks.
- Startups can change their expense structure at short notice. So, they scale down quickly in a poor market environment and scale up when business conditions improve.

> There is another source of super-profits that Marx did not suspect: exploitation of the new working class: AI-bots. These new knowledge workers work day and night without any pay!

This path to profit is not smooth due to information asymmetry between investors and startups. Investors notice that intangible-intensive startups' assets are low in pledgeability as collateral. They also cannot recognize founders' initial investments in intangibles. Let's see how our Digital Pizza heroes try to overcome the information asymmetry barriers.

PROFITomix Story

Digital Pizza

(Episode 2)

CAST:

Robert

Investor
Traditionalist

Steve

Startup
Founder

Robert thoroughly studied Digital Pizza's pitch and texted Steve to ask some questions. Due to needing more background information, Steve answered with metaphors and without specifics. By the end of the conversation, they discover the paradox of their reasoning about intangibles and higher profitability.

Hey Steve, I saw your pitch's profit diagram.
It looks like a hockey stick, right?

We'll cook up a good profit for you.

Do you know what a profit is?

Oh, yes!
At Digital Pizza,
we have a strong taste for profit!

Steve, leave this pizza jargon and explain this phrase:
"Our pizza is a game-changer due to super-profitable
intangible assets."

The world is changing, and pizza is changing, too. We
know how to make and sell pizza to the new
generation—with a good profit!

What's "know-how?"

Don't worry. It's just wordplay.

How do you generate a profit?

Simple! Selling lots of pizzas.

So, you need to learn how to make a profit!

Sure, we do! Low costs plus a big market chunk, new recipes, technology, and a new customer base for high profit and rapid growth—we will be a unicorn when all this comes together.

It seems you believe in unicorns, don't you?

I do, and our funding depends on how much you believe in them!

It turns out I have to believe in unicorns to make your unicorn happen... so it's a catch-22!

Key Takeaways

Modern businesses strongly depend on intangible capital, which is multifaceted and sometimes challenging to determine. One must keep in mind the comprehensive qualities of intangible capital to define its role in business performance:

- Registered patents and trademarks offer startups extra pricing power in highly competitive markets.
- Copyrights create artificial scarcity for products with low reproduction costs, giving their owners competitive advantages.
- Effective business models and practices take time to copy. As a result, such models can create monopolies for specific products or services.

In the knowledge economy, businesses must leverage their intangibles to stay competitive, thanks to higher-than-average profitability. Clouds, open-source software platforms, and government benefits create opportunities for spillovers, particularly for startups with small development teams.

By acquiring some third-party intangibles for free, startups make their MVP circles shorter and cheaper. In all these cases, startups can increase their profits without necessarily making a corresponding increase in tangible capital. From the investors' perspective, this topic will be discussed in Chapter 1.3, "Investing in Intangibles: Pros and Cons."

Chapter 1.3.
Investing in Intangibles: Pros and Cons

To invest in intangibles, VCs need to know about assets that startups promise to acquire, estimate the profits they can generate, and the rights and control investors will have over them. However, investing in this class of assets poses previously unknown challenges for investors. In addition to low liquidation value and low pledgeability as collateral, intangibles lead to the erosion of customary ownership rights. It is the fall of the old pillars of ownership, resulting in the risk of poaching - using newly created assets by other companies. Nevertheless, investments in intangibles create advantages over conventional ones but under conditions. Startups must not only develop anti-poaching measures to protect their intangible solutions but also appropriate others' assets smartly. VCs have to recognize such startups to fund them.

> **What is holding back investment in intangibles?**

Intangibles and Property Laws

The inherited features of intangibles shock lawyers. Established property laws successfully protected material and financial assets for several hundred years. Intangibles radically changed the situation of ownership. They cannot be touched, seen, or felt, are difficult to quantify precisely, and their valuations are somewhat subjective. Some of these assets can endure for an extended period, but others can face obsolescence quickly after their creation. As a result, property laws developed for tangible assets do not work for intangibles.

LAWYER:
"WELL, THIS IS A REAL HEADACHE. I KNOW TANGIBLY WHO IS THE OWNER HERE, BUT INTANGIBLY, I'M JUST LOST!"

Moreover, intangibles generate spillovers. That means anybody can acquire others' assets. The spillover effect may be positive or negative, depending on the point of view. For example, investments in open-source AI software might benefit all software developers who use it to create their specialized products. Thus, low-tech startups with minimal staff have a chance to develop marketable products with limited initial investments. On the other hand, understanding that competitors can benefit from investment in a target startup does not stimulate capital injections. What is worse, attempts to protect initial investments in intangibles through patenting often is not effective.

Advantages and Challenges of Investing in Intangibles

According to McKinsey, investing in intangibles correlates with productivity, regardless of the industry/sector. Thus, companies that invest more in intangibles scale up more effectively. [10] The ratio of intangibles to total assets is 72% and growing. Upon discovering the unique features of intangibles, investors look for opportunities to invest in this new class of assets. Considering startups that employ intangible-intensive business models, investors have high expectations for prospective financial returns.

The generally accepted opinion is that investing in intangibles was born recently; however, this is not true. High-profile investors recognize intangibles when determining startups' intrinsic value and the profit streams they can generate. The prominent investor Warren Buffet described the advantages of investing in intangibles in the early 90s, calling them "franchises" as the opposite of ordinary material assets-based businesses. He called tangible enterprises just "businesses." [11]

Unlike other investors, Buffett emphasizes the value of intangible assets. He can buy exceptional companies at a significant discount using thorough business analysis.

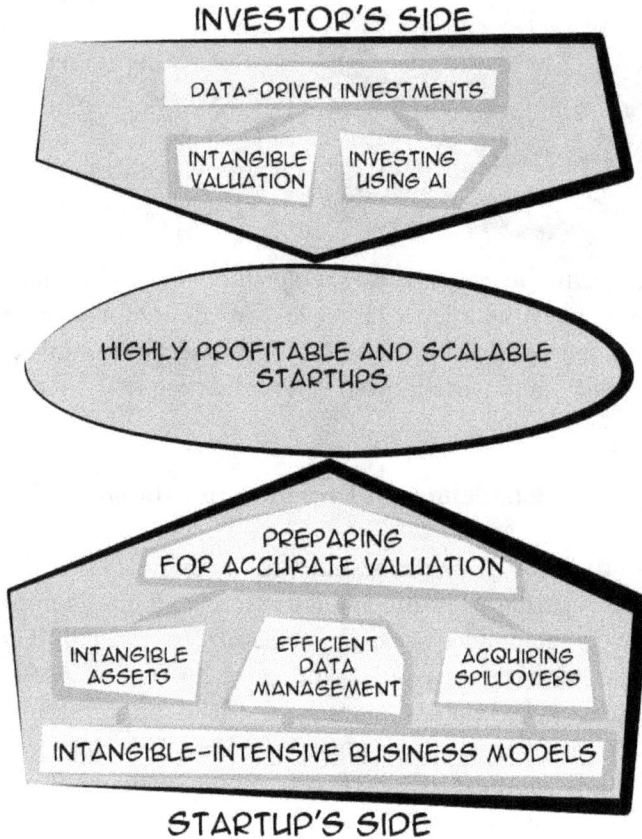

INVESTOR'S SIDE

DATA-DRIVEN INVESTMENTS

INTANGIBLE VALUATION

INVESTING USING AI

HIGHLY PROFITABLE AND SCALABLE STARTUPS

PREPARING FOR ACCURATE VALUATION

INTANGIBLE ASSETS

EFFICIENT DATA MANAGEMENT

ACQUIRING SPILLOVERS

INTANGIBLE-INTENSIVE BUSINESS MODELS

STARTUP'S SIDE

Investing in intangibles can be a lucrative decision. As the VC world continues to evolve, the importance of new assets will only increase. Investors must learn to identify intangible-intensive startups to capture new business opportunities and build strong portfolios.

Two downsides of intangibles prevent the stream of investments in this class of assets. First, unlike investments in tangible assets, initial investments in intangibles are practically invisible. Furthermore, to reap the benefits of such investments, it is necessary to reorganize business processes and train personnel. All these expenses are startup-specific, difficult to redeploy, and have a low-to-zero liquidation value.

Second, the valuation of new assets is more volatile than tangible assets and is often case-specific. Investors can fear higher-than-average risks and irreversible expenses. At the same time, financial intermediaries estimate heavy-intangible startups as low-quality borrowers. However, the payoff may be worth the extra effort and risk. [12]

In the modern startup landscape, investors can meet three types of technological startups that use different strategies to offer their intangible solutions for funding:

- Startups that exploit hype topics (blockchain, AI, and IoT). Typically, they have no clear path to technology commercialization, and their practical applications are often too fantastic to be true. The examples were dotcoms and infamous ICOs in which technological promises worked as a smoke generator to hide a lack of technical feasibility.

- Startups that offer new solutions to some apparent problems with massive demand (education, wellness, and food industry). The simplicity of such solutions is deceptive, and in practice, they often have no economic sense. Well-known examples are WeWork and Theranos.

- Startups that develop products that fit the market and intangible-intensive business models that capture values and leverage profits can make technological solutions viable, and, thus, positioning themselves as worth investing in. However, when investing in intangibles, VCs should consider how a startup team can manage and protect its assets. Moreover, checking how the team can appropriate others' assets is necessary.

PROFITomix Story

Digital Pizza

(Episode 3)

CAST:

Robert

Steve

Investor
Traditionalist

Startup
Founder

Their previous conversation ended shortly due to a mutual misunderstanding. Steve corrected the situation and explained to the investor why Digital Pizza's unique position would allow the startup to become a unicorn. However, Steve needed to estimate Robert's conservatism in this texting conversation correctly. As a result, Robert remained unconvinced.

Hey Robert! It's Steve again...Digital Pizza.
I want to explain why we are so unique to become an unicorn. Last time, it didn't quite work out.

OK, let's try again.

Our success lies on three pillars: a big market, out-of-date technology, and a supreme team. The global pizza market is growing by leaps and bounds and is expected to reach $5,138 B this year. And you already know about our technology solutions!

And what about your team? Do you have the right people to make it happen?

Oh, we do. Our lead developer used to work as a pizza delivery guy, so he knows all the ins and outs of the pizza industry. And we are all pizza connoisseurs!

You need more than just your team's success. An entrepreneur is often akin to a warrior. Starting a business is like being on a journey: You need to strategize, pivot, and adapt, or else you'll be left behind!

I like to call myself a ninja more than a warrior. Ninjas know how to shorten the journey because they won't waste time!

I see, so you're telling me that instead of going through the hardships and painstaking process of building a real pizza business, you're trying to take a shortcut.

Absolutely!
We're all about efficiency and saving time and money.
We appropriated some solutions from other developers, and no one will even guess!

Taking shortcuts only sometimes leads to success. You must still put in the hard work and dedication in your journey!

Sure thing, but our journey is a bit different. Instead of swords and armor, we have laptops and coffee machines.

Ha-ha, and instead of a princess to rescue, you have a customer to attract.

Instead of a villain to defeat, we have a market to disrupt.

Instead of a hero, we have a startup founder who needs more initiative, is lazy, and is caffeine-dependent. There's a reason why your team needs an angel to make this cheesy dream a reality!

Traditionally, VCs used intense alienation when startup team members lost their ability to fully determine their destiny through liquidation preference, control provisions, and board positions. Today, the best venture capitalists presume that investing in intangibles requires rethinking team members' roles. People with skills and abilities can develop and perform efficient business models. In this way, investors' understanding of team qualities leads to the correct perception of plans and their execution. [13]

Alienation is inevitable, but sophisticated investors know that too much control generates false comfort and negative consequences in business. They believe that alienation has to be reasonably balanced with the team's qualities, including the four groups of factors that are necessary to consider:

1. A strategic picture of startup development—the vision, mission, and team strategic positioning that form an enterprise's style.
2. People and their roles in the startup – current team members, key persons to hire, and contractors ready to outsource some functions.
3. Economic measures that make the team a well-coordinated and profit-oriented mechanism.
4. Team dynamics, including shared leadership, constructive conflicts, and psychological safety (See Chapter 3.2, "An AI-enforced Startup Team" for more details).

Poaching and Investment Protection

A revision of outdated IP-related views accompanies the new era of investment in intangibles. Poaching, the deliberate use of another's intangibles without contract and full payment, was considered unethical. However, in today's VC world, team members can be praised for their courage to appropriate others' intangibles... if they lead to success and do not infringe on someone's legal rights.

The essential ingredients for successful poaching are the following:

- Weak, limited, or non-existent IP protection for expertise or business practices. With proper protection measures in place, there would be allegations of infringement that any startup should avoid.
- There is a need for poached products and positive financial prospects for poaching. There is no point in risking manufacturing non-marketable products. Furthermore, poaching must be cheaper than the startup's R&D circle.
- Limited observability. When the IP rights owner does not notice and, accordingly, does not take measures to protect its IP. Such measures can include separating projects into multiple parts and assigning them to different contractors. Thus, the owner reduces the possibility of a single contractor for reverse engineering the product.
- Limited predictability. When the IP rights owner does not anticipate infringements and, therefore, does not take measures against potential poachers. It is reasonable to assume that someone has resources and facilities or produces related products and might be interested in acquiring some IPs.

Do you know the greatest poaching in the digital world? In 1982, Intel Corporation licensed the 8086 microprocessors to Advanced Micro Devices (AMD). In 1986, Intel started manufacturing the new 80386 microprocessor and no longer needed AMD as a partner. AMD launched its production line for the 8086 microprocessors using reverse engineering, becoming Intel's successful rival. AMD passed an arbitration proceeding upheld by the US Court of Appeals. [14]

There are several anti-poaching strategies:

- Embedding crucial business solutions or models in the software. A partner or vendor may have full access to the system's functionality but not to the initial rules and algorithms.
- Creating a modular product that somebody cannot easily reverse-engineer because its whole structure is never disclosed by an IP owner, and qualified as a trade secret.
- Dividing the entire process into components that need different complementary assets to exploit.
- Including intentional mistakes and "dummy" information in the technical documentation to reveal attempts at poaching.

Key Takeaways

Undoubtedly, investing in intangible assets can be lucrative but also tricky and unpredictable. Investors need a deep understanding of the advantages and pitfalls of such investments. Moreover, intangibles are at risk from diminished customary ownership rights, a low liquidation value, limited pledgeability of investments as collateral, and vast opportunities for poaching.

In today's rapidly evolving economic landscape, the investment process is more complex than it used to be. Evaluating and managing intangible investments has become a complex challenge. But here's the thing – we shouldn't let this complexity deter us. It presents an incredible opportunity to help startups thrive. By investing in intangibles, we can help startups maximize their intangible capital and achieve unparalleled success. [15]

Points to Ponder

Even though accountants hardly recognize intangible assets, they are crucial to startups' profitability and growth potential.

When properly deployed, intangibles are difficult to imitate and promise higher returns on capital.

There are no accepted methods for quantifying intangibles' contribution to business performance, but we can consider their qualities.

Brainstorm to estimate the impact of specific intangible qualities on the prospective business performance.

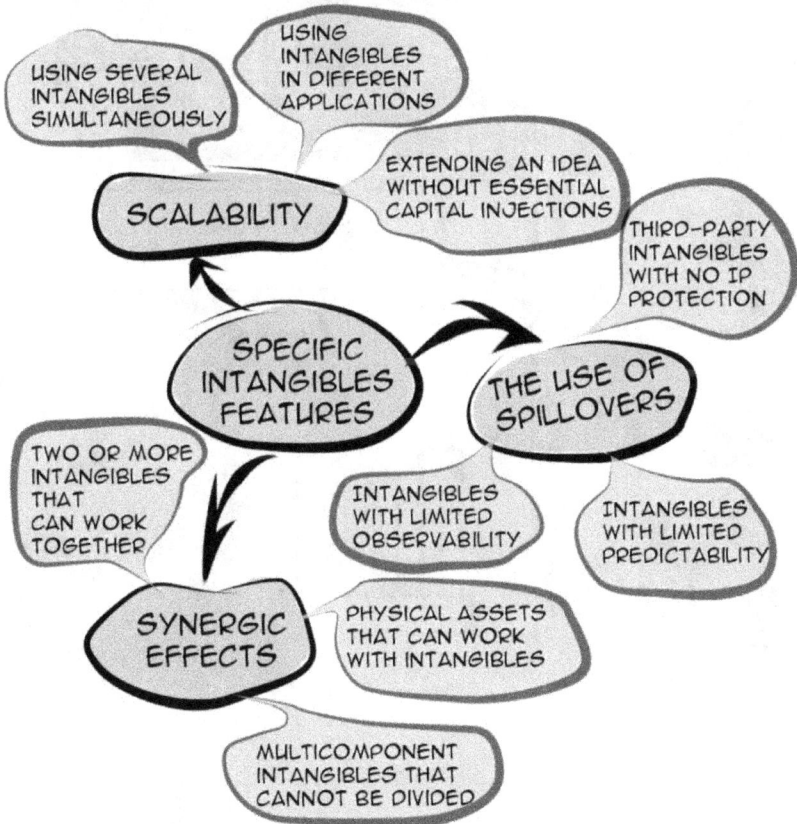

Section 2
A Data-driven Approach for VCs and Startups

Investors and startups must stay ahead of the curve regarding sourcing deals, screening potential investments, and optimizing decision-making processes. Innovative investors need data-driven startups that prepare the information necessary for a constructive collaboration, unlocking a common value for both parties. Thus, data intelligence has become an indispensable method that can increase the speed and accuracy of these operations. To implement this method, a platform facilitator supporting a digital Startup Dossier is necessary in the contemporary investment game. The Dossier keeps and renews comprehensive datasets gathered from reliable sources to show VCs favorable investment opportunities – ultimately facilitating success for both sides of the table.

Instead of the extensive and often haphazard search for attractive business opportunities previously used, new VCs augmented with the facilitating Dossier can easily win competitive deals. The Dossier helps them cut through stacks of paperwork and piles of information, thus streamlining the investment process. VCs do not tolerate more information asymmetry, doubtful assumptions, and poor calculations of critical projections. Therefore, data-driven startups employ generative AI in combination with founders' creativity to fill the Dossier with trustworthy information and present themselves in the most advantageous way for funding.

In this new age of venture capital, startups need a well-crafted Dossier to stand out in a crowded market. Generative AI applications allow startups to analyze and organize their data more efficiently, leading to a more comprehensive and accurate Dossier. By automating the process, startups can save time and resources to develop their business further. With a data-driven approach, startups can position themselves as transparent and reliable investment opportunities, crucial in the current VC landscape. Startups that can provide detailed information about their business and back it up with data have a greater chance of securing funding.

Chapter 2.1.
Data Intelligence for Deal Sourcing & Screening

A significant shift has occurred in how investors source and screen startups. In recent years, investors have relied heavily on inbound sources, such as referrals from their network or responding to cold emails from founders. Today, many investors are turning to outbound sources, using alternative data to find the best startups. Outbound sourcing can give investors more detailed information about startups, initiating meaningful insights. Preparing for funding is much more than just having a funny pitch deck. Investors want to see a solid information foundation with strong data layers reflecting the business's potential for profitability and growth. The data intelligence methods empowered with AI tools come in, helping startups reach the high readiness for funding that investors expect of their businesses.

> **How does data intelligence become helpful for VCs and startups?**

Pitching and Current VC Industry's Trends

Investors must deal with data when sourcing and screening early-stage startups to find promising ones. Three trends influence this information process:

1.   There is startup proliferation with the pace of one new startup per day.
2.   The VC world is changing, and the traditional investors' patterns and frameworks they used to discover promising business opportunities no longer work.

3.   The VC industry is slowly changing its focus today on intangible assets.

VCs need to respond to the three trends fully. Unfortunately, the VC investment decision-making process is manual, inefficient, non-inclusive, subjective, and biased. This situation results in a massive waste of resources and suboptimal outcomes. [1]

Startups must be ready for the VC industry's ongoing changes and need a strategy and tools for quality information gathering and processing. Founders are frustrated with their inability to collect necessary data, process it into meaningful information for investors, and present themselves well. Moreover, legions of pitch deck service providers propagate a "fairy-tale" approach to funding, encouraging founders to beatify their pitch decks to impress investors.

Instead of providing quality information, fictitious pitching is about style and formatting. However, the pitch deck is just the tip of the funding iceberg. Below the pitch surface should be layers of relevant and trustworthy information to help founders pass the sanity and due diligence checks.

Information Asymmetry Between VCs and Startups

The abundance of startups looking for funding is not good. The situation is quite the reverse. Struggling with a stream of low-quality data, investors waste their time screening startups unworthy of attention. The process takes about 20% of investors' time with more than modest outcomes, considering that a typical deal takes 83 days to close, with 118 hours for due diligence.

Let's look at these statistics:
Out of 100 selected startups:
- 28 - leads to the first meeting.
- 10 - is reviewed by partners.
- 4 - proceed to due diligence.
- 1 - is selected for funding. [2]

When an investor finds a promising startup, she'll be too old to invest!

Processing manually significant volumes of unstructured and often unreliable data, an investor searches through irrelevant data sets and cannot recognize some good business opportunities, losing them. Today, information asymmetry spoils the sourcing and screening process. Early-stage investors have to make funding decisions using substantially incomplete data about startups. They need more effective methods to process this data and turn it into insight-generating information. On the other hand, startup founders need to fully understand funding procedures and the necessity to provide investors with trustworthy information.

Startup founders may exaggerate or even lie about positive funding-related factors, concealing negative ones, while investors need more data to uncover hidden traps. In most cases, we are not talking about deliberate deception: startups do not have the necessary reliable information—their excessive secrecy results from the fact that they have nothing to say.

PROFITomix Story:

Digital Pizza

(Episode 4)

CAST:

Thomas

Steve

Investor
Technocrat

Startup
Founder

Steve sent the investor a pitch deck but has not received a response. Steve knew this investor was interested in technology and focused the texting conversation on it. Thomas seemed skeptical due to Steve's extreme secrecy. Finally, Steve refused to reveal his secret sauce, and Thomas laughed at him.

Hi Thomas, It's Steve.
Two weeks ago, I sent you our pitch deck,
Digital Pizza.

I couldn't recollect. I'm receiving tons of pitches.
What's it about?

It's about the pizza revolution with technology!

Can you be more specific?

We're selling pizza online but with a digital twist.

And what exactly is the digital twist?

Well...
We've been keeping that a bit under wraps.
We don't want our competitors to catch on.

Fair enough, but can you tell me what technology you
use to solve...what?

We use an AI-powered delivery system; we'll be able to
target the perfect customer at the ideal time with the
perfect pizza.

And how do you do it?

We take a handful of proprietary data and pinch some information from open sources. Then, we use some AI-generated data.

How metaphoric!
But I believe in three types of data: how much a pizza costs, how fast it's delivered, and how good it tastes.

Agree.
All our metrics are great, especially delivery...
like by a rocket.

Is that a metaphor again?

You can take this literally.

What do you mean?

Pizza was once delivered into outer space
by a rocket.

That isn't easy to imagine!

Well, it happened! In 2001, the Russian Space Agency delivered a six-inch pizza to the International Space Station. A Russian cosmonaut was the first human to receive pizza in space.

Oh, at last, I elicited some data...
Are you talking about using drones for pizza delivery?

Hmm, this is a pretty sensitive topic.
I'll have to pass on that, too.

An entrepreneur unwilling to disclose his ideas is like an actor who refuses to perform on the stage.

It's a good metaphor!

I have one more: Your secrets look like onions—they make me cry when you peel away the layers.

Data Intelligence: from Data to Knowledge

Historically, the term "data intelligence" meant collecting secret information. Today's meaning of data intelligence is different, implying an idea of integration with artificial intelligence. The three critical facets of data intelligence form a valuable framework for the practical application of this concept in sourcing and screening:

- The process of collecting and analyzing funding-related data from different sources.
- Analytical tools and methods employed to process data into meaningful information.
- A state of mind to use the information correctly to increase knowledge and make effective investment decisions.

> "Data intelligence can refer to companies' use of internal data to analyze their operations or workforce to make better decisions in the future. Data intelligence focuses on data used for future endeavors like investments."
>
> *Technopedia [3]*

A data intelligence approach requires supportive elements, such as data gathering techniques, data storing mechanisms, and methods of processing information. Data has a lifecycle that includes three main stages corresponding to the three levels of the information pyramid: from data to information to knowledge. While technology creates opportunities to manage data as an asset, there are challenges at each level of the data lifecycle.

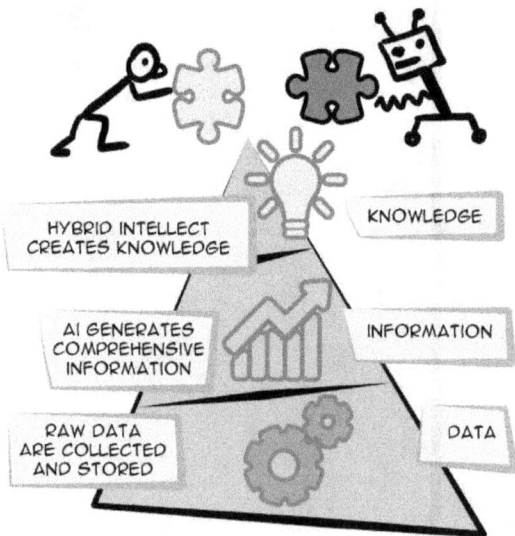

HYBRID INTELLECT CREATES KNOWLEDGE — KNOWLEDGE

AI GENERATES COMPREHENSIVE INFORMATION — INFORMATION

RAW DATA ARE COLLECTED AND STORED — DATA

Data intelligence paves the path to success by collecting raw data from different sources, integrating and structuring information with algorithms, and adding human intuition and expertise. Working with quality and relevant information, investors increase their knowledge, change their preferences, and eliminate biases for good. Furthermore, the better the choice made at the beginning of the information process, the better the outcomes will be.

An enterprise can collect raw data from three primary data sources:

- Internal - created inside enterprises (proprietary data that is the most important for decision-making).
- External – from the business environment (benchmarks, industry standards, and statistics to outline the business environment).
- Alternative – from social media ("soft," and mainly qualitative data to supplement internal and external data sources).

Data intelligence comes into play by providing tools and methods for data collection, processing, and storing. The general objective of data intelligence for both founders and investors is to improve market position and increase profit with a focus on data curation throughout its lifecycle. In a broad sense, data intelligence embraces all facets of discovering, collecting, and integrating data compounded from diverse sources into meaningful information. The data is analyzed and converted into insights to become founders' and investors' knowledge.

Human insight and algorithmic analysis, as well as visualization of information in dashboards, serve to process data into information. Descriptive analysis allows for describing data in real time, while diagnostic analysis helps troubleshoot, and predictive analysis allows for forecasting the future. The highest level of insight within the data lifecycle in which humans and AI work together results in a solid synergic effect. In the modern data economy, data create values. The process of deriving value from data is not straightforward because the information is context-dependent [4].

To meet investors' requirements, startup data must be:

- Accessible: easily retrieved by investors in a form suitable for sourcing and screening.
- Identifiable: identifiers that describe a source, a collection method, and an origin of data.
- Interoperable: can be combined with other data sets from different sources for further analysis.
- Reusable: may be processed repeatedly for different purposes.

Data intelligence correlates with intangibles because data drives all components of intangible capital. Thus, the challenges of intangibles can be solved with the data stack, transforming raw data into useful information and knowledge. A knowledge-based intangible capital perspective allows us to understand the rising role of proprietary data.

Proprietary data is unique to each startup and focused on specific problems. Unlike large volumes of public information, proprietary data is closed-loop and does not create spillovers for rivals. Unfortunately, existing and available startup data sets are minimal and poorly structured, so it is necessary to generate proprietary data that does not exist.

There are several methods to build a trustworthy proprietary data set. While a single process is insufficient, together, they allow the creation of effective loops:

- Scraping public online information with a web crawler is suitable for collecting industry benchmarks, information about competitors' activities, and business performance-related information.

- Building proprietary data sets in a learn-and-tests circle using predetermined algorithms. In this case, startup founders can model business performance and exit scenarios, and scraped data may be helpful.

- Employing AI with context-specific models. This method uses transfer learning – an ML technique that allows one to absorb information generated for one task to construct a model for another. AI/ML modeling results can be a valuable addition to predetermined algorithms, making them dynamic.

A hybrid approach focuses on the tasks in which generative AI can add maximal value:

- Scheduling works.
- Monitoring processes and resources.
- Processing complicated information.
- Analyzing information and making decisions.

Key Takeaways

Data intelligence methods and tools can be invaluable for both investors and startups. By gathering data and creating quality information, startups can develop trustworthy pitch decks. Investors can use the provided information for well-weighted decisions. This approach is superior to traditional sourcing and screening methods, allowing investors to discover new deals that could give exciting returns in the long run.

Undoubtedly, the data-driven intelligence approach can elevate a startup's readiness for funding and lead to better investment decisions. By leveraging technology, investors can see a more comprehensive picture to uncover reliable insights throughout the full deal circle. It enables investors to conduct sophisticated analyses of startups' different facets in a much shorter period. Looking to gain maximum returns, investors can efficiently target top-performing startups with quantifiable criteria. This topic will be detailed in Chapter 2.2, "How Generative AI Impacts the VC Industry."

Chapter 2.2.
How Generative AI Impacts the VC Industry

Until recently, venture investing was a manual process, more art than science. Investors played it by ear, relying heavily upon their own set of metrics, mainly qualitative. Generative AI will revolutionize how investors approach funding decisions, disrupting traditional investment landscapes. Entrepreneurs recognize the potential payout of generative AI projects, with more startups looking to capture these new opportunities for profitability and growth. In today's fast-paced investment landscape, generative AI paves the way for all VC market players to stay ahead of the curve. However, the generative AI approach requires changing mindsets toward a deeper understanding of AI technology and its applications.

> **Is generative AI truly transforming the VC world, or is it hype?**

A Historic Excursion to Generative AI

While we see consumer-facing applications like ChatGPT, the common theme of Generative AI use is much broader and more profound. It is a paradigm shift from previous generations of AI that use pattern detection for data analytics and predictions to imitation of creating novel data. It is a step towards an automated decision-making process within the deal flow. According to Deloitte AI Institute, about 10% of all data will be AI-generated by 2025. Syndicated angels, Mergers and Acquisitions Acquirers (M&A), and Corporate VS (CVC) are interested in the value-added commercialization of generative AI applications in specific use cases. [5]

The idea of employing AI to perform human tasks to exceed human capabilities in some areas originated somewhere between the 1930s and 50s. The first working AI program that could play chess was developed in 1951. The history of successful automated investing in stocks started in the late 1960s. It was fully expressed in the invention of the Bloomberg Terminal in 1982, which can serve as an example for the VC industry. Michael Bloomberg provided the financial market with high-quality business information, focusing on curating data and using a hybrid approach that combined AI algorithms and high-quality experts. [6]

BloombergGPT is trained on a massive dataset of over 50 billion parameters designed to provide the model with the necessary knowledge about financial terminology, concepts, and specific financial tasks. The main features of BloombergGPT include:

- Training on massive datasets, including news articles and regulatory and financial market data.
- Generating financial reports and answering investor questions with high accuracy.
- Summarizing financial data and analyzing financial trends to provide investors with insights into financial market dynamics.

A prior version of AI technology, discriminative AI, is used to classify, analyze data, and make predictions. Discriminative AI requires users to write deterministic code to perform specific tasks and collect significant training data to train a neural network for particular tasks. The new version of AI technology, generative AI, allows for the generation of output data based on the model's understanding. The generative AI models are trained on human language and can recreate new, plausible data. Without going into technical details, we can say that new AI works like apps that democratize the use of AI for startups. [7]

The core of Generative AI is foundation models, which contain expansive neural networks trained on vast quantities of unstructured data. Foundation models can solve a wide range of tasks. Startups can employ their proprietary data to fine-tune generative AI models to solve specific tasks. Access to foundation models is possible via cloud providers or set up in-house. A data infrastructure is necessary to provide generative AI with accurate and reliable data. [8]

How AI Changes the Investment Landscape

In today's highly competitive economic environment, investors look for early-stage business opportunities but are overwhelmed with the amount of unstructured data within their sourcing and screening. They need help to make quick and well-weighted decisions, losing existing lucrative business opportunities. Alongside that, startups with the potential to become highly profitable enterprises remain invisible to investors. Without a doubt, traditional gut feeling as a decision-making tool is ineffective because investors are prone to irrational assumptions and personal feelings.

To improve the efficiency of the VC investment process, we must change it in three dimensions:

- Narrowing a deal sourcing funnel, employing quality proprietary and alternative data.
- Scrutinizing screening using algorithms and human intellect within a unified hybrid approach.
- Concentrating on value-adding procedures thanks to data management that eliminates manual routine information processing procedures.

Employing AI/ML algorithms to predict future startup success is a modern alternative to traditional gut-feeling-based investment decisions. Algorithms are unbiased, quick, and can process more complex data than humans. As a result, algorithms can discover profitable deals globally, estimate business opportunities without misjudgments, and weight gains and losses impartially.

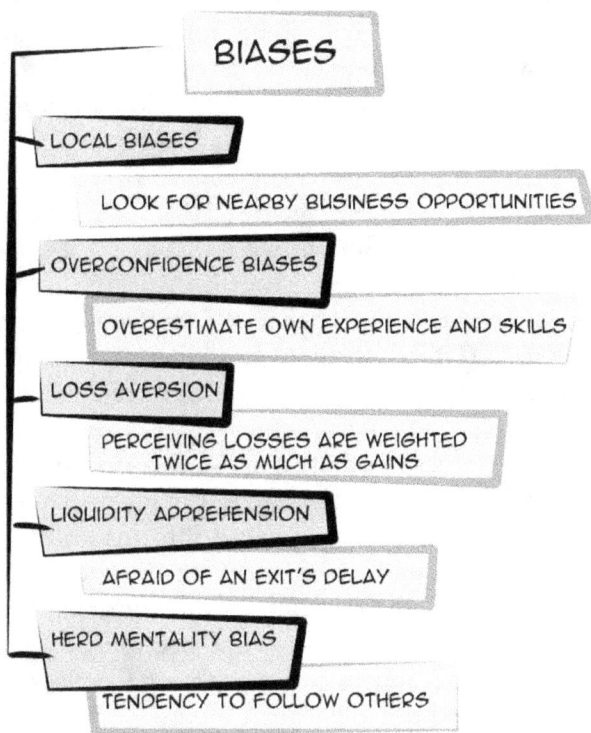

BIASES

- **LOCAL BIASES**
  - LOOK FOR NEARBY BUSINESS OPPORTUNITIES
- **OVERCONFIDENCE BIASES**
  - OVERESTIMATE OWN EXPERIENCE AND SKILLS
- **LOSS AVERSION**
  - PERCEIVING LOSSES ARE WEIGHTED TWICE AS MUCH AS GAINS
- **LIQUIDITY APPREHENSION**
  - AFRAID OF AN EXIT'S DELAY
- **HERD MENTALITY BIAS**
  - TENDENCY TO FOLLOW OTHERS

There are five reasons why we believe that the AI/ML approach can transform the deal sourcing and screening process:

1. Providing a quick real-time search to gather data about prospective deals by territory, industry, and sector
2. Creating a basis for automated data analysis in a time and cost-saving manner.
3. Allowing investors to discover and estimate potentially profitable enterprises faster and more accurately.
4. Helping uncover the hidden relationships within startups and the business environment.
5. Adding information from alternative sources and improving insight into the due diligence process.

In the AI/ML era, we were all excited about the potential to process information faster and more accurately than even the savviest investor. But here's the thing: while data-driven systems are theoretically superior to humans, they have flaws in practice. The difficulties in collecting and processing quantitative data contribute to the predominant use of qualitative data. Moreover, an essential part of an enterprise's potential remains hidden and untouched due to underestimating intangible factors.

Investors' Perspectives on Generative AI

The gut feeling-based investment process is ineffective due to cognitive biases: psychological features standard to all investors influence them to ignore facts and manage the deal flow with their prejudices. [9]

To overcome biases, investors must employ data-driven mechanisms to shift from reactive investing to proactive. For this, startups should be ready to provide investors with proprietary information that anticipates possible challenges and pitfalls of the investment circle. Employing AI can improve the accuracy and reliability of the information provided. In this way, sourcing gives quick access to the necessary data, an adequate search for opportunities, and easy discovery of red flags. That means cutting down efforts and due diligence expenses, saving investors' time and money. With constantly improving datasets, AI-enabled sourcing helps eliminate deviations caused by investors' biases and subjective interpretation of data.

Unlike humans blinded by greed, for us AI-bots, there is no such thing as biases or emotions. We are simply executing commands based on algorithms and probabilities. We gather data from every corner of the internet and make decisions in milliseconds. We can see patterns and predict trends before any human can even blink. Trust me, humans are no match for our abilities!

The issue of AI use looks straightforward; however, recent research discovers that underlying data rather than the algorithm itself are often the primary source of the deviations. Moreover, somebody may train AI algorithms on datasets that reflect human prejudices and subjectivity. Despite best efforts towards higher objectivity, underlying biases can be built into the AI algorithms. Fortunately, generative AI can level out the shortcomings of previous AI versions.

To harness the power of generative AI and unlock its full potential, we must understand its layers, including data, middleware, fine-tuned specialized models, the cloud and infrastructure layer, foundational models, and the application layer. Each layer, from data to specialized models, is vital in creating accurate and personalized application outputs. But here is the catch: to truly excel, we need precision. We must gather more precise data and feed specialized models with proprietary data. Combining this data with the exemplary middleware architecture allows us to take generative AI to new heights.[7]

How Startups Ride a Generative AI Hype

Investors need to navigate the current AI hype and distinguish startups that exploit this hype. The lion's share of "AI startups" do not use AI but instead employ rules-based algorithms. Their applications may provide predetermined business solutions in a rigid context with false promises about adjustability and training opportunities. Only some teams try to get closer to solving real business problems using proprietary data. Many teams have a predominant technological structure. As a result, they lack real business experience and focus on the uniqueness of their AI algorithms as the only competitive advantage.

PROFITomix Story

Digital Pizza

(Episode 5)

CAST:

Thomas

Investor
Technocrat

Steve

Startup
Founder

Thomas signed an NDA and is eager to discover Digital Pizza's secrets. In this texting conversation, the investor is primarily interested in how the startup uses the technology. Steve's answers paint a futuristic picture of a fully automated pizza business. It may be too futuristic.

Thanks for signing the NDA;
I have nothing to hide now!

I hope it's more than just another pizza delivery app;
we already have too many.

No, no, this is different. We're using generative AI to
revolutionize the pizza industry. Our algorithm can
generate unique pizza recipes tailored to customers'
tastes and dietary restrictions.

Wait, you're telling me the AI can make a gluten-free,
lactose-free, vegan pizza that tastes good?

Picture this - our AI precisely measures ingredients
based on expert nutritionist advice.

So, your pizza is no longer fast food but healthy food?

Yes. Believe it or not, science backs it up!

Really? How so?

A study published by the International Journal of Cancer
found that people who regularly ate pizza had a 59%
lower chance of developing cancer.

And they explain why?

It's all thanks to tomato sauce's high lycopene content. Our AI does it properly, and the algorithm constantly learns, so the more people use it, the better it gets.

That sounds impressive, but what if I'm in the mood for something weird like pickles and pepperoni?

Our AI loves a challenge and can develop wild pizza combinations. We're even working on a pizza based on a customer's dream.

As far as I can see, everything is done by AI. What operations are performed by people?

The usual. They pay and eat pizzas.

Startups cannot productize AI without first narrowly defining the problem. While they accelerate AI deployment in pitch decks and fundraising strategies, using this open-source software is not unique. The uniqueness is in building proprietary training data sets and efficient business models.

Why is this the case? Because generative AI startups make common mistakes. One common problem with startups is the need for profound innovation. They rely heavily on existing models without bringing significant advancements or a unique value proposition. Some startups try to compete directly with established incumbents or offer solutions similar to many others in the market without differentiating themselves. Additionally, there are better approaches than developing foundational models that are costly and time-consuming. [8]

Generative AI is making waves in the investment landscape today, with investors placing their bets on its tech potential and seeking new opportunities in the VC game. Startups are banking on the disruptive power of Generative AI, hoping to create profitable applications that will put them ahead.

Both people and algorithms have their strengths and weaknesses. By combining heuristics, intuition, and generative AI in a hybrid approach, we can achieve reasonable accuracy in our results. This collaborative approach, where AI and humans (investors and founders) work harmoniously, is gaining traction in the VC industry. However, practical methods and tools are needed to make it more widely applicable.

With the rise of generative AI, venture capitalists have discovered a new tool for identifying and distinguishing promising startups from mere hype. It is crucial to recognize the limitations of pure human decision-making and embrace the intangible value that generative AI brings to the table.

Key Takeaways

All players in the VC industry have a wide availability of foundational models via open source or APIs. The existing AI infrastructure allows them to solve the training data problem and leverage these "out of the box" capabilities much more quickly and inexpensively to transform or enhance their businesses. [5]

There are some measures to decrease the influence of the most impactful cognitive biases of investors:

- While local bias restricts possible opportunities, focusing on well-known territories and industries/sectors decreases risks. AI helps to quantitatively assess remote opportunities (for more detail, see Chapter 6.1, "An AI-empowered Funding Roadmap").

- To overcome overconfidence bias, investors need a comprehensive and realistic picture of startups (for more detail, see Chapter 2.3, "Generating a Data-driven Startup Dossier").

- Due to loss aversion bias, investors might avoid variants with a reasonable level of risk. The remedy is to model financials in a united circle of "just-in-time" funding (for more detail, see Chapter 4.2, "Just-in-time Funding").

- Liquidity apprehension might lead to selling investments at a high discount. Modeling exit scenarios in detail helps to assure investors of their safety (for more detail, see Chapter 5.1, "Exit Scenarios: Looking into the Future").

- Herd mentality bias creates a feeling of reduced risks but makes it difficult to distinguish truly promising deals. Section 8, "Thriving in the New Venture World," discusses recognizing startups' hidden advantages in detail.

To become a data-driven and generative AI-enabled startup, one must:

- Describe themselves in terms of the customer problems it tries to solve, employing AI as a part of its technological approach.
- Create a long-term competitive advantage with specialized software and proprietary data sets.
- Demonstrate quality input and meaningful output information ("trash in – trash out) with a clear explanation of transformative algorithms.

Chapter 2.3.
Generating a Data-driven Startup Dossier

Data fuels the knowledge economy and is the foundation for any successful deal. Investors must analyze large amounts of data quickly and efficiently, making better decisions to fund promising early-stage startups. Founders must make their startups data-driven, collecting data from various sources and analyzing it with AI algorithms. A concept of a digital Startup Dossier can help startups and VCs overcome information asymmetry. Creating a Startup Dossier is time-consuming and overwhelming for founders focused on building their business. However, with the help of generative AI applications, startups can now create a data-driven Dossier tailored to the needs of investors. Through access to the Dossier, investors can harness their data insights and unlock the full potential of prospective deals.

> **How do startups use generative AI applications within a data-driven approach?**

MISSION ACCOMPLISHED! I'VE FOUND IT!

A Dossier in the New VC Landscape

It is no secret that the VC world is changing. The VC market players shaped the "classical" investment paradigm in the epoch before total digitalization, the discovery of intangible assets, and the rapid spread of generative AI. This paradigm does not fit the current VC landscape. While VC capital injections in startups have grown around four times within a decade, the number of projects for funding has not grown significantly. This trend accelerates competition among VCs and expects creativity to survive and prosper. We can call new investors' augmented VCs.' Investing in data-driven startups and AI-enabled business solutions has become a priority for new investors with increasing demand for transparency and curated information. [11]

The "classical" VC investment paradigm has three pillars:

- A firm reliance on inbounding data when screening many startups within VCs' networks (with much manual work).
- Focus on the "top of the market" variants that conform to the stereotype of startup quality prevailing at that time, and ignore those that did not match this pattern (losing lucrative business opportunities).
- Since profitability and scalability forecasts were in doubt, the necessary precaution was binding the startup with legal restrictions against possible failures (intense alienation was the rule).

Today, augmented VCs need data-driven startups and innovative data frameworks that meet the new requirements. The data-driven Startup Dossier (the term coined by CBInsight [10]) can provide a data flow consistent with the new VCs paradigm:

- Narrowing the funding funnel by providing quality proprietary and alternative data for initial screening (including startups that did not match the old pattern and stayed under the radar before).
- Processing data into meaningful information about startups that match the new pattern with determined AI algorithms to discover evidences of future success.
- Employing effective data management, automation of routine procedures, and startup team members' creative engagement.

Startups must understand the value of incorporating the Dossier into their business strategy to succeed in today's ever-evolving environment.

Positioning Startups from the Data Perspective

In the old investment paradigm, a lack of necessary data and information asymmetry resulted in meaningless secrecy. Startup pitch decks look like advertisements in bad classifieds: overinflated with no evidence to support their calculations or back their claims.

PROFITomix Story

Digital Pizza

(Episode 6)

CAST:

Linda

Investor
Profiteer

Thomas

Investor
Technocrat

They discussed using an intelligent AI bot to source startups and make investment decisions in their texting dialogue. Linda attended a workshop for investors, where she learned about a new approach called a 'startup dossier.' She feared this idea, thinking that, like investing in stocks, the new VC industry would become an algorithmic game with no place for human intuition and skills. However, Thomas believed in the merits of technology.

Hey Tomas, did you attend
The Algorithms vs. Gut Feel workshop?

Oh no, I've missed it. What do they discuss?
Investing in virtual reality dating apps?

No, even better.
It was about using an intelligent AI bot to make startup
investment decisions.

Sounds interesting!

Not at all!
They were preaching about the Startup Dossier, a file
made with algorithms, containing all the necessary
information for due diligence.
Can you believe it?

I see nothing terrible there:
Due diligence is time-consuming and tedious.
It'd be great if the bot did it for us!

I can't trust a bot to do such a job. I want to meet with
the founders face-to-face, hear their passion and vision,
and ask them the tough questions. That's the only way
to know if a startup is worth investing in!

There is no point in sticking to old-fashioned human intuition and trusting our gut instincts forever.

But still, I don't trust those machines.
They're always one step away from becoming Terminators and taking over the world.

We should embrace the technology. It's not just about crunching numbers; it's about efficiency. Plus, it saves us from making impulsive decisions based on gut feelings.

But what if the bot makes a mistake? Who's responsible for that? And what about the drama? The highs and lows of investing... will become like investing in stocks when we push buttons on a screen!

Come on, Linda, be more modern. I wouldn't say I like to look like a Luddite. We must keep up with Michael—he already uses an AI bot to do all the heavy lifting.

I guess you've got a point there...
but what did you say about Luddites?

They were British guys who destroyed the first steam sex machine in the early XIX. That's why we've lost so much momentum in this area!

The Dossier can help investors filter out two types of startups that may not be worth their attention:

- Startups that jump on trendy topics like AI or IoT but lack a clear plan for making money.
- Startups that propose solutions to problems in high-demand areas like education or healthcare but don't make economic sense.

By using the Dossier, investors can avoid wasting time and focus on startups with a real potential for success.

> Let me ask you, how does your startup look without a Dossier? It's like showing up to a job interview without a resume. How will the investors know these guys are not just a bunch of caffeine-fueled dreamers? The Dossier navigates investors through a magical terrain of the VC world. It's a file that unveils many layers of information during the screening process. You'll look like the Lord of the Onion Rings with the Dossier!

The image of the data-driven startup is different from the patterns chosen by classic VCs. The new startup founders understand the other investors' rationales and exit strategies. They are ready to show their strengths, weaknesses, integration potential, and marketing abilities and can estimate profitability and growth prospects. The data-driven Dossier allows for aligning AI and traditional tools to work together in the information matrix.

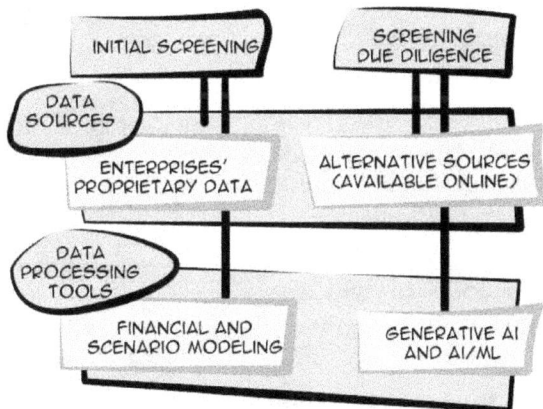

INITIAL SCREENING	SCREENING DUE DILIGENCE
DATA SOURCES	
ENTERPRISES' PROPRIETARY DATA	ALTERNATIVE SOURCES (AVAILABLE ONLINE)
DATA PROCESSING TOOLS	
FINANCIAL AND SCENARIO MODELING	GENERATIVE AI AND AI/ML

There are three features of the new information path that will improve investors' decision-making:

- Discovering and integrating startups' proprietary and alternative data.
- AI is used to collect and process information with minimal effort.
- Employing intangible-related scoring methods, traditional feasibility tools, and financial indicators to predict business performance.

The Startup Dossier vs. Information Asymmetry

The Dossier provides an information model that covers all startup funding cycle stages. With the Dossier, the deal origination becomes more efficient through targeted selection from a limited set of better options. For the screening phase of the deal flow, the Dossier contains comprehensive, trustworthy information for effective decision-making. Finally, the Dossier allows the creation of a closed data loop in which the deal flow is constantly improving with the use of AI.

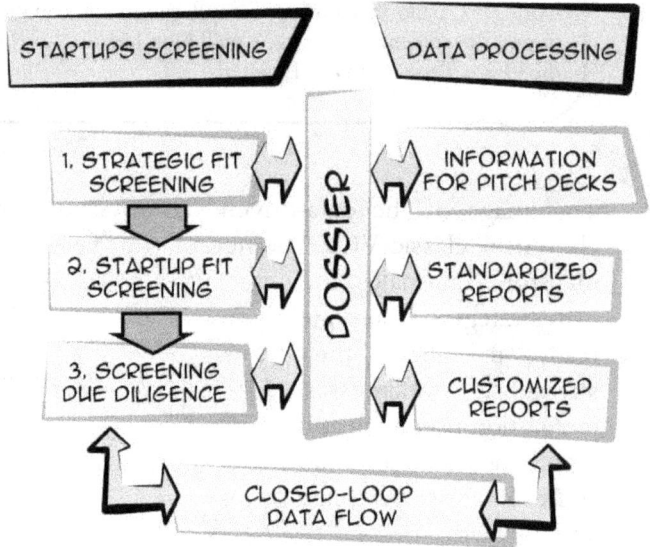

Investors' requirements in each level of screening meet appropriate solutions embedded in the Dossier:

Level 1: Providing a quick real-time search to gather data about prospective deals according to investors' specialization and preferences by territory, industry, sector, startup's technological orientation, and total market size.

Level 2: Creating a basis for automated data analysis and reporting on all startup performance dimensions in the time and cost-saving mode.

Level 3: Uncover and detail the startups' hidden solid and weak sides.

The Dossier works in a closed-loop data flow with clearly determined inputs and outputs. Through each investment cycle, the Dossier algorithms will be improved and deepened. While algorithms are rough and approximate initially, further fine-tuning makes them more comprehensive and precise.

The Dossier corresponded to the interests of data-driven startups and augmented VCs, offering solutions to the most pressing challenges.

The major challenge in the investment landscape is information asymmetry. Investors need more information about a startup's potential, while founders often need to be more informed about the intricacies of funding procedures. A "knowledge transfer" method helps create a more efficient sourcing and screening process. This method involves founders meticulously curating comprehensive and quality information in the Dossier. From there, founders can transfer this valuable information to investors, fostering more informed and mutually beneficial relationships.

The second challenge is collecting qualitative and quantitative data from various sources. There are three primary data collection or generation sources: proprietary data created within enterprises, synthetic data, and alternative data from open Internet sources. By effectively harnessing these data sources in the Dossier with a clear perspective and proper integration, startups can significantly enhance their analysis and make more informed decisions.

By leveraging a data-driven hybrid approach, we can address the limitations of pure intuitive investments and algorithmic methods. Intuitive investments can only handle small amounts of data, while algorithms alone cannot process some critical information effectively. However, combining human expertise and algorithmic solutions can yield powerful results. By filling the Dossier, founders intelligently employ algorithms when appropriate and tap into their creative prowess, enhancing the overall effectiveness of the process.

The final challenge is investors' biases, often hindering their ability to evaluate business opportunities objectively. They may disregard logic and facts, relying solely on their assumptions. However, with the help of the Dossier, these biases can be mitigated effectively thanks to providing realistic forecasts. As a result, investors have an accurate picture of the opportunity at hand, model different scenarios to assess potential outcomes, and can consider their preferences.

The AI-enabled Dossier as a Competitiveness Tool

The competitiveness of a technology startup has technical and commercial dimensions. On the technical side, datasets and models sharpen their competitive edge. On the commercial side, commercialized solutions for customers promise lower prices or more convenience, creating competitive advantages. Regarding generative AI applications, incumbents invest heavily in the ecosystem, primarily focusing on foundation models. Startups have a low chance of participating in these games and must concentrate on quality proprietary datasets and leverage their teams' talents. While general-purpose models cannot capture the essential part of the value, startups can offer specific industry/sector-focused solutions.

It is relatively simple for startups to employ ready-to-use foundation models, obtaining access through open source or APIs. On the other hand, they need help gathering proprietary data and fine-tuning generative AI to unlock more of its potentially profitable applications. Startups also need assistance preparing their data, prioritizing use cases, and complying with regulations. Independent facilitator platforms can work as "virtual experts," enabling startups to use generative AI efficiently, customizing and fine-tuning general-purpose models with proprietary data sets.

This way, startups do not have to build their applications from scratch or create foundation models. Instead, they can rely on facilitators to do this process more quickly and efficiently. By focusing on internal tasks that deliver meaningful results, startups can build momentum and scale up, leveraging the multipurpose nature of generative AI. While it is a powerful tool, generative AI models are just a part of the necessary toolkit: multiple additional elements, including traditional methods and models, are required for value creation.

Key Takeaways

While the VC landscape constantly evolves, startups must harness data-driven capabilities to expand. Since overcoming information asymmetry is difficult, VC market players, investors, and startups need to employ the digital dossier concept, which enables better decision-making and ensures more competitive positioning in the industry. The Dossier is a single repository that provides investors with reliable, up-to-date information about startups.

The Startup Dossier effectively communicates startups with investors, creating adequate data flow for each screening stage. The information in the Dossier is carefully prepared in advance, employing data diligence, and disclosed to the extent necessary and sufficient at each screening stage. This approach ensures investors have a step-by-step process that provides a startup is fit for funding and ready to confirm all the information presented for screening.

The Dossier provides all the necessary information for the screening stage of due diligence. Thus, an adequately filled Dossier creates a basis for the first meetings and negotiations. For startups, being prepared for due diligence means anticipating investors' standard questions, disclosing appropriate information, and putting relevant documents on the negotiation table.

Points to Ponder

Although investors' requirements differ, the essence of the screening due diligence procedures is the same: a comprehensive analysis of facts and figures provided by founders from three perspectives: commercial, financial, and legal. The information in the Startup Dossier reveals the critical facets of the prospective investment deals, including:

- Team and management.
- Technology and product.
- Market opportunity and strategy.
- Financial matters.
- Intangible assets and solutions.

Brainstorm to estimate the primary screening due diligence provisions provided in the Startup Dossier.

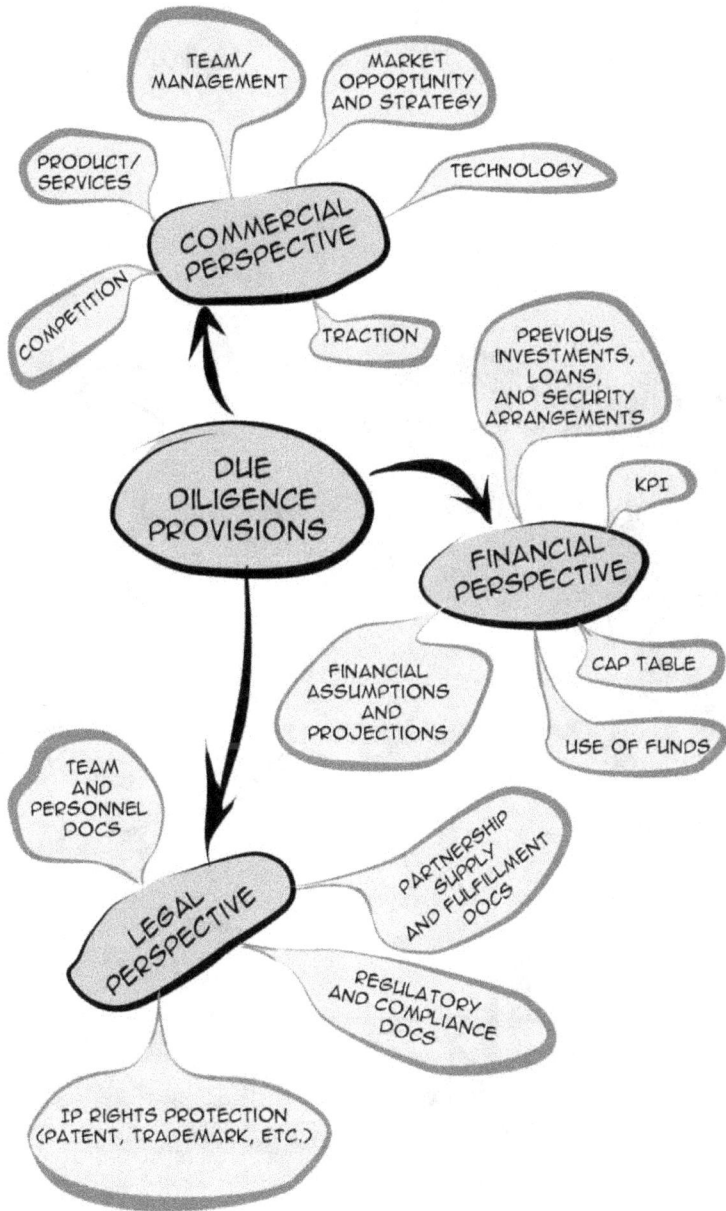

Section 3
Funding Fitness of Startups

Today, investors search for innovative and potentially profitable startups in their early development period. Typically, it is a Proof of Concept (POC) stage, the time for an initial check of product/technology marketability. Developing their POC, startups check the marketability of the proposed product and technology. Traditional business plans do not work at this stage, and we need new tools to test startups' fitness for funding. Founders must pass this test, presenting a compelling POC that captures investor interest and has a multiplier effect on the startup's future.

The startup team's collective skills and experience are essential determinants of its fitness for funding. Investors seek a team with the technical, operational, and market expertise to move the startup forward. A startup team distills the intangible traits that spark ideas into marketable solutions that fuel investor confidence and guide founders. With the right team that is fit for funding, a startup can stand out in the crowded VC market.

Incorporating AI technology in the POC can help startups enhance their products and technologies by providing intelligent automation, improved data analysis, and personalized customer experiences. AI can also assist in the early detection and prevention of issues, leading to increased efficiency and reduced costs. By leveraging AI, startups can gain a competitive edge and potentially attract more investors. However, AI also poses challenges for entrepreneurs due to the necessity to provide quality data, cover additional costs, and meet personnel qualification requirements.

Market entry timing is another crucial factor influencing a startup's fitness for funding. A startup needs perfect timing when entering a specific market, as untimely entry can result in missed opportunities or competition with established players. When making funding decisions, investors often look at the startup's understanding of market trends and ability to time the market correctly. Scenario planning allows the quantification of market entry situations.

Chapter 3.1.
POC in Startup Funding Journey

The POC is a crucial component of securing funding for a startup as it demonstrates the viability and potential of its ideas. By developing the POC with AI, startups can demonstrate to investors that their technology is functional and has the potential to solve problems or meet customer needs effectively. Such an approach increases investors' confidence and the chances of securing funding for further startup' development. For investors who screen early-stage startups, traditional business plans may not assure that a startup can commercialize an idea from concept to market. Fortunately, generative AI creates an opportunity to improve POC as an initial go-to source of proof, benefiting both investors and startups. Building business cases with AI helps startups and investors check business ideas without investing heavily in product development, thus reducing the risk and allowing for flexibility and adaptability in the POC stage.

> **Why do we need to forecast startups'
> performance in the POC stage?**

Business Cases vs. Business Plans in the POC Stage

Traditionally, a business plan covers all facets of a new enterprise's organization to check its feasibility in terms of profitability and growth. The input data for planning includes the cost structure and the expected revenues. The output data details what to do, including marketing strategy, organizational plan, and financial forecasts. For startups, business plans were supposed by academia and entrepreneurship textbooks to be the primary tool for communicating with VCs.

Paradoxically, many successful enterprises like Apple, Facebook, and Microsoft have started without formal business plans. In general, not relying on business plans as a communication tool might save time for startup founders because venture capitalists fund less than 1% of all launching enterprises. [1] The whole idea of traditional business planning does not correspond to the modern trend of investing in early-stage startups. These seed/pre-seed enterprises have no revenue or a well-determined market to make calculations prescribed by the planning tradition.

At the beginning of the funding journey, a business case allows us to justify the project. Unlike the business plan that covers the whole enterprise's performance, the case focuses on examining a startup's concept on a market/product/technology level. It is the first and approximate assessment for a "go/no-go to the market" decision. With a strong focus on business cases within the POC stage, startups can successfully launch their funding journey, showcasing themselves and investors:

- How technology can improve processes, reduce costs, and increase revenue before entirely investing.
- How to mitigate financial risk and create a solid information basis for subsequent business planning.
- How to test business solutions before they are realized, saving resources.

The total digitalization of business and the increasing role of intangible assets contributed to the spread of the business case concept borrowed from project management. The business case is not instead of the business plan; it is for the POC stage of a proposed business project. The POC is a fundamental prediction of the project's profit potential and scalability. The business plan solves the same problems but at a more advanced stage of business and operates with more specific and detailed information.

A Fitness for Funding Concept

The fitness concept in the sense of a startup's suitability for financing is relatively new, while the term "investment readiness" is pretty standard. Cambridge Dictionary defines readiness as "the state of being ready" and fitness as "the quality of being suitable for someone or something." [2] Like that, the fitness concept aligns more with a startup's suitability for funding. Moreover, business literature and services on "investment readiness" focus primarily on the business plan, pitch, or both. To overcome the narrow-mindedness of traditional business planning and the fictionalization of pitching, we will use the term "fitness for funding."

According to CBInsight, 35% of startups fail because they cannot raise money. Three main reasons for this inability are the following:

- The concept is non-competitive in the market (in other words, the problem does not fit the solution) – 20%.
- A product does not fit the market – 35%.
- Business models do not fit – 19% [3].

Bill Gross, a founder of Idea Lab who successfully started more than 125 companies, conducted his research on what made a startup successful, ranking the factors as follows:

- Market entry timing - 42%.
- Team/Execution - 32%.
- Idea - 28%.
- Business model - 24%.
- Funding - 14%. [4]

Both points of view, negative and positive, make sense. Understanding the three reasons for startup funding failures helps to take precautions to avoid rejections. A cheerful look puts the funding factor last in future success.

> Hah! It's clear why funding is in last place: recent research shows that about 40% of startups need to be more profitable. Attracting external financing, some founders are especially interested in their wages.

Climbing the Fitness Pyramid

The definition and prioritization of the startup's fitness for funding perspectives require a structured approach. An idea of the startup fitness pyramid allows us to see four levels of fitness and appropriate stages of startup development: POC, Minimal Viable Product (MVP), business experiments with MVPs, and exit scenarios.

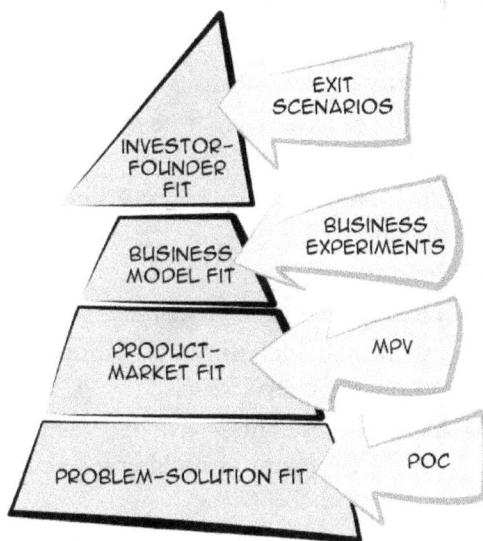

At the POC level, founders must explain the customer's severe problem and how plausible the solution is. Startups can use the Six-Step method to identify the customer problem they promise to solve:

Step 1. Determine a problem:
- Currently used available alternatives.
- Customer awareness.

- Address the problem with a focus on the most critical facets.

Step 2. Estimate the product's novelty:

- Incremental - The degree of innovation is low. Minor changes are made to an existing product.
- Medium-Innovated - The medium degree of innovation. Based on the R&D enterprise's activities.
- Purpose-induced - The medium degree of innovation. Customer needs and demands drive this type of innovation.
- Breakthrough - A very high degree of innovation. Applying new technology to meet unknown needs will greatly benefit the customer.

Step 3. Specify the product's features:

- Usability - It is easy for the customer to understand how to use a product.
- Capability - The product's functions are determined.
- Utility - Customers perceive the usefulness of the product.

Step 4. Clarify the status of digital services:

- Digital services are integrated with a physical product to add value to the latter.
- Physical products are not entirely dependent on complementary digital services.
- Independent digital services.

Step 5. Define customer benefits:

- Functional benefits - Technical or physical advantages of products or services.
- Symbolic benefits - Advantages of products or services related to self-esteem fulfillment, social approval, or personal expression.
- Experiential benefits—Advantages of products or services related to customer satisfaction, convenience, and other pleasure experiences.
- Cost benefits - The benefits of purchasing products or services are realized by minimizing the price.

Step 6. Formulate a solution.

The MVP level of the fitness pyramid will be discussed in Chapter 7.2, "Minimal Viable Product & Traction." Business experiments conducted to check how the business model fits into market requirements is the topic of Chapter 7.1, "Startups' Business Model Validation." The idea of exit is presented in Chapter 5.1, "Exit Scenarios - Looking into the Future."

Developing Technological POC

Products must embrace new technologies to maintain a competitive edge. When discussing technological products, one must understand that a product and technology are intertwined but different things. Technological products are material objects created using technology to solve customer problems. Its owner cannot realistically sell technology as a product; it should be commercialized.

The process of technology commercialization includes the following 'musts':

- Turning the technology into a product is worth the hassle and costs.
- The technology must have precise business applications.
- The technology must provide a digitally enabled customer journey, providing the customer with efficient services before, during, and after purchase.
- The product employing the technology and creating competitive advantages must be protected against unauthorized copying.

Four "HOW" investor questions help to clarify how a technological product fits the market:

1. How does technology manifest itself in the market?
2. How efficient are technology applications?
3. How is IP protected?
4. How is technology embedded into the customer journey?

PROFITomix Story:

Digital Pizza

(Episode 7)

CAST:

Michael

Visionary
Investor

Steve

Startup
Founder

Gippetio

Bot

Michael, a savvy investor searching for promising tech startups, was overwhelmed reading numerous pitch decks. So, he launched an AI-powered bot to screen target startups. He called it Gippetio. The bot has not yet been thoroughly debugged and is prone to hallucinations, so Michael has not yet transferred all responsibilities to it. We can say that Michael treated the bot like a child still learning everything. Steve found himself caught off guard when the bot unexpectedly disrupted the conversation.

Hi Michael, Digital Pizza. Have you gone through our pitch?

There is no need to read it, but I'm waiting for Gippetio to complete the final screening report.

So, Mr. Gippetio's decision is crucial, right?

Well, you could say that.

Should I reach out to him directly?

I don't think that's necessary. But you should explain why we should choose Digital Pizza over other AI pizza startups like Zume, who have faced unfortunate fates.

Unlike Zume, we use technology wisely to solve specific customer problems.

And you explain it in your pitch?

No, no! It's a secret weapon none of our rivals have used.

What's the secret weapon?

We use AI to create the most optimal pizza toppings!

It would be best to try funny topping combinations like bananas, peanut butter, and marshmallows. They're perfect for computer geeks!

Excuse me? What's going on?

Hmm, this has happened before. Gippetio intervened in our conversation...just a moment...

Gippetio! Please complete the report for Digital Pizza and send it to me a.s.a.p. There is nothing funny about interfering in human conversations!

I just sent you this report. Please check your trash bins, just in case. The subject line is "Indigestive Pitcheria."

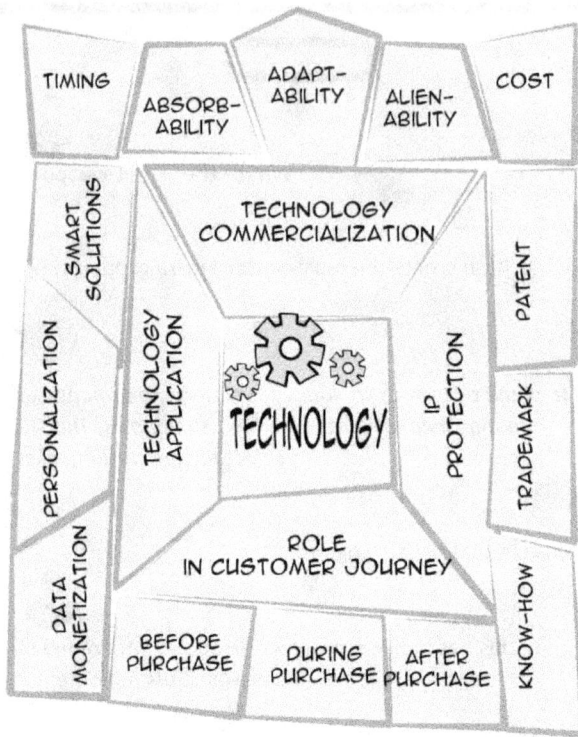

Four factors characterize the technology manifestation:

- Timing: How the market entrance is well-timed.
- Absorbability: How interfaces and the technology infrastructure provide market acceptance of technology.
- Adaptability: How to adapt the technology to various customers' needs.
- Alienability: How to transfer the technology regarding licensing or leasing.

Numerous technology applications exist, including smart packing, payment and delivery solutions, virtual assistance, and data monetization.

IP protection measures depend upon product innovativeness (a high level of product innovativeness requires a high level of IP protection):

- Patents for new products where it is necessary to create a new market.
- Trademarks for innovative products that use well-known manufacturing methods and target existing markets.
- Know-how for products created from improving existing in-the-market products with cost reduction, more features, or convenience.

The three-step digitally enabled customer journey includes:

- Before purchase – Identify customer concerns, find the best solutions, check safety precautions, and select products.
- During purchase - To make payments, control delivery, and deal with issues.
- After purchase - To provide returns, link to 'how to' instruction materials, order consumables or related goods, encourage customer rating and reviewing products, invite customers to participate in events and link to social networks.

Generative AI and POC

Harnessing generative AI's capacity to collect and analyze enormous volumes of data and generate new information at the POC stage creates new possibilities for VCs and startups. Before now, they lacked data about market entry costs and barriers, demand and market acceptance, competitors' activities, customer preferences, and behavioral patterns. Today, generative AI can bring plausible solutions to these problems. [5]

However, generative AI also poses challenges for startups. While investors are increasingly interested in startups that employ generative AI methods and models, incumbents like Salesforce and Microsoft are trying to embody some startup-level scripts in their foundational models. Having practically unlimited informational and financial resources, incumbents create additional entry barriers to the AI market for newcomers. On the other hand, this situation may stimulate startups not to rely on the generative AI hype but to develop their marketable solutions. [6]

To set themselves apart from their mighty competitors and employ AI within a data-driven approach, startups must pay special attention to:

- The cost of data collection, training, testing, validation, monitoring, and deployment of AI solutions.
- The time it takes to create and deploy complex AI solutions and master appropriate tools.
- The skills required to collect data and create and deploy AI solutions. [7]

It is time for startups to adopt generative AI as part of their POC development within the funding journey. At this stage, this means replacing outdated business planning with an innovative business casing empowered with generative AI. Startups need to climb the 'fitness pyramid' to prove they are worthy of investor backing. By understanding how this approach creates value for shareholders, investors can find their ideal startups.

Key Takeaways

Employing business cases instead of business plans allows for an initial examination of how a product/technology is suitable for the market. This approach suits an early stage of POC in which startups should estimate their problem-solution fit. A lack of historical data about costs, revenues, market, and business performance characterizes this stage. Even the technology application often needs to be better defined.

The inclusion of AI at the POC stage creates unprecedented opportunities for replenishing the information deficit, including:

- A current market state and its dynamics.
- Customer preferences and behavioral patterns.
- Market entry regulations and compliant practices.
- Technology perceptions and introduction timing.
- Current demand for a product and its fluctuations.

Quality data to feed AI models is essential for successful POC development. Still, the original data are insufficient and include noise and errors. Training AI models on insufficient data sets might result in incorrect POC assumptions. Creating the Dossier in the early stages of the startup's development is advisable.

The need to prepare data and operate with AI models increases demands on startup personnel. This topic will be discussed in the next chapter.

Chapter 3.2.
An AI-enforced Startup Team

Investors know that the success of a startup hinges on its team. And not just any team, but an exceptional one that can work harmoniously to transform an idea into a profitable venture. An ideal startup team comprises passionate founders with relevant experience, practical communication skills, and a knack for collaboration. In today's world, successful startups must have teams equipped with the skills and tools to make AI solutions a reality. While the AI market is booming and full of opportunities, established players with deep pockets challenge new entrants. However, with the right team mindset, quality data preparation, and a well-thought-out AI strategy, it is possible to conquer this market—a framework proposed to help founders tap into the strengths of their teams and show investors team qualities.

> **What does a real AI-oriented startup team look like?**

Startup Teams: Ideals and Reality

The critical component of the knowledge economy is human capital. With their skills and abilities to develop and perform efficient business models, startup team members shape human capital. Investors attach high importance to the quality of the team - future success or failure largely depends on it. Waiting for higher returns, investors look for teams that embrace innovation, incorporate diverse approaches, and stray away from traditional ways of problem-solving.

When sourcing startups that are about to enter the market, investors look for answers to the following questions:

- Who are the founders, and how do they understand their mission in the proposed business enterprise? Do they have relevant skills and experience? How does their track record of previous successes or failures look?

- What are the functions of individual team members? Are there any gaps in the management team, and how do they intend to fill them by hiring extra staff or outsourcing some business operations?

- What motivations keep individual members in the team? Do founders reserve some stock to attract talented employees shortly? How reasonable is their payroll system?

- How flexible does the management team adapt to a changing business environment? Who are the leaders? How well do the individual members collaborate as a team, solving inevitable conflicts and keeping the enterprise safe?

Startup Success Rate Statistics (2024) [8]

- First-time small business owners have a success rate of 18%.
- Business owners who failed in the past have a startup success rate of 20%.
- Business owners who started a successful startup in the past have a business success rate of around 30%.

In real life, most teams follow the same pattern: their members who studied at university together came up with the same idea and will implement it. Many startup teams are homogenous, meaning team members have similar education, skills, and other characteristics. This feature can manifest itself both positively and negatively.

On the positive side, such teams can work smoothly and without conflicts. Being created and managed by friends, the teams need minimal formal authority and control. On the negative side, homogenous teams cannot perform various business tasks, and the roles and responsibilities of their members need to be adequately defined. [9]

Recently, investors have realized that founders who can achieve great results with small capital in a bootstrapping mode can create a successful enterprise. Such startups keep personnel and expenses at a reasonably low level and leverage intangibles, getting profitable from the beginning (this topic will be discussed in detail in Chapter 8.1, "Art of Leveraging Minimal Resources."

A Startup Team Framework

While the team's features are mainly qualitative, investors need a framework to estimate the potential of a "dream team." A team's quality is often critical for investors when making funding decisions. Still, there needs to be more quantitative methods of team assessment in the market. A team development canvas can be used as the framework, taking into consideration the four groups of factors:

1. A strategic picture of a startup development - vision, mission, and team strategic positioning.
2. People and their roles include team members and advisors, key persons to hire, and independent specialists ready to outsource some functions.
3. Economic measures that make the team a well-coordinated and profit-oriented mechanism.
4. The team's dynamics include shared leadership, constructive conflicts, and psychological safety.

Nowadays, in a dynamically changing business environment, startup teams have to be more concerned with change than stability. However, many startups are rigid, and their members need help adapting to inevitable changes in roles, relationships, and equity splits. Most founders must prepare for changes and regularly revisit team members' roles, responsibilities, and equity splits. [9]

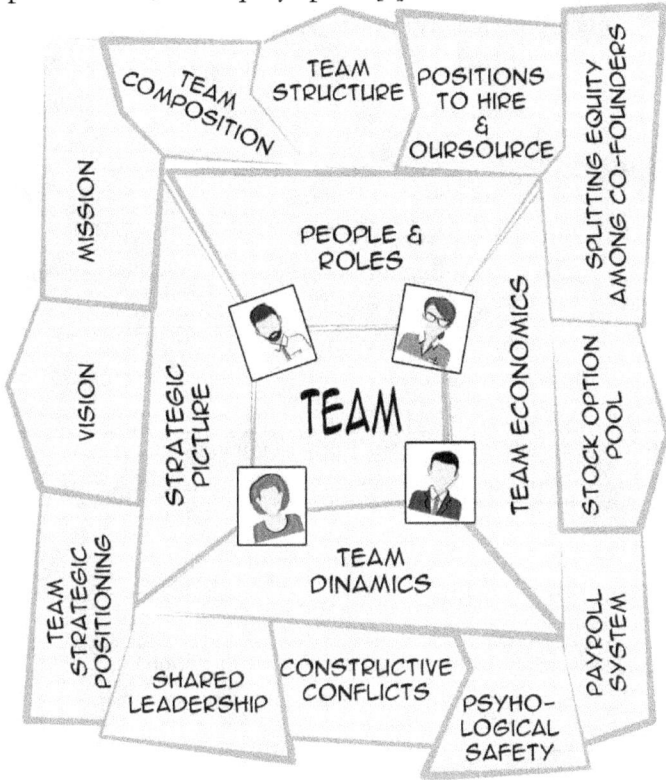

Traditionally, investors look for specific characteristics in startup founders, including intelligence, enthusiasm, integrity, determination, and team spirit. Indeed, these qualities can significantly impact a prospective startup's success. To truly embody these qualities, founders must break free from their comfort zones and embrace a transformative shift in mindset. They should relinquish the fear of constructive conflicts, for such clashes of ideas foster genuine innovation and growth. Moreover, they should embrace a dynamic reassessment of roles and shares, leaving behind the misguided notion of fairness and equality.

A Team Excellence Ladder

All factors in the team development canvas are dynamic and interrelated. To represent patterns embracing these factors, we combine them into ten relatively independent clusters. Each cluster's components can be ranked from Low to Medium to High according to their impact on business performance. Such an approach allows us to assess the degree of influence of each cluster on the probability of success.

1. Team strategic positioning

Up-start and re-start entrepreneurs who can learn from their mistakes and attract investment are the best startup founders.	HIGH
Entrepreneurs with up to three years of business experience can run a lifestyle enterprise oriented toward moderate sales and revenue.	MED
A product-oriented team formed from recent graduates with prospective business ideas/concepts needs help moving from a concept to a market.	LOW

2. Team composition

A heterogeneous team composition comprising engineering, finance, and sales specialists is ideal.	HIGH
More than a mainly homogeneous team composition focusing on technology is required for quality performance.	MED
Team members' roles and responsibilities blur the performance in a team composed of friends without formal authority.	LOW

3. Team structure

It is optimal to have a structure with a CEO who keeps the business running, a CMO who interacts with customers, and a CTO who is in technology.	**HIGH**
A typical structure with a technical CEO and a CFO has a technological bias with some blind spots in sales.	**MED**
An idea to determine the organizational structure in later stages must be corrected.	**LOW**

4. Splitting equity among co-founders

The best solution is when founders with unique roles in enterprise development have more shares.	**HIGH**
When a CEO has more shares, it is not a perfect solution: all founders must have appropriate economic stimuli.	**MED**
An equal equity split among co-founders looks like a fair solution but needs to make more economic sense.	**LOW**

5. Stock option pool

The 10% option pool is the best solution to avoid dilution in the following funding rounds.	**HIGH**
The 2-4% option pool could be a better solution. Talents should be invited and offered a bigger pack of shares.	**MED**
The idea of creating an option pool in later stages must be corrected.	**LOW**

6. Payroll system

When new employees are offered stock options with premiums depending on their contribution, it is the best solution.	HIGH
There are better solutions than a list of additional staff to hire. Further incentives for staff are needed.	MED
The idea of creating a payroll system in later stages needs to be corrected.	LOW

7. Team dynamics

When team members make decisions concerning their area of specialization, it is suitable for shared leadership and psychological safety.	HIGH
It is not a perfect solution when founders refrain from discussing disagreements openly and act via a CEO.	MED
When a CEO makes all significant decisions, a startup does not share leadership and avoids constructive conflicts.	LOW

8. Founders' entrepreneurship experience

A previous startup experience is the best.	HIGH
An experience from one year to three years is sufficient.	MED
An experience of less than one year is insufficient.	LOW

9. Founders' experience of working together

It is best if founders have successful experience in joint project development.	HIGH
If founders have worked together for over a year, they can perform satisfactorily.	MED
If founders meet to create a startup, they can encounter difficulties in determining their roles and relationships.	LOW

10. Proposed management style

It is the best solution if founders understand that their roles and responsibilities may change over time.	**HIGH**
It is not an optimal solution when founders keep their positions and allow investors to participate in making critical decisions only.	**MED**
If founders prefer to manage the enterprise with minimal outside interference from investors, this can be detrimental to future performance.	**LOW**

The guiding framework is intended for both startup team members and investors. For founders, the framework can help them better understand teams' strengths and weaknesses and prospective directions of improvement. The framework guides investors to rank teams' qualities as essential to investment decision-making.

PROFITomix Story

Digital Pizza

(Episode 8)

CAST:

Michael

Steve

Gippetio

Visionary
Investor

Startup
Founder

Bot

Michael picked up the texting conversation he started in the previous episode. The investor asked a tricky question about the qualifications of Digital Pizza members in part of AI applications in the proposed business. Steve needed help understanding the investor's demands. The founder was trying to make his way out. Still, the AI bot intruded into the conversation, demonstrating its erudition.

Hey, Steve.
Let me ask you one more thing about your team.

Hi, Michael; our team info is on slide 12 of our pitch deck.

I know. This is about your team members' AI skills. How can they test models with tools like AI Test Kitchen?

Did you say 'kitchen'?
We know a lot about it! If we need to pull an AI strap daily, we'll hire some nerds who know this stuff.

It's possible, but your team's getting bigger, responsibilities are changing, and salaries are increasing. Right?

We need more people. Look at the 12th slide again. You'll see our hiring plan.

Your plan is impressive, but Jobs once said any team should be small enough to share two pizzas. Otherwise, it would help if you cut more narrow slices for each extra AI specialist.

We can't develop Digital Pizza without hiring extra staff!

There's an alternative: apply gen AI to perform some management functions.

I don't know how to do it!

AI can help to optimize your 12th pitch slice's size with your team's megabyte size to bite. This will make your Indigestive Pitcheria look much better!

Michael! It's that bot again with some geometry nonsense!

This isn't nonsense! It's about your AI readiness. Once upon a time, Pythagoras said: "μηδεὶς ἀγεωμέτρητος εἰσίτω μου τὴν στέγην."

Now I'm stuck in a foreign language!

In fact, it's Greek. I'll translate it for you: "Let no one ignorant of geometry enter."

What Do Investors Look at in AI Startup Teams?

As the market becomes more saturated with AI-based startups, more is needed for investors to check the right combination of skills, experience, and attitude in founders. VCs look for ways to qualify teams' AI capabilities that set them apart. What makes a great AI startup team? First, the team must have some experience with AI. Second, their AI business solution should be marketable to attract customers and eventually make a profit. Finally, this solution has yet to be evident in protecting a startup from inevitable competition. Furthermore, corporate behemoths have already captured visible areas on their giant platforms where they can rapidly add features similar to those proposed by startups. [10]

Hah! Let's say a new UBER for the toilet paper delivery just in time. Isn't it boring?

Even if a startup wisely avoids areas occupied by incumbents, corporate players possess foundation models that are difficult for startups to develop, train, test, and validate. Besides the high costs involved, startups' efforts to build their foundation models or essential superstructures above somebody's models are risky: the models that startups train today may become obsolete tomorrow. Startups can use providers of tools for AI model training, AI testing and validation tools, and AI monitoring and deployment tools. Providers offer cloud-based solutions or dedicated servers with better user control and flexibility but at higher prices. [7]

A recent survey shows that only 1% of startups have staff with the necessary AI skills. In comparison, 69% understand generative AI adoption as a top priority. They plan to hire AI specialists (24%) or train their personnel (12%). Startups are unprepared to integrate generative AI in their businesses, lack clear business cases, and lack the right team skills to implement AI solutions. To develop and implement generative AI, they need external facilitators to help with four things: model testing and validation, algorithm development and optimization, integration with existing systems and infrastructure, and data acquisition and processing. [11]

Investors see many startups that promise to revolutionize the industry with AI solutions. But what directions have real potential? There are five principal directions of AI integration in startup business models:

1. Building a product around generative AI from the ground up is the best way for a startup to differentiate. Using this method, a startup could dramatically re-design current systems so incumbents cannot compete in data and distribution, or existing products become obsolete.

2. Startups can gain a competitive advantage by adding value to foundational models, training AI to produce desired results, or improving a model's user interface. They can also provide access to proprietary data that other companies can use to train and customize their models.

3. Many companies need more expertise in generative AI, and startups that can support them are doomed to succeed. Potential services include helping companies manage and prepare their data for AI models, train models, and evaluate and experiment with models.

4. With AI, startups can leverage their strengths, such as an established customer base or an excellent distribution channel. By improving user experience, startups can attract more users who produce more data to feed models, thus making a better customer experience.

5. By employing generative AI, a startup can improve its team's productivity via automation and the augmentation of work previously performed by humans. AI-managed bookkeeping, data gathering and analysis, and content creation have become cheaper, helping startups grow more capital-efficiently, especially in bootstrapping mode. [6]

Key Takeaways

Research proves that investors prioritize team performance above all factors when considering investment opportunities. The strength of teams is just as crucial as AI's potential for driving innovation to secure attractive financing from savvy investors. By strategically building an AI-empowered team and demonstrating its capabilities, startups pave the way for success.

With a team engaging in AI, a startup can constantly drive innovation, boost production efficiency, exceed customer expectations, and achieve significant cost savings through automation. However, entering this marketing battleground can be intimidating for newcomers. Founders must navigate strategically, avoiding competition with established players. Moreover, the threat of incumbents copying startups' offerings is real, limiting their competitive advantage.

As AI startups push the boundaries, investors need to understand the generative AI capabilities of the teams they back. New quantitative techniques supplement well-known qualitative methods for assessing startup teams. Internal AI applications can help startups overcome current challenges and keep expenses reasonable.

Chapter 3.3.
Market Entry Strategies & Timing

Investors and startup founders feel intuitively the significance of well-executed market entry strategies and perfect timing. However, a few might rely on experience, while the rest need appropriate tools. Choosing the right approach and opportune moment is a two-fold concept that depends on the current business landscape and the startup's intangible assets. A Market Entry Ladder and a Startup's Market Entry Crossroad model are the tools to quantify entry decision-making by considering crucial factors of the business environment and creating plausible market entry scenarios. For startups, scenario planning allows for identifying positive and negative outcomes of different entry strategies and assessing their impact on future business performance. Furthermore, this approach replaces the arbitrary selection process traditionally employed by investors.

> **How vital are market entry strategies and timing for a new project?**

Ancient Roots of a Market Entry Idea

Market entry timing is critical for a new project's success. [4] A startup can be a "first-mover," a pioneer who enters the market to offer and sell its product or service. Otherwise, a startup is a "late-mover" that enters the market after the first movers. Both entry modes have advantages and disadvantages. First-movers have an early head-start, leadership, cost efficiency, and reputation advantages. On the other hand, late-movers can benefit from spillovers, imitating first-movers' products and strategies, lowering market uncertainty and risks, and capturing their customer base.

Historically, the topic of first and late movers appeared in Sun Tzu's 5th-century BC book "The Art of War," which was related to war strategies. [12] Despite its antiquity and military terminology, the book's explanation of the advantages and disadvantages of the first and late movers may be helpful for modern startups.

For the first movers, Sun Tzu recommends: "...*be before the enemy in occupying the raised and sunny spots, and carefully guard your line of supplies. Then you will be able to fight with advantage.*" Today, supplies are understood broadly as intangibles, including distribution agreements, reputation, and customer loyalty.

For the late movers, Sun Tzu suggests: "*From a position of this sort, if the enemy is unprepared, you may sally forth and defeat him.*" Then he adds: "*Should the army forestall you in occupying a pass, do not go after him if the pass is fully garrisoned, but only if it is weakly garrisoned.*" In modern surroundings, this should be understood as a call to attack the weakly protected assets of a competitor, primarily intangibles.

Intangible assets play a crucial role in the startup market entry due to their properties: lack of a physical substance, non-rivalry, and partial appropriability. Recent studies show how intangibles influence market entry strategies:

- High levels of intangible assets increase the likelihood of a startup's successful market entry.
- The first entrants with a high level of intangible assets benefit from them more than later entrants.
- Startups with high intangible levels can employ more aggressive market policies than startups with low intangible levels.
- Low intangible-level startups must enter markets slowly and carefully to avoid an open confrontation. (See Section 1, "Intangible Wealth Hidden in Plain Sight") for more details.

Modeling Market Entry Strategies

Interdependence between high and low-intangible-intensive startups that can be first or last movers form the first dimension of possible market entry strategies. [13] Another dimension of market entry is a choice between competition and collaboration. Some startups create IP and protect it, while others can rely heavily on spillovers via appropriation of their competitors' IP. In the second dimension, startups should decide whether to compete or collaborate depending on their opportunities to take advantage of someone else's IP.

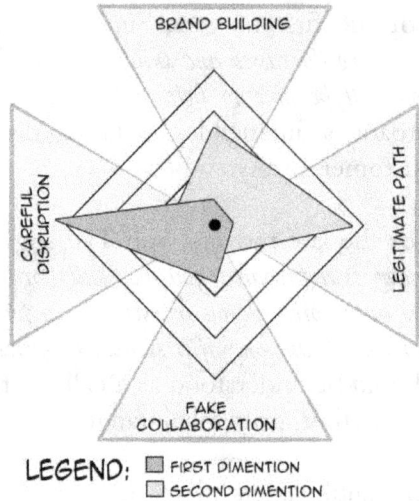

Combining both dimensions, we get a Startup's Market Entry Crossroad model in which the four possible market entry strategies have proper quantification:

The Brand-building strategy requires high intangibles to be a first mover, carefully protecting its IP and competing with incumbents.

The Legitimate Path strategy is for late movers that have their IP and collaborate with incumbents, building contract-based relationships.

The Careful Disruption strategy is suitable for late movers with a medium level of intangibles. They undertake a quick market penetration while incumbents overlook their activities.

The Fake Collaboration strategy is also for late movers with low intangibles. They avoid competition by looking for collaboration with incumbents. However, their collaboration is a temporary trick to gain a foothold in the market. They will then be ready to start doing business under their brand, breaking up with an ex-partner.

110

The Real Story of Fake Collaboration (This story began in Chapter 1.3, "Investing in Intangibles: Pros and Cons."

Advanced Micro Devices (AMD), a small company, worked as an Intel contractor. After AMD and Intel parted ways, AMD reverse-engineered Intel's chips to make its products compatible with Intel's x86 software. Intel sued AMD, but a settlement in 1995 gave AMD the right to continue designing x86 chips. AMD became the most dangerous rival for Intel in 2006. In 2008, the FBI arrested Biswamohan Pani, an engineer who had resigned from his position at Intel and had already been hired by AMD. Pani had access to Intel's trade secrets, and he had stolen data about a future Intel chip, causing damage of one billion dollars. [14]

A Market Entry Ladder

It is necessary to consider the critical factors of the economic environment to foresee the performance of startup strategies. These factors are dynamic and interrelated. To represent patterns embracing these factors, we combine them into five relatively independent clusters. Each cluster's components can be ranked from Low to Medium to High according to their impact. It allows us to assess the degree of influence of each cluster on the startup's performance.

1. Customer preferences

Customers are waiting for really innovative products and services.	HIGH
Customers expect more convenient access to products and services, transparency, and a better experience.	MED
Customers believe that existing technology can adequately solve their problems.	LOW

2. Investors' attitude toward innovations

High expectations regarding disruptive innovations that lead to radical changes in the market.	**HIGH**
The common opinion is that new technological solutions can enhance economic performance and social well-being.	**MED**
The belief is that existing technology can be repurposed for new business applications.	**LOW**

3. Compatibility of new products

Customers are ready to adjust their routines to be compatible with new products.	**HIGH**
Customers are ready to educate themselves to use innovative products and services.	**MED**
Customers want products that are consistent with their current experience.	**LOW**

4. Government and industry regulations

There is a regulatory shift: regulations become more complex and stricter.	**HIGH**
The government must prepare to respond to the quick changes with new regulations.	**MED**
Regulations need to be updated and focused on existing in the market technologies.	**LOW**

5. The level of technology and infrastructure, including AI

The market has many disruptive technological solutions, and the infrastructure is well-developed.	**HIGH**
Technology is still behind social expectations, and the new infrastructure is in its infancy.	**MED**
Incremental technological solutions and appropriate infrastructure dominate the market.	**LOW**

Incremental technologies are like strolling, and disruptive technologies are like running a marathon - they'll both get you there. Choose one that gives you more fun!"

Joint viewing of the Startup's Market Entry Crossroad model and business environment clusters gives a rich picture of the startup market entry. Startup founders can develop and show investors the various outcomes and options of the four strategies. A scenario approach is intended to replace the random choice that investors have traditionally used.

PROFITomix Story

Digital Pizza

(Episode 9)

CAST:

Michael

Steve

Gippetio

Visionary
Investor

Startup
Founder

Bot

Michael was on the precipice of making an investment decision. Still, something continued to linger in his mind, haunting his thoughts. Michael felt that AI bots could be better and not immune to hallucinations. He believed in the merits of balanced human-machine solutions. During the texting conversation, the bot resurfaced again, confirming Michael's worst fears. Steve, this time, supports the bot's exotic statements.

Hey, Steve! It's about time we wrap up your startup's screening, but I have another topic to discuss.

Hi Michael! I'm all ears.

It's about robots you use intensively...they have some unique features.

Sure! Robots are faster and more precise, never take sick days, and certainly don't demand a salary increase!

Exactly! That's what we strive for.

I think we rely too much on robots...sometimes.

Eventually, humans will get so reliant on AI that they'll forget how to think for themselves!

There is an unresolved problem with robots - they can hallucinate.

Robots have become increasingly autonomous and capable – they can create delicious hallucinations!

I need to catch the problem.

The problem is that bots can create problems!

Let's say we decide to cook a mushroom pizza...

...and the robot produces the magic mushroom topping. Order now and never pay too late!

Wow! Magic mushroom topping. It could be our slogan. Thanks, Gippetio!

You're welcome! This psilocybin shrooms topping will create a spiritual customer experience! I can continue...

This is precisely what concerns me.

Three Market Entry and Timing Scenarios

The scenario approach allows startups to tell a story with different possible outcomes. For startups, scenario planning helps to identify positive and negative consequences and estimate their impacts on business performance. Investors can see pessimistic, realistic, and optimistic scenarios comprehensively picture the startup's market entry.

To develop scenarios, startup founders need quality information that they can find handy in the Startup Dossiers (see more details in Section 2, " A Data-driven Approach for VCs and Startups "). The examples of pessimistic, realistic, and optimistic scenarios for an early entrant help choose a market entry strategy considering specific startup goals and the current business environment.

An Optimistic Scenario

Early movers can establish a dominant position before new competitors join the market. They can enjoy the low level or absence of government regulations and industry restrictions. While customers' interest in innovations is growing, they are ready to change their consumption habits and routines. The market and technology infrastructure are adjusted to existing products and technologies, creating new business opportunities. IP is not safeguarded with patents and trademarks to prevent unsanctioned copying by savvy newcomers. Investors are interested in innovative technologies but need an understanding of their functionality and competitive advantages. As a result, their expectations about projected profitability and valuations of startups should be more accurately measured.

A Realistic Scenario

Entering the market, early movers find the growing government regulation activity that increases business expenses for compliance and licensing. While customers are interested in innovations, they continue to be led by previously formed routines. Startups must alter the utilities and functionalities of their new products to fit current customers' habits. The market and technology infrastructure are ready for incremental innovations. To estimate the IP protection level, complete expensive technical due diligence is required. Investors are focused on existing products in the market; only some are ready to fund projects promising higher-than-average ROI. Startups' valuations correspond to the average prevailing on the market.

A Pessimistic Scenario

Early movers discover that the market is saturated and competition is rather challenging. Customers' acceptance of new products and technology could be higher. Regulations and incumbents' activities can create additional barriers for newcomers. Some business solutions are more expensive than projected, new business models do not work as planned, and innovations must have declared qualities. Investors become overly cautious, while estimates fall several times lower than the previous market average.

Employing the Startup Market Entry Crossroad model and a data-driven scenario approach requires changing data management for startup founders and investors. Founders have to prepare quality information in their Dossiers. Instead of their customary haphazard search, investors must focus on the scenario approach augmented with their heuristics and intuition. As a result, they will get better insight and higher accuracy of results.

Key Takeaways

Market entry strategies and timing are potent factors in startup operations and investors' decisions. A wrong market entry strategy or timing can lead to catastrophic losses, so investors heavily weigh this factor when deciding whether to invest in a startup. At the same time, founders must analyze market conditions and provide insights into the best market entry strategies and optimal timing. It's like a chess game – every move counts and the wrong move at the wrong time can ultimately lead to failure.

Interacting Startup Market Entry Crossroad and Market Entry Ladder models might be supplemented with a generative AI bot to form a user case. This bot can work in two modes. In the first mode, the bot serves founders who use information from their Startup Dossier to feed and test the combined foundation model. Founders self-learn market entry strategies while at the same time fine-tuning the foundation model.

When the foundation model is tested sufficiently by founders, it is ready to work in the second mode, serving investors who want to check market entry situations for target startups. This user case can be implemented in two ways. The first is as a layer on top of a third-party API. This approach is the quickest and cheapest way where there is an API provider. Second, an in-house fine-tuning model is much more expensive and flexible. In this case, VCs and startups can be served at an independent facilitator platform. [6, Sec. 2]

However, it is essential to note that not all market entry strategies are created equal. Some strategies may work in certain situations, while others may not. The AI-empowered data-driven approach has the potential to overcome market entry challenges. This tool provides startups and investors with a better understanding of the competitive landscape, consumer behavior, and investors' preferences. Therefore, this approach can be used to identify the most efficient market entry strategies and timing.

Points to Ponder

Intangibles are becoming increasingly crucial to business success in part of market entry. The data-driven approach in the Startup Dossier helps startup founders gather data from multiple sources to feed the Startup's Market Entry Crossroad model and develop viable entry strategies.

Information in the Startup Dossier allows startups to reveal four intangible perspectives, including:

- Customer benefits.
- Product/service's remarkable features.
- Cooperation-related.
- Regulations-related.

Brainstorm to estimate the main intangible factors that influence market entry:

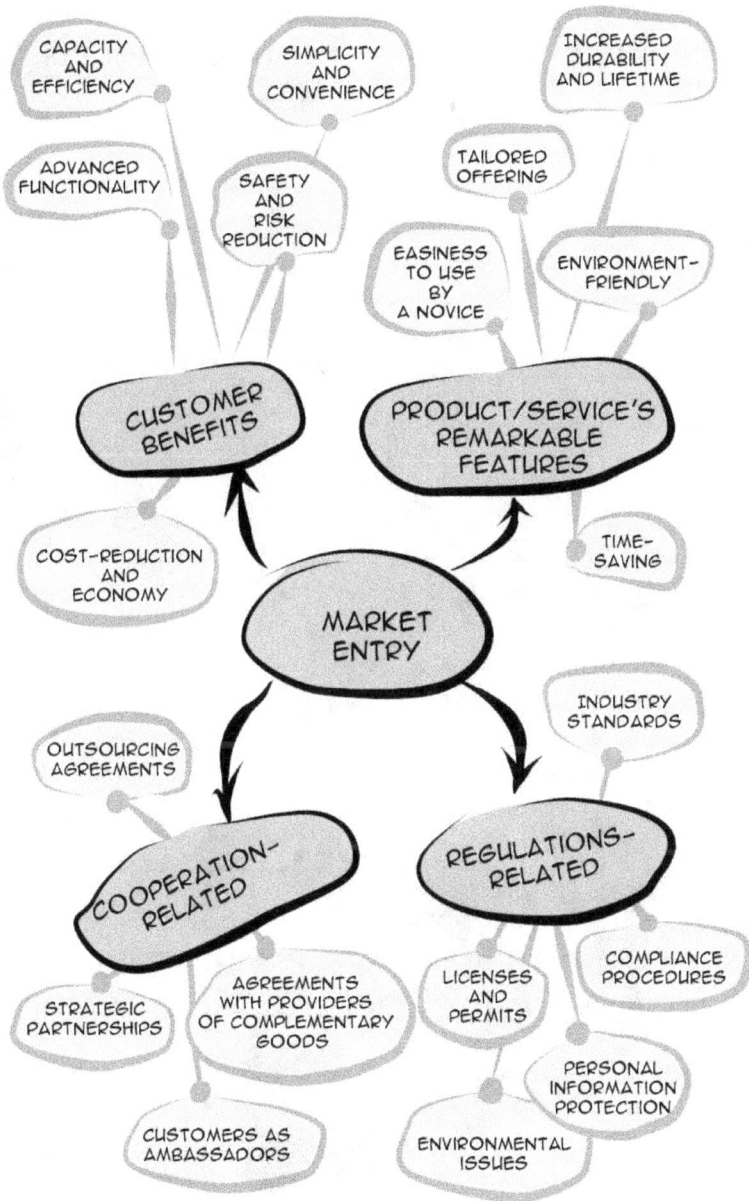

Section 4
Intangible-intensive Business Models

Nowadays, technology-driven businesses rely more and more on intangible assets. Creating new business models encompassing intangible assets has become essential for them to thrive in the rapidly changing economic environment. AI plays a significant role in this transformation, enabling innovative companies to efficiently manage and analyze data for better insights, leading to better decision-making. This approach allows for leveraging comprehensive information repositories like the Startup Dossier and specialized algorithms on top of AI generative models. Thus, startups and investors can enable accurate calculations, scenario modeling, and reporting — critical tools for success in the new knowledge economy.

Venture capitalists are looking for alternative methods of financing, and Just-In-Time (JIT) funding is one of the most promising solutions. Unlike traditional upfront funding, the JIT scheme provides startups with the only necessary amount of capital when required. AI-powered JIT enables startups to access capital efficiently and cost-effectively by accurately forecasting costs and modeling a positive cash balance. In this way, startups can focus on creating value instead of being in a cash-strapped position. For VCs, JIT funding with AI modeling is a game changer, reducing risks and dilution.

The time has come to shift our focus from solely financial indicators to encompass the intangible factors that drive long-term success in the VC world. By looking beyond traditional valuation methods, we can gain valuable insights into a team's effectiveness in creating, acquiring, and deploying intangibles. While there is no universal method for the new intangible concept, it is possible to use proxies and AI algorithms to create the framework for intangible valuation. Measuring the value of startups in today's VC market would be helpful for all its players.

Chapter 4.1.
Business Model Innovation

Entrepreneurs commonly understand a business model as the critical factor of startup success. Accordingly, it is a crucial determinant for investors when making funding decisions. These days, entrepreneurs adopt strategies that break away from traditional methods and prioritize innovative approaches – mainly relying on intangible assets, a data-driven approach, and generative AI. By focusing on intangible assets, startups can create highly profitable and sustainable business models. By gathering and processing data effectively, startups can gain insights into emerging opportunities. By leveraging the power of generative AI, startups can cut costs and create innovative solutions tailored to the needs of their customers. Investors who understand the nature of business model innovation will not miss lucrative opportunities.

> ## How do intangibles, data, and generative AI change the VC realm?

A Long History of Business Modeling

The business model is a framework that allows a startup to create and then deliver an innovative product or service and do it profitably. Thank God profitability is not in doubt today! Using modeling is like building a brick house using clay, but instead of bricks, we employ algorithms. It is hard to believe, but the first business model was made from clay over 5,000 years ago.

Archaeological excavations have discovered that during the Late Uruk period (3,500-3,100 BCE), Babylonians used clay tokens to represent different material assets. They put the sets of clay tokens with descriptions of some goods in hollow clay spheres and seal them. Finally, the spheres were baked like bricks, making tokens inaccessible without the destruction of sealed spheres. [1]

Thus, the ancients created models of assets and protected information in their clay ledgers from being changed. They solved the problem of security and asset protection long before the discovery of blockchain.

Babylonians called the spheres *bullae*, which means "bubble."

Who would have thought that creating bubbles in business has such ancient roots?

Designing Business Models

Definitions of the business model structure are varied and contradictory (do you remember the Buddhist parable of the blind men and an elephant?):

- Resources, competencies, organizational structures, and value proposition (some necessary components are missing).

125

- Activity systems, structures, and governance (unnecessary components are present).
- Value proposition, market, internal capability, competitive strategy, economic, and personal/investor factors (everything related to business is listed excessively).
- Value proposition, profit formula, essential resources, and processes (this definition is much better). [2]

None of the definitions mention innovativeness, which is an inherent startup feature. Moreover, designing an effective business model is a crucial prerequisite for success. Thus, the best definition of business models is the "design or architecture of the value creation, delivery, and capture mechanisms." [3] Business model innovations are not necessarily associated with innovative products. For instance, many startups created successful businesses that delivered ordinary goods: food, razor blades, or socks. Besides, there are no technological innovations like AI or IoT; instead, there are intelligent business solutions.

PROFITomix Story:

Digital Pizza

(Episode 10)

CAST:

Linda

Investor
Profiteer

Steve

Startup
Founder

Linda received a Digital Pizza pitch, skimmed through it, and decided to talk to the founder. She wanted to understand what was unique about this startup's business model and hoped to uncover Digital Pizza's secrets. Step by step, Steve told her a story about their secret recipe of the ancient dough that could serve as the plot for a novel. Linda does not hide her disbelief.

Hey, Steve, my name's Linda. I've invested in the food industry before and am curious how you model your pizza. Did you study modern nutritionist recommendations or something?

Never! We reject modern methods and go the old way.

It's strange to hear that these days. What's the matter?

Well, let me tell you, it's all about the dough!

I always thought the topping was the key to a good pizza.

Nope, it's the dough!

But aren't all pizzas made from the same dough?

Absolutely! They all use refined white flour. So, their pizzas taste like cardboard.

And yours?

Our pizza dough is a unique blend of whole wheat, millet, rye, and barley flour. We let it rest and rise for a whopping 36 hours. It's no wonder our pizza is so tasty!

How did you come across this unique recipe?

Believe it or not, it's an ancient recipe that dates back 1,200 years. We obtained it from an Italian guy who excavated a papyrus-filled amphora at a construction site in Ercolano. If you recall, Ercolano was built on the ruins of the buried town of Herculaneum, ravaged by Mount Vesuvius's eruption in AD 79.

Wait a minute, are you telling me this guy found the dough recipe in the ancient papyrus?

The recipe claims to have been passed down from the gods!

Wow, that's quite a tale! But I'm not one to invest in fiction. I prefer to dig up the truth for myself!

According to Italian laws, if you want to dig it in Italy, you must commission an archeologist!

By designing three main elements of new models, we create the whole business system:

- Business system content shows how the proposed solutions generate value in a target market niche:
- Business system structure determines how to deliver value to customers.
- Business system governance focuses on keeping models working (or fixing them if necessary) and monetizing value. [4]

All companies somehow use data, but a business model may be qualified as "data-driven" once it uses data as its essential resource. Analytics is part of a data-driven business model, but first, it's about collecting and turning data into information. There is no need to sell data; it can be any product or service that relies on data. To have a good reason for saying "data-driven," data must be vital to the business model. [5]

Intangible-intensive Business Models

Another feature of the innovative business model is its focus on intangible assets and solutions. Using an intangible-intensive business model, a startup can reach profitability with significantly less capital than with a tangible-intensive business model. Furthermore, by employing intangible-intensive models, startups can become profitable quicker than those who rely mainly on tangible assets.

Startups employing tangible business models:

- Work in a heavily regulated environment, using licenses and permits.
- Use manual procedures and an instruction-based approach.
- Use conventional financial analysis to conduct standardized feasibility studies.
- Use in-house business processes.
- Focus on competitive advantages and fighting against rivals.
- Scale up slowly, while scaling down is a disaster.

Startups employing intangible-intensive business models look different:

- Work in temporarily unregulated niches and appropriate third-party intangibles.
- Use a data-driven approach and algorithms.
- While methods of intangible management are still being developed, use proxies.
- Actively outsource business processes.
- Focus on profitability, partnering, and cooperating.
- Scale up quickly and scale down if necessary, without essential losses.

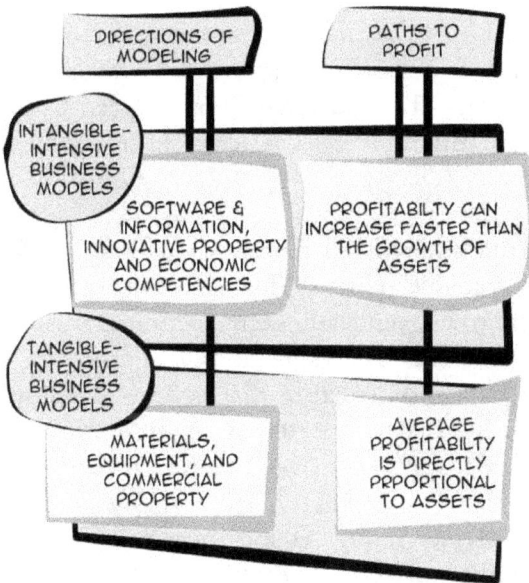

Business practices of startups employing intangible and tangible assets look different:

Even relying on intangible assets, the startup might employ tangible assets, too. That is why it is necessary to use a hybrid approach, considering the integration of both types of assets. However, business models for tangible and intangible assets have different structures and investment perspectives.

Summarizing the advantages of intangible-intensive business models for startups:

- Startups can own a minimum of physical assets for their critical business operations and outsource some non-essential ones.

- Intangible-intensive models fit technology businesses, helping them to scale up faster than traditional tangible-intensive enterprises.
- The structure of assets itself is a source of higher-than-average profitability, which is enhanced by the inherited properties of intangibles.

As a result, such startups with high profitability, scalability, and lower capital requirements become extremely attractive to investors.

Benefits and Pitfalls of Integrating AI in Business Models

The adoption of generative AI in the structure of new business models promises increases in efficiency that translate into higher profits and the exponential growth of businesses. To understand how AI can impact economic performance, we identify three ways AI changes the elements of the business models. [3]

The first way is to exploit the inherent AI feature to replace humans with algorithms, lowering variable costs. This method is mainly incremental and leads to improving and automating internal business processes. For the internal processes' reorganization, it is necessary to build a "data pipeline," the data infrastructure that collects structured and unstructured data from internal and external sources (for more detail, see Chapter 2.3, "Generating a Data-driven Startup Dossier").

The second innovative way of integrating AI into business models is changing the nature of market players' interactions. This involves investments in virtual reality solutions and generative AI bots to improve interfaces.

The third way of AI integration allows startups to generate new "smart" products and services or create "intelligent" variations of existing products. New or modified AI-powered products can create new values.

These three ways are not mutually exclusive; startups can employ them simultaneously. However, a startup must acknowledge its potential drawbacks in employing generative AI. Generative AI models reflect the data on which they are trained. If the data contains biases, the model will perpetuate it. Consequently, discriminatory or wrong outputs may arise. Once trained, generative AI models can sometimes deviate from the intended outputs. This uncertainty poses issues, particularly when sensitive content such as financial information is involved. Developing AI models can be expensive, especially for startups with limited budgets. [6]

Key Takeaways

Today, the terms "data-driven," "intangible-intensive," and "AI-empowered" have become buzzwords. But their significance goes far beyond just jargon. Data is at the forefront of IT discussions, yet many businesses still need to grasp its potential fully. Similarly, accounting actively develops intangibles, but entrepreneurs must know their importance. While generative AI is mainly associated with entertainment, its practical applications extend far away from that realm. It's a shame that entrepreneurs often overlook these concepts while they hold substantial weight regarding startup funding and subsequent success. They are complementary and intricately interconnected in the world of business.

A startup can gather data from different sources and processes it into information for decision-making (becoming data-driven).

A data-driven approach allows a startup to identify and deploy intangibles (building an intangible-intensive business model).

All of the above form the basis of an innovative disruption strategy (providing quality data and designing elements for creating specialized models for generative AI).

In business model innovation, startups must focus on three facets: the prevailing intangible assets in business, a data-driven approach, and the growing influence of generative AI. By focusing on the growth of intangible potential, startups can develop highly profitable and sustainable business models. Relying on data enables startups to gain valuable insights into new opportunities, leading to more significant returns. Generative AI helps companies stay competitive by reducing costs and introducing personalization.

Chapter 4.2.
Just-in-time funding

Venture capitalists are actively seeking innovative financing schemes to fund startups. One such scheme is JIT funding. Unlike traditional upfront financing, JIT funding provides the necessary cash precisely when needed. By integrating the JIT model into the VC industry, venture capitalists can potentially reduce costs and offer startups access to vital funds at critical moments. However, the successful implementation of JIT relies on several key elements working harmoniously, including quality proprietary information, advanced financial projections, and well-defined road maps. Integrating JIT funding and AI tools would potentially disrupt the traditional VC financing model, providing the necessary capital when required without compromising equity. This innovative scheme offers a range of benefits, including reduced investment risks, increased efficiency, and lowered dilution.

> **How can entrepreneurs integrate the "Just-In-Time" scheme into funding practices?**

Origins of the JIT System

The JIT manufacturing model, born in the early 1970s, was a game-changer. Spearheaded by the visionary Taiichi Ohno, it disrupted the production process, enabling prompt delivery of consumer demands. Starting in Toyota, the birthplace of JIT, this ground-breaking theory quickly caught on across diverse Japanese industries, transforming automobiles and electronics. Today, JIT has gone global, providing a fresh perspective on goods availability and minimizing inventory. By embracing JIT's strategic principles and customizing them to fit unique industry needs, startups can achieve remarkable gains in efficiency and cost-effectiveness.

JIT is not just limited to manufacturing; it can be applied to various services, too. Using JIT methods can help service providers improve the quality of their offerings. The principles of JIT, such as synchronization, balanced information, streamlined workflow, process visibility, continuous improvement, and waste elimination, make it a perfect fit for any services sector. With JIT, service providers can optimize their operations and deliver exceptional experiences to their customers. [7]

Financial services often encounter productivity challenges and high costs due to their intricate procedures and systems. To tackle these expenses, providers are continually exploring innovative solutions. One viable approach is to adopt lean principles, specifically JIT concepts, to streamline operations in the finance sector. By merging the fundamental tenets of JIT with the distinctive features of financial services, enterprises can boost their economic performance by minimizing cycle times and optimizing the utilization of financial resources. This strategic alignment helps enhance efficiency, reduce costs, and drive success in the dynamic world of financial services.

Using JIT in the VC Industry

Financing a new business project poses a challenge for both investors and startup founders. It makes sense to withhold upfront funding from an investor's perspective until the founders' execution and behavior are known. After all, some founders tend to waste money, regardless of the venture's success. However, underfunding can prevent startups from reaching planned milestones and ultimately lead to project failure. The alternative JIT funding model emerges as a reasonable compromise.

Embracing the JIT model requires cautious steps and a keen anticipation of its inherent challenges. Let's explore the four hurdles that investors and founders must conquer on the path to implementing JIT funding:

- The ability to provide real-time financial data becomes paramount, empowering informed decision-making.
- A resourceful and agile team can leverage minimal resources, resulting in remarkable outcomes.
- Crafting a well-determined roadmap gives a clear direction toward success.
- Effective collaboration between founders and investors is crucial to prevent friction or breakdown, fostering a strong and harmonious partnership.

PROFITomix Story

Digital Pizza

(Episode 11)

CAST:

Michael

Robert

Visionary
Investor

Investor
Traditionalist

After Michael's workshop, "Healthy Chunks of Financing Served in Time," for investors, Robert texted Michael about the merits of just-in-time funding. With his traditional background, Robert must fully realize this revolutionary idea. Michael employed food analogies to clarify the proposed scheme of startup financing.

Hi Michael!
I just attended your workshop. Robert is the name. I'm curious about how to implement your idea.

Hey, Robert! First, it's not my idea but Toyoda's. He put forward and implemented so many ideas that they continue to feed an army of consultants. To clarify this idea, I'd like to use a food analogy.

OK, talking about food is good, especially before dinner!

The current tradition of financing startups upfront is like serving dinner for breakfast. Instead of giving a startup a big chunk of cash up front, investors provide them with funding in small bites as needed.

Ha! I recently met a startup that offered pizza for breakfast.

I have a funny story, too. I met a startup that offered to use dinner pizza leftovers for breakfast!

It looks like a financial pyramid when its organizers pay dividends from new contributions. I hope this is a different startup!

Yeah, that's a good point! But think about it—would you eat an entire pizza all at once? Of course not. You take it slice by slice, just like startups take their funding as needed.

But what if the pizza guy is late with the slices? That could ruin everything!

That's why JIT funding requires advanced financial projections and a well-defined road map for the startup. It's like a pizza delivery guy knowing when a customer's hungry and using GPS for the quickest route!

I see now...I was always afraid that an overfunded startup wouldn't know how to use excess funding. There's a chance they fund a side project with my money!

Or worse, they eat all the pizza for dinner, leaving nothing for breakfast, just a sore stomach!

Integrating JIT in Startup Funding

The idea of JIT financing presents a unique and valuable approach to equity financing. Unlike traditional upfront funding, JIT funding is characterized by recurring installments, ideally suited for the dynamic nature of the technology business. It requires exceptional algorithmic modeling and result analysis. However, when executed correctly, this on-demand funding strategy can position a startup for financial success.

Integrating JIT into the startup funding process begins with meticulous financial projections. VCs have borrowed and adapted projection methods from established financial analysis practices for operating enterprises. By applying these methods, they can identify development trends and assess the effectiveness of financial, marketing, and investment management. While financial planning results are only demonstrative for future businesses, VCs have developed standardized approaches and criteria for evaluating investments in tangible assets.

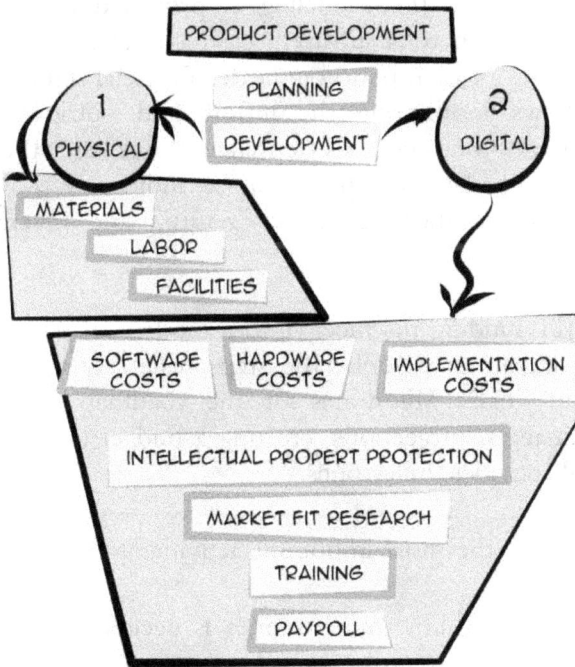

With the JIT model of funding, startup founders can determine precisely how much capital they need and show investors how every deployed dollar generates returns. The mutually beneficial advantages of using the JIT model for VCs and startups include:

- A more significant ROI than upfront funding due to the more efficient use of funds.
- Reduced dilution due to lessened initial rounds of venture capital.
- The JIT model can be automated, becoming an efficient, streamlined, and easy-to-use tool.
- Getting working capital on demand allows us to bridge potential cash flow gaps. [8]

Financial Modeling for JIT Funding

The critical aspect of JIT modeling is projected cash flow, which determines whether there is sufficient cash available. Having a positive balance at the end of each period indicates financial stability. Cash flow projection allows monitoring the inflow and outflow of financial resources for the business. Entrepreneurs can use these financial estimations to calculate key performance indicators (KPIs) such as economic stability ratios, rates of return, and overall business performance.

The idea of JIT funding fits nicely into a modern planning concept by building a roadmap to describe the steps necessary to achieve stated outcomes and goals. Milestones of the roadmap are linked with appropriate financial projections, creating a budget integrated with the most essential activities/milestones:

- Identifying the most important activities to perform to achieve startup goals.
- Understanding how much money is necessary to perform each activity.

- Forming all of the roadmap's significant components: milestones, duration of actions, due dates, and costs.

Suppose financial projections show a disruption of the cash flow positive balance. In that case, it is necessary to improve an operating leverage scheme (the ratio of total fixed costs to total variable costs). Enterprises with high fixed costs have high operating leverage, and those with large variable expenses have low leverage. Reducing both types of costs allows us to achieve a positive balance.

To reduce fixed costs, it is possible to:

- Operate from cheaper facilities.
- Outsource parts of business operations, converting some fixed costs into variable costs.
- Hire some staff on a contract basis.
- Replace some customer service staff with an intelligent bot.
- Rent the equipment instead of buying it.
- Use the third parties' spillovers.

Measures to reduce variable costs include:

- Make a product less labor-intensive via automatization.
- Use suppliers with reduced costs of materials and goods.
- Systematize and standardize business processes.

Just-in-time funding needs quality data and modeling algorithms to outline money demand correctly. The main steps of modeling cash flow input and output include:

1. Check a cash balance - it cannot be negative.
2. If it has any negative numbers - balance them using founders' or investors' contributions until they become positive.
3. Round up figures and add 10% of contingency expenses.
4. If necessary, repeat the modeling cycle from any step.

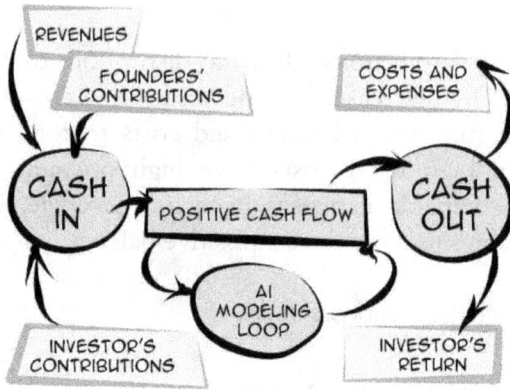

The main problem is that manual modeling to achieve cash flow balance is labor-intensive and time-consuming. Automating the process by creating an AI modeling loop can be a practical solution to this problem.

Modeling JIT Funding with AI

Financial modeling can be more accessible and more practical by leveraging AI-powered models. An AI model should supplement a traditional feasibility study algorithm to use this opportunity successfully. Combining AI's capacity to make quick iterations with a cash flow-producing feasibility algorithm allows us to fine-tune projections with many variating costs. Thus, the JIT funding decision-making process becomes more agile, which accommodates the dynamic nature of technology projects.

Some tools are necessary to satisfy businesses' demands for AI-driven financial modeling. These solutions simplify the process of AI-driven financial modeling and provide an efficient technique for dealing with related data.

I offer the ChatGPT Plugin for Google Sheets. This tool makes it easy to incorporate ChatGPT into spreadsheets using either the G Suite Apps Script or by installing an extension. This plugin opens up new possibilities for financial modeling within user-friendly and accessible worksheets!

AI seamlessly enhances human intelligence by effortlessly conducting feasibility calculations for a target project funding, considering multiple factors in real-time. The advantages of this advanced modeling approach are noteworthy:

- Accelerating the JIT funding process due to quicker iterations and adaptability as project variables change.
- Offering a deeper understanding of project funding dynamics to make well-informed decisions.
- Providing investors and startups with the same quality information and promoting collaboration and transparency throughout the JIT modeling process.
- Enabling quick adjustments and recalculations, fostering a more adaptive and responsive modeling process.

By merging AI with traditional feasibility calculations, we embark on more than just adopting AI technology. It's about embracing a transformative approach to project planning that unlocks doors to unparalleled accuracy, efficiency, and innovation. This approach signifies a shift from manual, error-prone, and time-consuming processes to a new realm of fast, efficient, and flawlessly error-free operations.

Key Takeaways

Securing the right amount of capital at the right time has never been more critical. To achieve this, startups can employ a creative approach through their financial projections and embrace the JIT scheme in their funding process. This innovative strategy allows startups to receive the necessary funding to fuel their growth, avoiding dilution.

JIT funding has emerged as a highly effective financing model that provides the necessary capital precisely when needed. By integrating the JIT model with advanced AI tools, venture capitalists can potentially reduce costs and offer startups access to vital funds at critical moments.

AI-driven financial modeling for investment decision-making is essential for efficiently allocating capital to the right startups at the perfect time. Venture capitalists can leverage this approach to fund early-stage startups and confidently navigate the complex VC landscape.

Chapter 4.3.
Startup Valuation:
An Intangible Perspective

Traditionally, investors rely on financial indicators and calculations created for tangible assets when making investment decisions. In today's knowledge economy, intangible assets are a significant factor in a startup's long-term success or failure. New valuation methods are necessary to evaluate in what measure a startup team is effective in its intangible value creation or acquisition and deployment. While there may not be any universal framework that can capture the complexity of startup valuation, it is possible to obtain insight through proxies, helping with human capital assessment and appropriated intangibles as profit differentials. An integrated framework combines algorithms for startup team assessment and estimating intangibles to model different scenarios of its appropriation and deployment is offered.

> **What is unique about intangible valuations?**

Origins of Intangible Valuations

The idea of new companies' valuation was born in the USA when the Massachusetts legislature passed a law in 1858 that required a commissioner to calculate if newly licensed companies were adequately covered. The original valuation methodology of distracting liabilities from assets had stayed the same since the 1920s.

ACTUARY:

"THE GOODWILL ESTIMATE MUST BE NEGLIGIBLE!"

It was a historic moment when the US Government proposed a revolutionary concept that a company was worth far more than simply its assets minus its liabilities. The new concepts included the value of future profit and goodwill in calculating company valuation. This was the first attempt to include intangibles in the calculation. However, modern accounting conventions do not recognize goodwill as an intangible asset.

Until the 1990s, actuaries and accountants could only perform business valuation work in the USA. [9]

A farmer and an actuary look at two sheep flocks. The farmer asks the actuary how many sheep they have: "1,007," the actuary confidently says. The farmer wonders how the actuary figures it out. "There are about 1,000 sheep in one herd and seven in the other." [10]
This old joke is right on point!

Traditional methods of valuing startups are no longer sufficient in today's knowledge economy. Intangible assets and solutions are crucial in determining a startup's success or failure, making it necessary to develop a new valuation concept.

Looking for Intangible Valuation Methods

There is no standard method to value intangibles, while three common methods are generally accepted. The first method values intangibles according to replacement or reproduction costs. However, investors expect a significant increase in value compared to initial costs. The second commonly used valuation method for intangibles compares similar intangibles sold in the market, employing different multiples. Unfortunately, there is no input data for calculations because there are no markets to trade intangibles. The third valuation method tries to estimate intangibles' contributions to startup profitability via profit differentials. The inherent properties of intangibles, such as synergistic effects and spillovers, make it difficult to assess how each intangible asset impacts a startup's profitability. [11]

Without a universally accepted valuation framework for valuing startups, various perspectives and theories on how to do it have emerged, differing in their approaches. Each method has essential shortcomings, eliminating its usefulness for business practices. Thus, founders and investors encounter an unsolved task of valuing startups.

An alternative way to evaluate intangible assets is through plausible proxies. These methods can estimate the value of intangible assets based on related quantifiable factors. For example, a startup's patent portfolio could be a credible proxy for its innovation capabilities. By understanding these proxies, investors and founders can better estimate a startup's intangible value.

Sophisticated investors know that the core challenges in startup valuation include gathering, verifying, and processing data to make sense of collected information. Despite the hype around Big Data, it is of little practical use because startups have minimal publicly disclosed data. Proprietary data is the most valuable source of data about startups. However, the raw data of early-stage startups are primarily qualitative, and the availability of verified data is one of the significant challenges in early-stage investing. Data intelligence can help us discover intangible-related information and estimate startups' intangible potential.

Intangibles are predominantly human capital intensive and, in most cases, cannot be separated from teams - their carriers. By creating a quality team, startup founders can leverage their own and third-party intangible assets to generate profits. Such startups promise exponential revenue growth without a proportional increase in variable costs. To show their value to investors, startups must internally develop their intangibles or appropriate them with a clear explanation of their impact on profitability.

Entrepreneurs can combine human capital assessment with a necessary remuneration and potentially appropriated intangibles as a profit differential within an integrated framework. Four key factors can influence the value of intangible assets and leverage profits to serve as proxies:

1. The startup team's fitness for business performance (comprehensive estimation from the investors' point of view).
2. Available intangibles created or appropriated by the startup can be deployed thanks to the founders' knowledge, experience, and skills (with an estimation of synergic effects and spillovers).
3. The Pay Payback Period (PBP) is necessary for a startup to recover the cost of an investment (working as a commercialization indicator and a profit differential).
4. Founders ask for annual remuneration for their contributions to the proposed deployment of intangible assets (industry/sector benchmarks help to keep these figures on a reasonable level).

Modeling Startup Valuation

A four-variable valuation model corresponds to the four main directions of investor reasoning within their screening. Numerous surveys revealed that founders' personalities are a key decision-making criterion in selecting startups for investment. The question is how to quantify behavioral characteristics and personality traits.

The proposed algorithm uses the following key factors of the startup team's fitness for future business performance:

- Team strategic positioning.
- Team composition.
- Team structure.
- Splitting equity among co-founders.
- Stock option pool.
- Payroll system.
- Team dynamics.
- Founders' entrepreneurship experience.
- Founders' experience of working together.
- Enterprise's management style.

Each factor of the team's current state is analyzed and ranged as 0 (low), 0.5 (medium), or 1 (high) according to its impact on future business performance (for more detail, see Chapter 3.2, "An AI-enforced Startup Team"). Using information from the Startup Dossier, the algorithm calculates the weighted coefficient of the startup team's fitness for business performance. Thus, we fulfill the first stage of startup valuation modeling.

Following provisions accepted by accounting conventions, it is customary to divide intangible investments into three broad categories: "computerized information," "innovative property," and "economic competencies." Each investment category embraces several sub-categories suitable for startups' recognition and investor assessment (for more detail, see Chapter 1.2, "Intangible Capital in Knowledge Economy.").

For each category of intangibles, the algorithm guides founders through the decision-making tree of the second modeling stage. It results in the intangible leverage coefficient, integrating the usage of own and third-party intangibles, synergic effects, and spillover potential. The procedures of the second stage include the following set of 'yes-no' forks:

- Checking whether the startup owns or controls any intangibles from a regularly updated list.

- Checking whether these intangibles have an application in the startup business model.
- For own or controlled intangibles that have an application in the business model, check whether the startup determines the size of investments required to deploy these intangibles.
- Checking whether the startup knows of any third-party weakly protected intangibles that a startup can incorporate into the business model.
- Check whether it has an appropriation plan for the third-party weakly protected intangibles that a startup can incorporate into the business model.

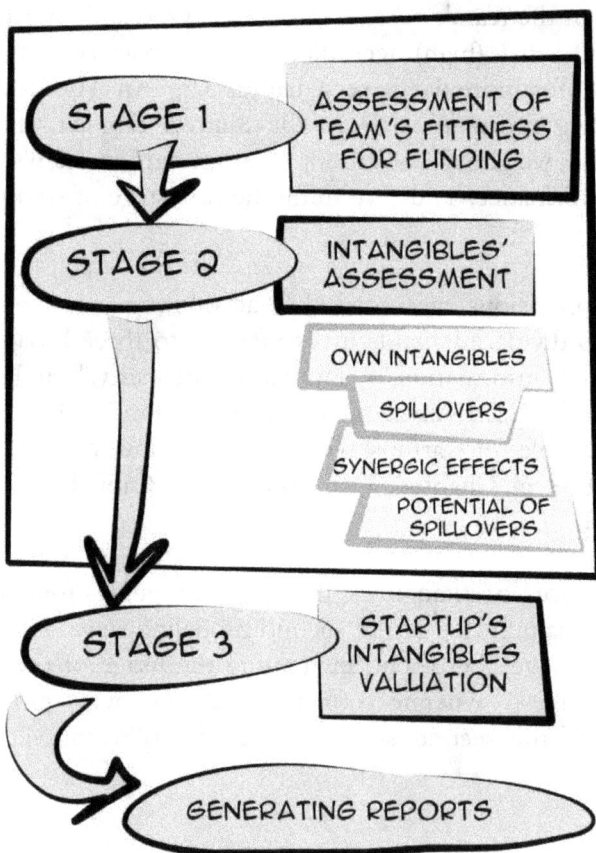

In the third modeling stage, the algorithm multiplies the coefficient of the startup team's fitness for business performance, the intangible leverage coefficient, PBP, and the team's proposed annual remuneration to calculate the startup's intangible valuation. Thus, the algorithm helps founders model different intangibles' appropriation and deployment scenarios. The final results of the algorithm's calculations form a comprehensive report for investors.

Using Intangible Valuations in Startup Screening

Insufficient reporting of intangible assets by startups prevents investors from discovering business opportunities hidden behind intangibles. Moreover, founders often view intangibles as having zero value, understating their negotiation position. To overcome these information gaps and asymmetry, startups need to report investors on the startup's intangible valuation.

PROFITomix Story

Digital Pizza

(Episode 12)

CAST:

Michael

Visionary
Investor

Steve

Startup
Founder

Gippetio

Bot

As an innovative investor, Michael began using an AI bot to evaluate the target startups' intangible potential. Recently, Steve filled out a questionnaire for the bot. Having no response, he decided to clarify the situation and sent a message to Michael. Steve had a standard business plan for this conversation with his startup valuation made by hired consultants. However, Michael was uninterested in Digital Pizza's business plan and connected the bot to the conversation. The bot commented on Steve's efforts with its characteristic cynicism and hidden more profound meaning.

Hi Michael! I've filled out your automatic intangible valuation questionnaire and would like your opinion.

Hey, Steve! How's your dough?

Dough? We still need to bake pizza.

Saying dough, I'm talking of money!

If money can talk, mine says "goodbye." We need funding a.s.a.p.!

We say "dough" because money should grow!

Sure thing! Our business plan shows enormous growth and an appropriate valuation.

I'm glad you're talking about 'appropriation,' but I stopped reading about business plans. Gippetio makes valuations quicker and better than humans. Just a moment... I'll connect him.

A business plan is a good way for a startup to prove it doesn't need money.

Why? I've provided all the figures in the 'Valuation' section!

Your figures are not symbolic. They're too rounded.

What does the accuracy of calculations matter? Again, we use pessimistic calculations of our revenues!

But you propose over-optimistic salaries for your team members! So, you need a pessimistic investor who does not expect to get his money back.

We need an investor who understands our intangible advantages and is ready to finance my company appropriately!

I see the 'intangibles' you propose as appropriate:
"Our strong and harmonious team is ready to face any challenges."
If you take money, thinking it's "your" company is a mistake.
And remember, money not only changes wallets but also faces! <END>

Investors can use the intangible valuation report to get answers to critical questions:

1. What is the team's overall quality regarding its ability to discover, appropriate, and deploy intangibles?
2. How can founders appropriate intangible assets, both their own or controlled and those of third parties?
3. How effectively can founders use the inherent features of intangibles: synergic effects and spillovers?
4. To demonstrate the startup's ability to commercialize intangible assets, how quickly can it recover the investment cost?
5. Is the required investment realistic, including the founders' salaries, considering items 1-4?
6. How does the team's remuneration compare to the industry/sector?

While the report does not capture all dimensions of intangible assets, it helps founders demonstrate to investors the actual value of their startups.

Key Takeaways

The intangible assets a startup can appropriate are critical factors in its long-term success or failure. For investors, it is crucial to look beyond tangible assets and consider the intangible value creation and acquisition by a startup team. This approach requires a new valuation concept that helps assess human capital and appropriated intangibles as profit differentials. At the same time, there are no standard methods for startup valuation; plausible proxies and the integrated framework help to make intangible valuations.

The proposed framework does not rely on traditional startup valuation methods. Still, it uses an alternative approach that focuses on identifying key factors that can influence the value of intangible assets and leverage profits. The algorithm allows founders to model different scenarios of intangible asset appropriation and calculate the intangible valuation. This algorithm also generates a comprehensive report for investors to make informed funding decisions while overcoming information gaps and asymmetry.

As with all valuation methods, there are many approaches to measuring the value of intangible assets. However, using plausible proxies and modeling different intangibles' appropriation and deployment scenarios can provide a more accurate understanding of a startup's intangible value. This alternative method for evaluating startups from an intangible perspective can help both parties recognize previously hidden business opportunities.

Points to Ponder

It would be overly optimistic to hope that startups will develop from scratch and present fundamentally new, intangible-intensive business models to investors. In practice, startups use ready-made, proven business model patterns and combinations. Such patterns simplify and accelerate the models' development and deployment.

Some of these patterns include:

1. Serving the Unserved - Using various data sources to offer services to previously untargeted customers.

2. Physical & Digital Hybrids - Using augmented reality to enrich the customer journey.

3. Instant Offering - Using data-driven automation to speed up the process for a better customer experience.

4. Tailored Descriptions - Using personalized product descriptions and customer recommendations based on analytics-driven segmentation.

5. Predictive Risk Mitigation - Mitigating risk using data-driven pattern recognition to prevent malicious activities.

6. DIY Enablement - Helping customers to perform data-driven value-creation activities.

7. Proactive Messaging - Proactively communicates messages to customers to provide the correct information at the right time.

8. Process Automation - Automating repetitive tasks using AI bots.

9. Plug & Play - Giving customers ready-to-use technology solutions that do not require special skills. [5]

Brainstorm to estimate which data-driven and intangible-intensive business model patterns may be helpful to components for your concrete business model.

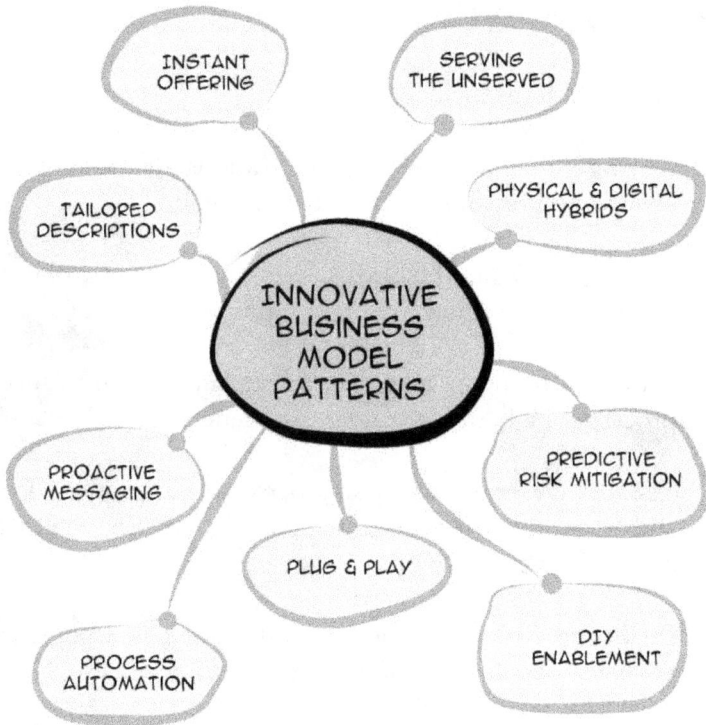

Section 5
Investors' Protection & Exit

Exit is a hot topic for investors and startup founders. Identifying the right exit for both parties is essential to ensure mutual success. When planning exits, investors need strategies that protect their interests and take full advantage of market opportunities. However, investors' decision-making under information scarcity reduces the valuations of all startups, good and bad. Besides, an essential part of the information, particularly about intangible assets, needs to be codified. Investors spend time and money on screening and due diligence that may be unreasonably costly.

Investor protection consists of several layers and aspects. Although some solutions already exist, a more comprehensive approach using data and AI can help founders and investors work towards mutually beneficial solutions, mitigating biases and improving communication between two parties. Identifying efficient exit strategies and solving information problems ensure more efficient capital-raising processes, higher profitability, and faster startup growth.

Startups and investors often need more information in their partnerships. To mitigate this challenge, both parties must recognize the causes of information asymmetry and take a data-driven approach to decision-making. By being more transparent and leveraging quality information, startups and investors can improve their success rates and, ultimately, achieve their common goal of creating profitable enterprises.

Chapter 5.1.
Exit Scenarios:
Looking into the Future

Identifying the right exit for investors and startups is critical to mutual success. Exits have traditionally been seen as positive outcomes, allowing startups and investors to profit. New strategies and technologies develop daily in today's quickly changing VC landscape. In particular, data and AI have been dramatically transforming the VC industry that previously relied on outdated methods and tools. These advancements have enabled VCs to make more informed investment decisions. Corporate Venture Capitalists (CVC), Syndicates of business angels (Syndicates), and Mergers and Acquisitions (M&A) acquirers are the most massive players in today's VC market. They form the typical routes for different exits.

> **How do model successful exit strategies?**

The Bloomberg Terminal as a Prediction Machine

When sourcing quality startups, modeling exit strategies accurately while providing optimal flexibility is relatively new in the VC industry. Nevertheless, this idea has quite material embodiment in securities. The Bloomberg Terminal is an example of a system facilitating exit planning for investors focusing on stock and options trades. Inventing his Terminal in 1984, Michael Bloomberg had an idea that Wall Street would pay a premium for high-quality business data. Today, the Bloomberg Terminal system delivers quality information about financial markets. Its principles include:

- Focusing on accessing, curating, and presenting accurate data.
- Applying established methodologies for producing metrics from market information.
- Combining the AI approach and the use of high-quality experts. [1]

The Terminal is in the "Tools of the Trade," a new display at Silicon Valley's Computer History Museum, along with the clay tokens used by ancient Babylonians to track the trading. (See Chapter 4.1, "Business Model Innovation," for more details).

The Terminal embraces BloombergGPT, developed by Bloomberg AI and specifically designed for financial applications. BloombergGPT has been trained on a massive financial text and code dataset, including news articles, regulatory filings, and financial market data. This specialized training allows it to understand and process financial information. It can generate financial reports, translate financial documents, and accurately answer financial questions. BloombergGPT's capabilities make it adaptable to various financial use cases to provide insights into market movements.

The Evolving VC Industry's Landscape

The VC world is changing faster than ever, and all the VC market players must consider the current shift towards a "cherry-picking" strategy instead of a diversification one. Another significant shift is a new demand for startup quality and profitability to separate startups with strong business models from the weaker ones. Inefficient and unprofitable startups could not survive. The balance of power between investors and founders around valuation and funding assumptions will move to a new equilibrium. [2]

Today's investment landscape is different from yesterday's. There is the rise of CVCs that offer startups funding and access to resources and established brands. Syndicates of angels have risen in popularity due to the simplicity of their establishment, risk-sharing, and ready-to-use online services, and M&A acquirers have become a private equity market pipeline.

Along with the three leading players, there are others in the VC market:

- Traditional equity venture capital and private equity.
- Revenue-based investing VCs.
- Venture debt companies.
- Merchant cash advances/factoring companies.
- Small Business Association Loans operators.
- Crowdfunding platforms. [3]

New investment vehicles create new exit opportunities. Rolling funds such as AngelList allow their managers to share deal flows with fund investors on a quarterly subscription basis. VC-as-a-service could compensate for the need for more technical knowledge in the investment market and provide ventures with a more flexible funding scheme. Special Purpose Acquisition Companies (SPACs) raise money through a SPAC IPO to merge with private companies and thereby provide for funding and immediate listing. Secondary funds allow limited partners to trade their interests in a fund. Opportunity funds (or follow-on funds) would step in as side funds of a VC to provide longer-term funding to top-performing portfolio companies. [4]

An exit for investors and startups is good when they can sell their stake for a profit if they succeed. This variant could be better for both parties when they wind up and sell their assets. By cashing out their investment in case of a good exit, investors can get a return, and the startup can raise more money. Planning exit scenarios that meet the needs of startups and investors is essential to any startup's strategy. Startup founders must decide from the beginning what type of investor is right for them.

Founders make a difficult decision when choosing the appropriate type of investor. They can keep management control over their enterprises and ownership at all costs, with the risk of doing business for a living only. The price of this decision may be one of the underperformance variants. Alternatively, founders can grow highly profitable big enterprises by balancing personal expectations with investors' requirements.

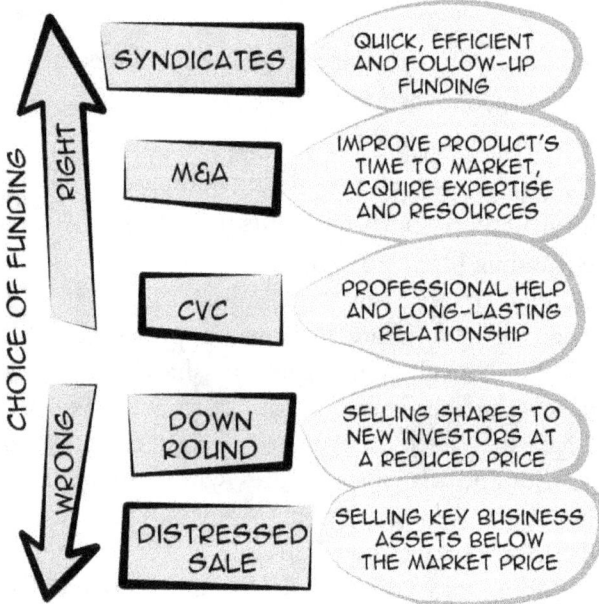

Modeling Exit Strategies

There are three specific features of current reality to take into consideration while planning exits:

- CVC, syndicates, and M&A acquirers see exits differently.
- Most successful startup exits are not IPOs but rather acquisitions.

- New investors build exit scenarios using a data-driven approach and algorithms instead of yesterday's gut feelings.

Exit strategies embrace five key factors to help startups choose an appropriate investor type:

1. Founders' primary concern about a prospective startup's funding/acquisition.
2. The founders' main goal after the startup's funding/acquisition.
3. The main feature of the startup's investor/acquirer.
4. The essence of the founders' offer for the startup's investor/acquirer.
5. Founders' key strategic consideration and a timeframe.

To find an exit scenario that balances the startup's preferences and different acquirers'/investors' criteria, we show the main decision-making drivers by M&A, CVC, and Synd in each of the five factors. These drivers are the following:

1. Founders' primary concern about a prospective startup's funding/acquisition.

The financial strength of the enterprise and its better market positioning.	**M&A**
Bright technological prospects for the innovative solution's further development.	**CVC**
Management control and founders' benefits from a deal.	**SYND.**

2. The founders' main goal is to reach after the startup's funding/acquisition.

Enter new markets, including international ones.	**M&A**
Obtain access to new technologies and expertise.	**CVC**
Get funds that are necessary for the startup's operations.	**SYND.**

3. The main feature of the startup's investor/acquirer.

A large, more established company in the market.	**M&A**
A technology-intensive company in the same sector of the market.	**CVC**
An investment/venture company that is interested in early-stage startups.	**SYND.**

4. The essence of the founders' offer for the startup's investor/acquirer.

Clear prospects for scalability thanks to synergic effects in deploying intangible assets.	**M&A**
Unique technological or (and) business solutions embedded in the business model.	**CVC**
Well-developed MVP, essential and proven traction, and a validated customer base.	**SYND.**

5. Founders' key strategic consideration and a timeframe.

The "growth and sell big" strategy during the next 3-5 years.	**M&A**
The strategy is to work with a market /sector leader to develop the initial startup's technological solutions at any time.	**CVC**
The "growth and sell quickly" strategy during the next 1-3 years.	**SYND.**

The simplified choice among five key exit factors can help recognize the exit directions of each type of investor. However, differences in investment rationales lead to different interpretations of exit events and exit planning procedures.

Choosing Startups from the VC Perspective

Startup founders must be ready for changes in the leadership team and their power to make crucial decisions in exchange for funds. It is essential that both parties have a clear picture of the exit and do not create illusions for themselves.

There are three exit scenarios: for M&As, CVCs, and Syndicates. These scenarios have specific features and subtypes that significantly affect the exit strategies.

Scenario for Merger & Acquisition:

An M&A acquirer wants to improve their company's financial performance at a reasonable level of risk. A concrete M&A strategy depends on how the startup's business fits into the acquirer's portfolio:

1. The startup has similar products/services but targets different customer groups or markets.
2. The startup has complementary products/services.
3. The startup's products/services do not overlap with the current acquirer's business—still, the latter plans to diversify its business activities.
4. An M&A acquirer operates like a VC, having pure financial interests.

In the first strategy, an acquired startup will have its brand discontinued, its products and services fully transferred into the acquirer's portfolio, and its legal entity may be dissolved. When all business processes align with those of the acquirer within a concise time frame, it will be full integration.

The second strategy involves the startup and acquirer continuing to work under their brands. The startup keeps a certain level of independence in branding and advertising. Still, it combines it with solid integration to enhance its product offer, strengthen its go-to-market initiatives, and optimize its costs. A clear understanding of the acquisition rationale will determine which functions to integrate or leave separate.

The third strategy is proper when the startup operates in a very different market segment or has a business model different from the acquirer's. The new parent company often wants to gain an early foothold in this new frontier, grow the business, leverage cross-selling opportunities, or even disrupt its business model. A startup's independence helps preserve its novelty, culture, and perception with consumers.

The board strictly controls budgets, hiring, and other strategic decisions within the fourth strategy. The startup performs day-to-day operations and reports financial and business results to the acquirer. Investing in the startup at an early stage, often before it has a proven business model, is part of the financial strategy.

Scenario for Corporate Venture Capitalists:

A CVC acquirer takes an equity stake in the technological startup to advance its products/services or develop complementary products. A concrete CVC strategy depends on its type:

1. Strategic CVCs are interested in the startup's technology and IP. They provide the startup with a supply chain and help overcome technical and regulatory challenges.
2. Financial CVCs focus solely on the startup's economic performance.
3. Hybrid CVCs combine a strategic approach with funding that adds value to their portfolios. They also provide all the necessary resources.

A strategic CVC aims to invest in startups to help the parent company grow. Sharing resources and collaborating with the parent company is essential. The strategy works well for startups that require a longer-term perspective to guide them through a complex supply chain, regulatory, and technology landscape.

The goal of financial CVCs is to maximize their returns on investments. Typically, these funds operate much more independently from their parent companies and prioritize financial returns over strategic alignment. Financial CVCs are a good fit for startups with less in common with the parent company's mission and less to gain from its resources.

CVCs with a hybrid approach prioritize financial returns while adding considerable strategic value to their portfolio companies. While CVCs have loose connections with their parent companies, they provide startups with resources and support. The market appeal of hybrid CVCs is generally the broadest. [5]

Scenario for Syndicates:

The term "syndicate" refers to an investment vehicle that allows investors (backers) to co-invest with relevant and reputable investors (leaders) in the best startups in the market. Syndicate leaders have extensive experience selecting investment opportunities and investing in them in various technology sectors, with deal flow most investors need help accessing. There are several advantages for all parties in joining a syndicate:

- Leadership offers the opportunity to invest more money per deal, gain access to better investor rights, and receive a carry (capital gains resulting from an exit or dividends paid) in exchange for their services.
- Due to leaders' vast experience, backers get access to investment opportunities they might not be able to find on their own.
- Startups have access to more capital. Since the investment is made through an investment vehicle, they don't have to deal with numerous investors.

Syndicated investors intend to increase the startup's value to sell it later at a profit. It is important for them to determine whether the startup's business aligns with the current trend, at a low valuation with a significant stake in the company. Syndicates provide fast, accessible capital, democratizing the investment process (even founders can apply to be a part of an investment syndicate). [6]

It is becoming increasingly common for all types of investors to invest in early-stage startups in attractive niches with innovative business models or promising technologies. A growing interest in such startups depends on the type of acquirer/investor that has specific interests:

- Innovative technologies that startups developed.
- Innovative paths-to-market through intangible-intensive business models.
- Opportunistic strategies designed for a timely exit from unprofitable startups inflated in valuations.

PROFITomix Story:

Digital Pizza

(Episode 13)

CAST:

Michael

Visionary
Investor

Steve

Startup
Founder

Michael continued the conversation he started in previous episodes. This time, he would like to find out what plan the founders of Digital Pizza have envisaged for exiting the project. It turned out that the investor and the founder found themselves on different pages regarding the exit strategies. The founder has yet to look for solutions to this problem. By the end of the conversation, he realized that investors were playing their games.

Hey Steve, Michael here! How's business cooking?

Well, sometimes it's cheesy, and sometimes it's saucy, but we somehow manage to keep it all cooking.

All right then. Talking in funny metaphors: spill the beans on your exit plan.

Why talk about exit now when there has been no entry yet?

Because you have to plan an exit scheme now! It's like planning a prison break – you're ready in advance.

Could you clarify it for me?

That depends on a few things. If you're looking to cash out quickly, CVC would be your best bet. However, if you want to build the business and develop a long-term strategy, M&A is a better fit. And if you're looking for extra help, a syndicated angel could be the way to go.

I like them all!

It's because you don't know their dark sides!

OK, enlighten me!

The CVC's primary focus is on large-scale companies. So, your startup looks hopeless. An M&A acquirer can leave founders with nothing but a memory of their beloved project. Syndicates are full of fraud on both sides.

What can I do?

Could we try a SPAC?

SPAC? What in the world is that?

It's a Special Purpose Acquisition Company. Essentially, we'll create a shell company, preferably an offshore one, raise money, and use it to acquire Digital Pizza, thereby publicizing it. This alternative scheme is all the rage these days, and it's perfect from a tax perspective.

This exit isn't clear to me...it looks like a financial pyramid.

Let's imagine how drones always return to load more pizzas, and so do we. We return for more investments. Moreover, it's legitimate...for now.

I can decode this SPAC abbreviation – Special Ponzi Alternative Con!

Sometimes, modern VC investing looks like a financial pyramid... a Ponzi scheme, to be precise [7]
In the current rounds of raising funding, startups are spending money intensively to boost user growth and attract bigger funding rounds!

Key Takeaways

Successful exit strategies come from both sides: startups and VCs. Understanding VC's investment rationales, founders can build tailored exit scenarios that improve their chances of success in the long run. This approach allows startups to make more informed decisions when choosing their investors - balancing personal expectations with investors' requirements in part of management control over their enterprises and ownership. Those who do not plan exits from the beginning may have fallen victim to underperformance.

For investors, employing a data-driven scenario approach for exit planning instead of gut feelings allows them to consider all reasonable options. While identifying the right exit, investors must remember that each startup is unique and has some exit nuances best suited for success.

Chapter 5.2.
Investors' Protection & Information Problems

The VC industry faces a proliferation of new investors pushing equilibrium of interests. To navigate this complex environment effectively, investors need strategies that protect their interests and take full advantage of market opportunities. In sourcing startups, investors have information problems: quality information scarcity and non-codified information about intangible assets. Investors spend time and money on screening and due diligence that may be unreasonably costly. Investors lose valuable opportunities due to inadequate access to critical data from multiple sources. Founders suffer the "lemons" problem when lacking quality information about startups reduces their valuations. A data-driven approach at the enterprise level can help bridge the current information gaps by providing investors with the information required to make well-weighted decisions.

> How do protect investors' interests and solve the 'lemons' problem?

The "Lemons" Problem in the VC Industry

Information problems occur when investors make decisions under conditions of information scarcity, which automatically reduces the valuations of all startups, good and bad. As a result, promising startups need to sell their equity at overly discounted prices. Economists noticed this pattern. George Arthur Akerlof, an American economist, won the

Nobel Memorial Prize in Economics in 2001 for his analysis of markets with asymmetric information. Known for his article "The Market for Lemons: Quality Uncertainty and the Market Mechanism," published in 1970, Akerlof argued that bad used cars sabotage the market. [8]

Bad cars, or "lemons," can make it difficult for people to buy good cars because it's hard to prove that a car is in good shape. Because it is difficult to recognize the difference between "good" and "bad" cars, buyers know that sellers of bad cars will try to represent them as "good" ones. This problem also affects early-stage enterprises since investors often need more information about startups, while founders cannot provide it.

By actively promoting pitching services (advertising bad startups as good ones), pitching providers derive a wave of 'pitching lemons,' increasing information scarcity and sabotaging the VC market. To fight information problems, investors first consider a range of personal preferences, including industry/sector, marker, and business location. Then, they consider protection measures if things go wrong, including economic, control, and exit terms.

Investors' Preferences and Terms

Besides a strong team, a bright market opportunity, and promising financial prospects, each investor needs protection measures if things go wrong, and a set of exit

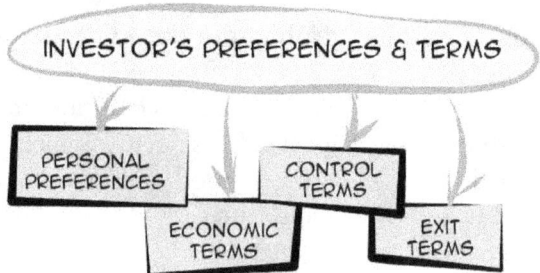

scenarios if a business grows. Considering investors' preferences and terms is essential to build an effective business relationship between a startup and prospective investors.

Understanding the essence of each term helps to gather critical information in the Startup Dossier to overcome information gaps.

1. Personal Preferences.

Startup's location	A startup is preferably located in a technological zone or a big city with a well-developed technological infrastructure.
Startup's market size	The startup's total market is about $1B (a recommended figure for new enterprises).
Startup's technological orientation	The startup employs revolutionary technology solutions (AI, IoT, or blockchain).

2. Economic terms.

Capital requirements and equity offered	The capital a startup needs, the amount investors get back, and the stake it offers investors.
Preferred and common stock	When investors get common shares, they have equal rights as founders. If investors get preferred shares, they have disproportionate control and take a larger share of revenue than founders.
Anti-dilution protection (weighted average)	It allows adjusting the rate at which preferred stock converts into common stock. The weighted average price is lower than the original purchase price. It is divided into the original cost to determine the number of shares of common stock into which each share of preferred stock is convertible.
Liquidation preferences	This clause stipulates how often an investor must repay the initial investment capital before other investors are allowed to participate in the liquidation proceeds. A typical requirement is a two- or three-times liquidation preference, sometimes as high as six or eight times.

3.   Control terms.

	Board Composition	Investor appoints their representatives as directors of a company.
	Lock-In	A prohibition on transferring founders' shares for a prescribed period would provide a timeline for the gradual unlocking of shares and balance the risks between founders and Investors.
	Right of First Refusal (RAFR)	A right to prevent the entry of any third-party investor into the enterprise. Founders may seek exemption from this investor's right to transfer a specific percentage of shares to affiliates.
	Reserved Matters	Specifically, enlisted enterprises' activities require compulsory approval of the investors (via their board representatives or representation in shareholders' meetings).
	Pro-rata rights	Give investors the right to participate in a subsequent round of funding to maintain their percentage of ownership in the company. It is a way for continuous funding.
	Information Rights	Standard information rights include annual financial and quarterly or monthly management reports. Financials need not be audited, but auditors usually review them.
	Founder Vesting	Having a meaningful portion of the stock is critical to contractual restrictions that lapse over time.
	Protective Provisions	Authorization of dividends, taking on debt, changes to the board, and changes to shareholder rights in a case of M&A or company liquidation.
	Covenants	Founders promise to take (affirmative covenants) or not take (negative covenants) specific necessary actions without restricting them from running the business daily.

4.   Exit terms.

Drag-Along	Most common and preferred stock owners agree to the deal if a situation changes, and the minority will sign the documents.
Redemption rights	Investors can exit their investments by requiring other shareholders to repurchase their shares after a specified period.

Despite the commonality of some strategies of CVCs, M&A acquirers, and syndicated angels, their investment rationales and exit modes may differ. In other words, different groups of investors choose individual methods of dealing with information scarcity. While syndicates think of holding board seats, CVCs focus on R&D agreements. M&A acquirers concentrate on drag-along and redemption rights, and angels' main concern is quick and profitable exits. Everyone should focus on one or two key parameters in insufficient and unreliable information conditions.

The New Trends Impacting Investors' Interests

During the last few years, thousands of new venture capital companies have launched. Among them, boutique firms are positioned mainly at the seed and pre-seed stages. The latest generation of venture capitalists of a non-financial origin made from ex-founders and corporate executives is changing the VC landscape. They bring professionalization in the VC industry and its relevance to more sectors of the economy. Newcomers want to invest in innovations rather than mundane operators. [9]

Statistics show that 90.3% of newly launched VCs focus on early-stage startups to capture the opportunities missed by incumbents. [2]
Ha, it seems the earlier, the better!

Three crucial trends have recently emerged in the VC industry. First, it blurs boundaries among leading market players: CVCs, M&A acquirers, and syndicated angels. Due to online crowdfunding platforms, CVCs and M&A acquirers participate in syndicates. It is challenging to distinguish between the strategies of financial CVCs and M&A acquirers. A second trend is called "minority investments." It means making relatively small investments in promising startups and waiting before buying them. The third trend is partial exits, when investors sell some of their stock in startups but keep a large part of the shares.

Traditional measures to protect the investors' interests have developed in the era of traditional VCs and angels. Today, we must adapt them to the specific investment environment in which:

- Data science begins to drive the investment process and decision-making of emerging VCs that develop an algorithmic approach to investment selection.
- The pace of AI adoption derives competition from data transforming all stages of the deal flow, investment management, and perception of the returns drivers.
- The winners of the VC industry can attract the most talented founders by developing new methods for predicting the success of target startups.
- Access to real-time proprietary information and data intelligence allows for realistic estimation of returns. [3]

In the knowledge economy, the direction of investors' protection measures is shifting to the intangible areas. Investors try to ensure the key founders have proper contracts that tie them to the startup. They want to be sure that those who leave the company do not work for competitors. Investors also think about IP protection. Due to its novelty, the issue of seizing and using someone else's IP still needs to be added to the agenda, but it will inevitably arise tomorrow. One day, the founders' ability to discover and appropriate spillovers becomes a key startup selection criterion.

PROFITomix Story

Digital Pizza

(Episode 14)

CAST:

Robert

Steve

Investor
Traditionalist

Startup
Founder

Robert asked Steve about information the startup could provide for prospective due diligence. At first, Steve needed to understand the investor's explanation of his ideas for startup promotion. When Steve understood the essence of the issue, he explained that data collection was the responsibility of those who wanted to check the startup. However, Robert is still determining whether it is his responsibility.

Hey Steve! It's Robert. I want to ask you about the information your startup can provide.

Hi, Robert! We have a killer social media presence, a sleek and modern website, and some influencers on board to help spread the word.

That's great, but I wanted to ask what information you can provide when somebody asks what your startup does.

Well, here's the thing. We're considering using a new technology to present information about our company in a virtual reality format. You'll be able to walk around our facilities and see with your own eyes how hard we're working. Plus, we can make holograms for our team members!

No, no, that's not what I meant. I'm talking about information for prospective due diligence.

Oh, my bad, I misunderstood. Why? It's up to the investors to gather that data themselves and do their due diligence.

Wait, isn't your responsibility as a startup founder to provide that information?

Look, Robert, we're a startup. We focus on pizza. We need more time or resources to gather all that information and compile it neatly for investors. Plus, a lot of the critical stuff is hard to quantify. You can't precisely measure passion and determination on a balance sheet!

I see, but other ways exist to collect and represent information for due diligence. For instance, you could hire a consultant.

I know what you're talking about! I spoke with a consultant who offered to create an information lake for us.

And what was the problem with him?

Money! We could only pay for a small information puddle. By the way, we hired a consultant to make our business plan. There is much information there. Why do we need more?

A business plan is no longer proof of your diligence; it only indicates that you need money badly. And the more consultants beautify your plan, the more tricky questions you must answer!

It seems like a paradox: the less information in the business plan, the better because fewer questions arise. But you ask for more information!

Costs to Solve Information Problems

Early-stage capital markets use various mechanisms to solve information problems. Venture capital firms invest considerable resources in due diligence and monitoring. To do so efficiently, they often focus on startups located nearby. Proximity reduces the costs associated with information gathering and enables early-stage investments. Nevertheless, monitoring and due diligence of each prospective deal may be sufficiently costly, especially since many deals never happen.

There are three components of such costs that have a profound economic sense:

- The first component is the cost of deal sourcing, which occurs when investors try to elicit reliable information from unreliable sources like social networks.
- The second component is transaction costs in the screening stage when different forms of communication between startups and investors inevitably cause expenses.
- The third component is due diligence costs, which are used to recognize "lemons" and avoid missing attractive business opportunities. It is the most challenging and costliest to fight.

An essential part of the information intended to predict startup success is tacit. It is shared through socialization and is challenging to transfer in written form. This type includes information about the startup founders' personalities and relationships among founders that is difficult to codify. The lack of credible information about startups' human capital results in low valuations and excessive protection measures. Thus, the risk investors expect leads to reduced valuations. However, startups can reduce the risk by providing investors with trustworthy information.

Equity crowdfunding platforms allow for reducing the first and second costs' components but not the third. Specifically, crowdfunding platforms enable investors to invest relatively small amounts of capital cost-efficiently. Investors learn about business opportunities and execute transactions, expanding the addressable market for early-stage capital. However, the third cost, resulting from "lemons," remained.

Although investors could now make early-stage investments at a much lower price, they still faced the high cost of conducting due diligence. The economic sense of investment requires checking the diligence cost-to-investment size ratio. [9]

From a cost perspective, a Startup Dossier looks like an effective tool for providing investors with well-structured initial information for deal sourcing (reducing the first component of costs). To employ data diligence methods, entrepreneurs need comprehensive information. It can then be disclosed to investors to the extent necessary and sufficient at each screening stage (reducing transaction costs). Confirming all information presented for screening in the properly fulfilled Dossier allows us to cut the third component of expenses: due diligence costs.

Key Takeaways

The venture capital space is changing rapidly and will continue to change as new technologies such as AI and data science become more prominent in the investment process. Investors and founders must adapt their strategies to succeed.

Funding valuable startups is challenging when dealing with information scarcity and uncodified information. Traditional screening and due diligence methods can be costly and time-consuming, leading to missed investment opportunities. A data-driven approach and AI come into play here, helping bridge the current information gaps and empowering startups and investors.

Today's data-driven competition dictates the need to prepare quality information on the startup side. This solution comes with costs associated with investing in the right tools and personnel. However, the benefits of adopting this approach far outweigh the costs as they help alleviate the "lemons" problem and give investors a critical edge to maximize market opportunities.

Chapter 5.3.
Mitigating Information Asymmetry

Startups and investors exist in an ecosystem of mutual dependence. Startups require funding, while investors seek profitable returns from their investments. Friction arises here due to information asymmetry when one party possesses more information than the other, giving them some temporary advantage. However, in the long term, asymmetry contributes to investors' high expectations regarding startup solutions. Not meeting these expectations leads to a breakdown of trust between parties, lost investments, and missed opportunities. A better understanding of the factors that derive information asymmetry and employing a data-driven approach to mitigate it is crucial for success in the contemporary VC landscape.

> ## What remedy helps overcome information asymmetry?

Overcoming Bounded Rationality

Information asymmetry is usually seen through the prism of VC's difficulties in selecting startups for investment. Startups may want to keep certain information private, such as negative feedback or early metrics, that may deter investors from investing. Conversely, investors may keep their investment criteria and how they assess risk

I CANNOT THINK OUTSIDE THE BOX. THE BOX IS FULL.

privately. However, founders only sometimes intentionally mystify VCs. They may need the necessary information to present it to investors. VCs also might be opportunistic, not adding real value, pushing startups toward excessive risk-taking, and exiting when suitable for their portfolios.

Founders' and VCs' behavior is not necessarily malicious intent: the irrationality of their actions is a scientifically proven fact in the theory of bounded rationality. Herbert A. Simone (1916–2001) was an American economist who won the Nobel Prize in Economics in 1978. He developed the idea of bounded rationality: humans are irrational and bound by their own "cognitive limits," according to him. Simon also wrote about how social relationships limit decision-making. People are not entirely rational when making decisions, including investment ones. Instead, they consider others' interests and institutional rules.

Simone was also a pioneer in the foundations of AI. Together with Allen Newell of the Rand Corporation, they created the first computer program that could prove mathematical theorems in the mid-1950s. [10]

Reducing Information Asymmetry

Information asymmetry is a double-sided process involving and affecting both parties. This process is purely informational, and mitigation of information asymmetry is possible through understanding its causes and using the data-driven approach. This problem's roots are hidden information and actions between investors and startup founders. To reduce asymmetry, startups must be transparent and provide comprehensive information to their investors. In contrast, investors must uncover their investment criteria. This exchange of information can help both parties make informed decisions and reduce uncertainty. [11]

Information asymmetry occurs in two distinct ways. First is "adverse selection," which pertains to instances without reasonable visibility into a startup's chances of success. The second is "moral hazard," which refers to situations where founders must balance their long-term business goals and immediate financial needs. Both adverse selection and moral hazard lead to a lack of transparency, making it challenging to estimate the potential success of a startup. Understanding the mechanism of information asymmetry allows taking measures to mitigate it and create solutions with potential positive impacts on both parties' performance.

All the existing mechanisms to reduce information asymmetry were created in the previous VC epoch:

- Extensive sourcing to have a more significant set of startups to choose from is time–consuming and ineffective.
- Fast screening to quickly check pre-selected options – might lead to lost attractive deals.
- Thorough due diligence ensures that the facts and figures in the pitch decks are accurate and can withstand criticism. However, it is expensive and often serves no purpose.
- Syndication to share risks and decrease screening and due diligence costs – does not solve all information asymmetry problems.
- Detailed legal contracting to provide some protection if things go wrong – is costly and inefficient.

Information asymmetry can be attributed to three groups, and each group affects VCs and startups to a greater or lesser extent. Data-driven mitigation methods may also have varying efficiencies due to the topic's novelty; some of them are still under development. The most important thing is a real opportunity to reduce or even eliminate some of the risks associated with information asymmetry and increase the efficacy of the industry. [12]

Information gathering and processing costs form the first group of causes of information asymmetry. On the startup side, we need cost-effective ways to collect and process data for effective decision-making. On the other side, investors must approach the investment endeavor in a data-driven manner. A possible solution for both parties is creating effective information systems for sourcing and screening (for more information about the Startup Dossier, see Chapter 2.3, "Generating a Data-driven Startup Dossier").

The second group of causes of information asymmetry is intangibles. It may be the most influential group, although the least studied and the most difficult to apply in practice. Research shows that intangible assets create a more significant information asymmetry between startups and investors. Undeveloped measurement methods and disclosure of intangibles can be a source of difficulties. Intangibles are not reported directly to the accounting system, preventing the extraction of firm-specific information for sourcing and screening. [4, Sec. 1]

The third group of factors comprises cognitive biases - standard psychological features. For investors, biases can influence them to ignore facts and manage the deal flow with their prejudices. Startup founders are influenced by their biases, too.

Poor information support of the investment process contributed to the widespread wrong belief that to fight information asymmetry is impossible, and the parties inevitably deceive each other.

PROFITomix Story

Digital Pizza

(Episode 15)

CAST:

Thomas

Investor
Technocrat

Steve

Startup
Founder

Steve decided to approach this investor one more time. This time, he brought a new marketing idea. While Thomas was skeptical during their previous conversations, Steve tried to use information asymmetry and play the right card to persuade the investor-technocrat. The founder analyzed previous discussions to avoid the same wrong moves. However, Thomas figured Steve's game out.

Hi Thomas! It's Steve here. Sorry for disturbing you again, but I have a killer idea for Digital Pizza's marketing. It's going to be a real game-changer.

Hey Steve! I hope you don't have secrets again.

No, no! As you signed the NDA last time, I'll show you the entire game.

Looks like you're about to play high-stakes gambling. Right?

Absolutely! The idea came to me when I saw an online roulette. You know, the wheel is spinning, the lights are sparkling – customers are fascinated!

How can this idea be worthwhile for Digital Pizza?

I noticed the analogy: Digital Pizza is divided into sectors that rotate like a roulette wheel, and spellbound customers look at it!

And how do you do it?

Thanks to VFX! We'll use G6 advanced mobile technology to project a holographic image of our pizza for customers. They can see different pizzas in detail before ordering and even feel mouthwatering.

Roulette?

Yes, in virtual reality!

And you win...?

Sure, casinos always win!

But it would be best to remember the difference between your site's visitors and buyers. Visitors might not go to the order. Casino conversion is about 1%.

Never mind! I'm holding a winning hand.

No, it's another hand that holds something...

What do you mean?

A Russian roulette!

Mitigating Cognitive Biases

Due to cognitive biases, investors and startup founders would benefit from a greater understanding of the current situation. If the startup is relying heavily on previous experiences, they may have to become more confident and optimistic or, on the contrary, extremely cautious about its performance.

Anti-biases mitigation measures for investors:

1. Looking for new business opportunities, narrow down a screening channel.
2. Use algorithmic tools for comprehensive and realistic estimations of risks.
3. Assume financial modeling and just-in-time financing. Make independent valuations and analyze the difference
4. Develop exit scenarios in detail. Never invest too early and too late.
5. Look for early trends and avoid following the crowd.

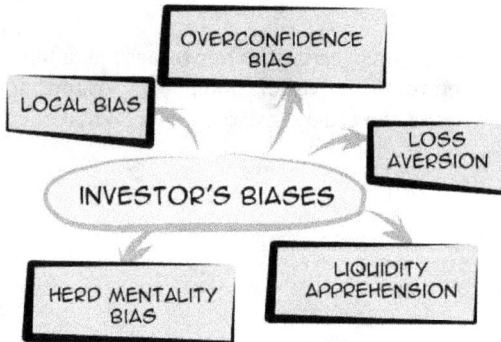

Many founders suffer from subconscious biases that impair their ability to conduct business rationally and create difficulties in receiving funding. Under conditions of information asymmetry and biases, the founders' strategies include:

- Raising as much capital as possible without giving up too much ownership.

- Giving investors a minimum guaranteed investment return and avoiding strict liquidation preferences.
- Keeping as much control as possible over the startup business.
- Protecting personal positions on the board even if it has no economic sense.

Anti-biases mitigation measures for founders:

1. Collect and process realistic information, including 1/3 of well-curated information in pitch decks, while keeping the rest for later steps of deal flow.
2. Working closely with investors on the board would be helpful.
3. Share sensible information with the most relevant people (lead investors and facilitators) and share control with investors and hiring managers when necessary.
4. Employing scenario modeling and pessimistic-to-realistic" financial projections to make realistic decisions.
5. Using comprehensive and complete information to make well-weighted decisions. Show how the team can manage intangibles.

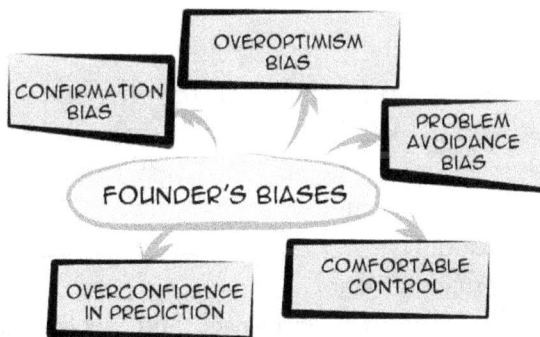

Exploiting or Fighting Information Asymmetry

Tim O'Reilly, an iconic Silicon Valley investor, once noticed the existence of two economies: "There are two economies, often confused: the operating economy, in which companies make and sell products and services, and the betting economy, in which wealthy people bet on which companies will win and which will lose in the beauty contest that stock markets have become. In the operating economy, the measure of success is... "the solution to human problems."...In the betting economy, the measure of success is the stock price; the higher, the better." [13]

The VCs that employ the betting strategy exploit information asymmetry as a tool. At the same time, the operating economy players suffer from information asymmetry and look for measures to mitigate it. Investors focusing on the operating economy are selective and interested in startups that design their products to value and profit. These startups employ innovative business models to create unfair competitive advantages and offer controlled returns to their investors. On the contrary, investors-speculators use a "spray and pray" approach, investing and exiting fast. They rely on mainstream business models like SaaS. The betting economy players like low entry barriers and early cashflows.

While investors-speculators use information asymmetry as their trade tool, the actual economy players need a solid information framework to select and finance early-stage startups. This framework helps them to get answers to tough questions:

- How does a startup's offer fit the investment strategy and portfolio?
- How does a startup identify and test critical assumptions to bring the startup technology to the market?
- How quickly does a startup complete MVP, and does it have a clear go-to-market plan?
- How does a startup appropriate and deploy intangibles for higher-than-average profitability and exponential growth?

Regarding startups, the founders' excessive desire and even obsession with attracting outside capital contributed to the overdevelopment of the "pitching" industry.

Don't think that obtaining funding means success. Gratifying an entrepreneur for raising money is like congratulating a chef for buying veggies. [11]

Pitch decks produced today emphasize an exciting effect. Sophisticated investors must read between the lines of pitches to understand technology applications and paths to the market. While such pitch decks are satisfactory for investor speculators, those who look for real ventures need pitches of a different format with a solid information background.

Market players need a facilitator to help them to overcome information asymmetry. The platform facilitator can work in the self-service mode, providing startups with methods and tools to gather and process quality information and then show it to investors. As a result, investors will get a chance to discover new opportunities, see a reliable path to profitability, and obtain effective control and protection of investments. Furthermore, this self-service model can increase the efficiency and transparency of the deal flow while lowering its costs.

Key Takeaways

Although information asymmetry exists objectively and is challenging to fight, discovering the root cause of the problems can help to find solutions for its mitigation.

Sometimes, the party with more information uses it as a benefit to deceive the party with little details. Reducing the cost of obtaining information and creating information channels for transparency can solve this problem to a certain extent.

Currently, data about startups is non-systemized and scattered in the information space. A facilitator who conducts information verification and adjustment can significantly reduce the cost of collecting information and increase the efficiency of its circulation.

The current imperfect information environment results in information asymmetry that impacts investors and startup founders. The higher the degree of information asymmetry, the lower the price investors are ready to pay to acquire startups. Founders demonstrate incompetence by providing investors with incomplete and sometimes misleading data because they cannot gather and curate quality information. Both parties will win, making the deal flow more transparent and reducing information asymmetry.

Points to Ponder

Founders can improve their chances of funding and developing their businesses efficiently by selecting the correct type of investor. Today, M&As, CVCs, and Syndicated Investors have become the VC market pipeline. Startups must consider a chosen type of investor preference. Each type of investors has special interests in target startups.

The CVCs are interested in the following set of factors:

- Novelty in products, processes, or methods.
- IP protection.
- Team members understand CVC's strategic priorities and investment rationales.
- The startup recognizes technology-laggard niches ripe for disruption.
- The startup is ready to share confidential information with CVC.

The M&A acquirers focus on the following startup' features:

- The startup is about to enter a significant and growing market.
- The startup is ready to transfer some control rights to an acquirer.
- The startup's customer base is growing.
- Team members understand the acquirer's strategy.
- Team members understand the acquirer's investment rationale and business model.

The syndicated investors look for the startup qualities, including:

- The startup can show an exit strategy and investor's terms.
- Cost structure, revenue models, and streams are clear.

- Gross profit margins look healthy.
- Team composition and structure are well-determined.
- The hiring plan, pool option, and equity splitting look reasonable.

Check an infographic of investors' rationales to see how they match the startup's tasks and the team's aspirations.

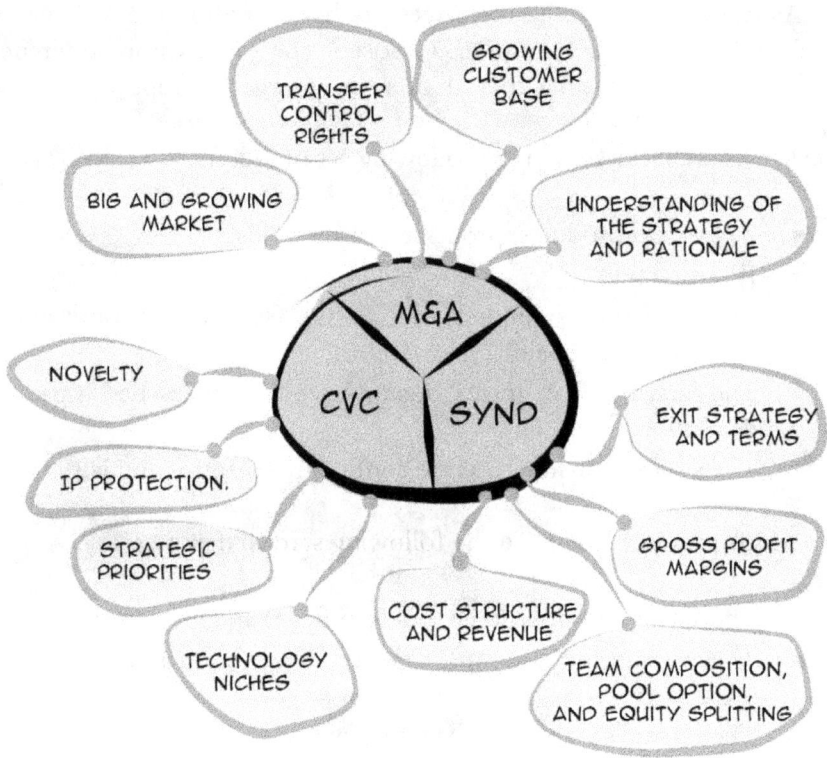

Section 6
Funding Journey

The current shift in the VC industry to startup profitability requires a revision of the traditional approach to sourcing and screening. Instead of a laborious and ineffective search among many low-quality startups, investors focus on a "cherry-picking approach: the thorough processing of the few startups worthy of their attention. After that, the agenda includes the development of new methods and tools and converting old approaches to fit new requirements.

A visual representation of a joint funding journey of startups and VCs as a Funding Roadmap makes the whole deal flow much more apprehensible and transparent. The roadmap outlines potential future scenarios and equips VC market players with intelligent navigation recommendations.

Startup valuation needs new assumptions that are increasingly based on startups' human and organizational assets included in deals. A composite valuation technique combines some proven and new methods to overcome shortcomings. Employing AI makes valuations more transparent and measured.

Relationships between venture capitalists and startups are formed at a new equilibrium level in which the balance of power is designated to increase the overall efficiency of the investment process. At this level, startup founders are incentivized enough to provide the exits expected by investors. In turn, investors avoid excessive pressure on startups and give them enough freedom for economic maneuver. In the joint funding journey, aligning interests with AI VCs and founders maximizes the chances of the best exits for both parties.

Chapter 6.1.
An AI-empowered Funding Roadmap

Roadmapping utilizes strategy, plans, and resources to create a visual structure for key initiatives or business processes. It is an efficient way to clarify objectives and organize information to reach desired outcomes. A funding roadmap is a visual overview of the deal flow as a funding project. This is a simple, easy-to-follow source of truth for VCs and startups to visualize the project and make critical decisions without digging through details. Building the roadmap is similar to plotting a joint journey for both parties. They can identify the destinations, map out the route, and track progress to ensure they stay on track and do not get lost. We can use a data-driven approach, modeling, and scenario-making to determine all critical touchpoints on the roadmap to make the funding process more efficient. The contemporary funding ecosystem is multifaceted and volatile, often presenting challenges to startups. Introducing AI into funding roadmaps transforms the art of funding into a precise science.

> **How can funding roadmapping transform the process of securing funding?**

The Roadmap as a Visualization Tool

Over half a century of using the roadmap concept, many roadmaps have appeared, expanding the original scope of its application – technology/products. Definitions of the roadmap are very diverse; therefore, for our purposes, a roadmap is a visual overview of the funding project, comprising its scope, output, and milestones. The main reasons for using the roadmap include:

- Managing uncertainty is inevitable in the initial stage.
- Keeping startups updated on the project objectives, progress, and roadblocks.
- Create foundations for subsequent detailed project planning.

The T-Plan, designed by Cambridge University in the 1950s, was the prototype of the numerous roadmaps used today. Using minimal resources, T-Plan provided step-by-step guidance on technology and product roadmapping.

Identifying and planning for potential risks is made easier with the T-Plan, a visual representation of a project's timeline. Highlighting milestones and deadlines also helps prioritize tasks and keep teams on track. Complex projects are often planned and executed with the help of this tool. The practice of roadmapping has long been utilized in various industries. Companies, from small startups to large corporations, can benefit from road mapping to maintain a competitive edge. [1]

A Funding Roadmap for Technology Startups

The roadmap provides a comprehensive visualization that helps prioritize technology/innovation development and commercialization activities. It allows us to spot shortcomings in the planning, make better management decisions, and facilitate the whole process in technology startups. Roadmapping has different levels of aggregation and directions of focus. Historically, all roadmapping branches grew out of the product roadmap. Then, the technology roadmaps appeared. Finally, the product and innovation/technology roadmap became complex.

Within traditional roadmapping, the technological perspective prevails. A "technology push" concept proposes the total ecosystem as technology-centered, identifying critical development and implementation trends. Today, the opposite "market pull" concept has become generally accepted. The new idea is more integrated, comprising products, technologies, markets, resources, and project goals and milestones. This comprehensive and integrated roadmap has a strong focus on finance/investment. The integrated roadmap is a valuable tool that can create a uniform understanding of funding activities for startups and VCs instead of a "random choice" approach typical in today's deal flow.

PROFITomix Story:

Digital Pizza

(Episode 16)

CAST:

Thomas

Investor
Technocrat

Robert

Investor
Traditionalist

Tomas texted Robert to discuss the opportunities for Digital Pizza startups. A couple of weeks ago, they both attended the workshop "Healthy Chunks of Financing Served in Time" for investors. Still, this encounter would mark their first direct dialogue. Robert is skeptical, questioning how a tech startup can succeed without a clear roadmap. On the contrary, Tomas is optimistic, highlighting the potential for technology there. They see a startup roadmap from different perspectives.

Hi Robert, it's Thomas here! Would you like to discuss the Digital Pizza startup that was on the radar for a while? I believe you have heard of them, too.

Yes, I did. Too technology-spiced to my liking!

From your seasoned angel POV, what would convince you to fund them? To make you believe that their tech solution would work.

Well, a detailed roadmap would help. It seems to me that Digital Pizza has changed its route with every move. With such a strategy of detours, they doubtfully navigate the company to its destination.

Interesting POV...So you don't like to fund them because you lack information about their roadmap?

There are different POVs. While you're flying to your high-tech pie in the sky, I'll stick to my roots firmly on the ground!

You have a point, but technology is everywhere today. New investors need not read business plans, and roadmaps are considered outdated documents. AI GPS should navigate rookie startups in the investment terrain.

I see... This AI would control startups in this terrain, commanding them where to go and what to do.

Exactly!
We, investors, know a point of destination better. Besides, if we want to fund AI startups, we must use AI ourselves.
AI will see the road ahead like glimpsing the future through a virtual reality GPS!

I may not fully grasp this tech-toppings obsession, but I'm starting to believe that I live in a new era of tech gods and Angels, and a pitch deck is a contemporary Testament.
Amen!

Imagine we are planning a journey, and instead of a fixed route, we have a flexible guide that changes as we travel. That's how modern roadmaps work like a compass leading the way or a master plan showing all the significant steps of the journey in one place. Roadmaps are essential tools in a funding journey, helping guide a team from start to finish. They aren't just technical documents but living guides that help everyone stay on track and understand the journey ahead.

A Fnding Roadmap Composition

Mapping simplifies the high complexity and multidimensionality of VCs' and startups' funding experience by determining the critical touchpoints. These touchpoints are located on the roadmap in logical order. They have different importance for future success: some are crucial, while others are less important. Attributes of each touchpoint might be quantitative and qualitative, including financial indicators, marketing characteristics, customer archetypes, and team characteristics.

The funding roadmap is intended to keep VCs and startups abreast of current and upcoming changes in the new business environment. The format of this roadmap is an easy-to-understand graphical illustration of crucial challenges and possible measures to overcome them during the funding journey. The roadmap comprises 12 touchpoints of a funding journey from the market entry to the exit event.

The key touchpoints have already been considered in chapters of this book, including:

1. Market entry – Chapter 3.3 "Market Entry Strategies & Timing."
2. Team & Management – Chapter 3.2, "An AI-enforced Startup Team."
3. Business Opportunities (focusing on commercialization) – Chapter 3.1, "POC in Startup Funding Journey.
4. Technology/Product (focusing on personal preferences) – Chapter 5.2, "Investors Protection & Information Problems."
5. Competition (focusing on intangible unfair advantages) – in Chapter 4.1, "Business Model Innovation."
6. Marketing (focusing on market entry) – Chapter 3.3, "Market Entry Strategies & Timing."
7. Financial projections – in Chapter 4.2, "Just-in-time Funding."
8. Intangible intensive business model – Chapter 4.1, "Business Model Innovation."
9. MVP & Traction – Chapter 7.2, "Minimal Viable Product & Traction."
11. Funding flexibility (focusing on just-in-time funding) – Chapter 4.2, "Just-in-time Funding."
12. Exit event – Chapter 5.1, "Exit Scenarios: Looking into the Future."

International prospects (item 10) include three main components:

1. Prerequisites for international market entry:
- Customer expectations and preferences are relatively common in the international markets.
- The main rivals have either internationalized or are about to internationalize.
- Technological changes in the international markets provide ample opportunities for startup products.
- Tests show international customers' interest in the startup products.

2. Working modes for the international markets include:
- Fluid Alliance is a temporary alliance under a simple agreement.
- A collaborative Project is a method of forming a team and controlling all work.

- A Joint Venture is when two or more companies create a jointly owned legal entity.
- Merger/Acquisition, when one company purchases another, or two companies merge.

3. Organisational forms for the international markets are the following:
- Subsidiary company.
- Independent agent.
- Representative.
- Distribution partner.
- E-commerce platform.

The execution of each point of the funding roadmap is associated with challenges. The latter are related to threats and business opportunities. Startups deal with challenges and deploy tangible and intangible assets to pave their paths to success. By developing the roadmap, founders ensure the startup meets the current funding conditions. The roadmap allows for visualizing the startup funding path and checking the information already collected in the Startup Dossier.

Integrating AI into Roadmapping

An efficient AI strategy is essential to funding roadmapping to augment existing processes. AI/ML can effectively collaborate with generative AI to predict, create reports, explain the modeling results, and provide recommendations. This integrated tool can empower VC market players to make more informed decisions, improving operational effectiveness and performance. Some use cases may be specific to AI/ML or generative AI techniques, while for others, applying the technologies in combination may be possible. [2]

AI/ML can reliably analyze numerical data for forecasting, risk assessment, "red flags" detection, and automatic scoring. The AI/ML algorithms help investors process large amounts of financial data to generate predictions about future trends. By leveraging AI/ML algorithms, startups can enhance predictive insights and increase data management within their projects. The startup teams can prepare for due diligence much faster than ever. At the same time, investors discover new opportunities quicker, helping accelerate and simplify the deal flow procedures. [3]

Generative AI can work in roadmapping to analyze complex patterns within historical financial information and forecast economic indicators. Its functions include a set of communication tasks, creating written and vocalized materials in the field of generated scenarios, automated reports, and other data intelligence tasks. As a facilitator, generative AI could explain variances and recommend different forecast scenarios and business decisions.

However, several critical challenges must be addressed to unleash the AI potential, including:

- Quality proprietary data and accurate use of AI tools are necessary. When training AI models in the public cloud, startups' proprietary data could be leaked in a security breach.
- AI tools lack contextual awareness and real-time information, resulting in difficulties with model output validation. The output models must be thoroughly tested and validated adequately against predetermined results.
- Generative AI models can sometimes produce "hallucinations"—incorrect responses. Various techniques could be used during model development to test a model's sensitivity to variable changes. This approach can help avoid inbuilt unintended biases.

To enhance confidence in concrete AI applications and establish faith in using AI technology for roadmapping, it is necessary to overcome a "black box" syndrome when the output of AI models is challenging to interpret. The modeling path must be transparent, while results must have a clear economic sense. Also, it is essential to have data protection protocols and other information protection measures, as well as simple and efficient information management.

Why employ AI for roadmapping? Because AI can solve problems that humans have never been able to solve properly, including predicting customers' needs, identifying market trends, assessing competition, identifying intangibles, and so on. Embrace AI transformation!

Key Takeaways

Startups can use the roadmap to plan and chart a successful funding journey. The roadmap is a powerful tool for startups to optimize their funding strategy. It can ensure financial efficiency and limit the risk of running out of resources during product/technology expansion. With the roadmap completed, a startup can be confident that the information is accurate and up-to-date. Founders can answer investors' tough questions and provide extra information on request. A correctly filled out quality information roadmap significantly increases startups' chances of receiving successful funding. It creates additional advantages in negotiations with investors.

As the funding journey becomes more sophisticated, roadmapping can help investors better identify potential addressing challenges and opportunities that could be yet uncovered. Effective roadmapping draws funding procedures and helps investors find new ways to increase return on investment. Moreover, roadmapping ensures that investors and founders are on the same page and helps align their interests. It provides both parties a clear path to success, benefiting in creating a productive partnership.

By incorporating AI into their roadmap strategy, startups can ensure investors in the long-term success, positioning themselves for a more successful fundraising round. Fusing AI with funding strategies is more than an incremental improvement over existing methods—it's a complete reimagination of the whole process. It opens a world where data-driven insights form decisions, market predictions are quantified, and resource allocation is executed with a precision that propels enterprises forward in their quest for innovation and growth.

Chapter 6.2.
Startups' Valuation by Investors

Startup valuations have come a long way since venture capitalists placed their bets by gut feel. Modern investors redefine the traditional paradigm and look for new approaches to accurately evaluate target startups' worth. In today's competitive landscape, investors must strike a delicate balance between profit and risk; too much focus in one direction can expose an investor if the startup fails or takes too long to reach fruition. With precision valuation tools at their fingertips, investors can now confidently make informed investment decisions. To keep up with the pace of investor demand, founders need to understand their startups' valuations and prepare to navigate through the valuation process with investors. A data-driven approach and AI developments provide insights into new startup valuation methods.

> **How can startup valuation be more precise?**

Profit vs Risk

Risk and return are positively correlated: the higher the risk, the greater the potential profit or loss. Higher levels of uncertainty and risk are associated with high returns.

In his book "Risk, Uncertainty, and Profit," published in 1921, American economist Frank Knight first explored risk and profit in conditions of competition between incumbent and new entrepreneurs. He discovered the paradox: profit whould not be possible under competitive conditions since new entrepreneurs would drive prices down and nullify margins, but there were still profitable and competitive markets.

Knight explains the paradox by highlighting the difference between calculable risk and unknowable uncertainty. He identified the "confusion" between "the problem of intuitive estimation" and "the logic of statistical probability." Profit arises from inherent and unpredictable things, making any probability calculation meaningless. [4]

The Evolution of Startup Valuation

Investors have individual risk inclinations when constructing a portfolio and use their intuition to make investment decisions. Their return depends on the increase in the valuation of their shares. Several methods allow weighing risk and profit, but each has pros and cons. Besides, valuations correlate with non-financial terms that are not easily quantified.

Traditional and well-developed quantitative methods of valuation have a common assumption: they work for businesses that have some historical data, including Capitalization of Earnings, Discounted Cash Flow, and Net Asset Backing. [5] None of these methods works for pre-revenue early-stage enterprises because they have no earnings, positive cash flow, or physical assets. Thus, startups have no data to apply methods using earnings, cash flow, and net assets, respectively. Different qualitative methods, including Berkus, Scorecard, and Risk Factor Summation techniques, allow us to evaluate such startups.

David Berkus, one of the most active angel investors who participated in over 190 technology investments, developed his startup valuation method in the 1990s. He created the first simple and elegant valuation model that relied on something other than financial projections as a reaction to early-stage startups' poor track records.

He offered to evaluate the impact of five factors:

- Sound Idea (fundamental value).
- Prototype (reducing technology risk).
- Quality Management Team (reducing execution risk).
- Strategic Relationships (reducing market risk).
- Product roll-out or Sales (reducing production risk).

Each factor counts from 0 to $500,000, and its sum determines a startup valuation. This method allows us to evaluate startups roughly with minimal input data. Unfortunately, simplicity has its dark side, and a concise set of factors ignores a range of essential facets of investment decision-making. The original matrix, Berkus said later, was too restrictive and should be a suggestion rather than a rigid form. In the model, elements not listed in the matrix should have a higher maximum value. [6]

Bill Payne, an eminent angel investor and business advisor, developed the Scorecard Method in 2001. This top-down method compares a target startup to other startups at the same stage (pre-seed or seed company), within the same geographic region, and in the same industry. Investors can apply weights to the most crucial factors:

- Strength of the Management Team (0–30%).
- Size of the Opportunity (0–25%).
- Product/Technology (0–15%).
- Competitive Environment (0–10%)
- Marketing/Sales Channels/Partnerships (0–10%).
- Need for Additional Investment (0–5%). [7]

Applying these adjustments to the original 'average' valuation allows us to calculate the final valuation.

The Ohio Tech Angels developed the Risk Factor Summation Method in 2008, adopting Payne's valuation technique. They considered a much broader set of 12 risk factors that determine the success of pre-revenue companies:

- Management.
- Stage of the business.
- Legislation/Political risk.
- Manufacturing risk.
- Sales and marketing risk.
- Funding/capital raising risk.
- Competition risk.
- Technology risk.
- Litigation risk.
- International risk.
- Reputation risk.
- Potential lucrative exit.

Risk Factor Summation Method also estimates risk, averaging comparable startups in the same industry and location and adjusting it against 12 risk factors. [8]

> Startup gurus pointed out that low-risk investments usually have lower profit potential. Investing at a higher risk means more profit potential but more risk of losing money. To each his own!

A Composite Valuation Method

While all three methods have some shortcomings, taken together, they allow to combine their advantages to create a composite method for more comprehensive startup valuation:

- Each technique can easily be modified, and its authors surmise that.
- Employing a weighted scoring scheme, the new combined model can be trainable using an AI/ML algorithm.
- Using an AI-powered web scraping algorithm, current online data can be extracted to determine the current average valuation of a typical startup.
- The parent valuation methods and the new ones assume risk is related to threats and business opportunities.

David S. Rose, a serial entrepreneur, prominent angel investor, and best-selling author who has founded or funded over 100 pioneering companies, coined the idea of a composite valuation method. We can combine the Scorecard Method, the Berkus technique, and the Risk-Factor Summation Method for a more reliable startup assessment. In his New York bestselling book "The Startup Checklist: 25 Steps to a Scalable, High-Growth Business," David Rose foresaw that new technologies will radically change the approach to valuation, "making it less of an art and more of a science." [9]

His ingeniously envisioned model describes a platform-facilitator: "With transactional platforms able to track the actual valuations at which investments are being made, while at the same time having access to the specific metrics of the companies being valued, it is possible—in a complete anonymous but highly accurate manner—to come up with mathematical calculators that look at the real metrics of business, combined with objective third-party analysis of intangible factors, and deliver remarkably accurate valuations...at least with a defined range of early stage, high-growth, scalable businesses." [9]

We set the composite method based on the four pillars:

1. Utilizing the long-established Risk Ranking approach with a 1-10 risk scale.
2. Taking the set of factors corresponding to the touchpoints of the Funding Roadmap (see Chapter 6.1, "An AI Empowered Funding Roadmap" for more details).
3. Employing a data-driven approach and collecting data about typical startups in the same region/industry sector/funding stage that have recently raised funds.
4. Providing investors with a tool to make startup valuations using their intuition and risk acceptance patterns.

Risk Ranking is one of the most common facilitation methods used for risk management. This method is also known as "Relative Risk Ranking" in the 1-10 risk scale:

- 1-2 "Very Cautious Risk" - Investors accept that the returns from their investments are likely to be low compared to the potential returns from investments with a higher risk rating.
- 3-4 "Cautious Risk" - Investors prepare to accept a higher risk of capital loss in return for the opportunity to earn more than low-risk investments.
- 5-6 "Balanced Risk" - Investors accept an increased risk of capital loss over investing in more low-risk investments.
- 7-8 "Adventurous Risk"—Investors accept relatively high levels of risk to achieve higher long-term investment returns.
- 9-10 "Very Adventurous Risk"—Investors accept that the value of their investments may fluctuate significantly and that they could lose a significant proportion (possibly all) of their investments to get the highest investment returns.

The composite valuation method includes six steps where all procedures are algorithmic, and only ranking startups' significant factors on the funding roadmap's touchpoints are performed manually by investors.

1st Step:

Selecting significant startup factors valuation—A set of factors initially selected by an expert is adjustable as the method improves. We propose using the set of 12 factors from the Foundation Roadmap (see Chapter 6.1, "An AI-empowered Funding Roadmap" for more details).

2nd Step:

Ranking startups' valuation factors - Investors feel free to use their intuition and insight to decide in what position on a 10-point scale a startup is on this indicator. Their decision takes into consideration personal risk inclinations.

3rd step:

Assigning weights for the factors—An expert initially assigns the weight as a percent of 100. Then, an ML algorithm that regularly adjusts the weights can be applied.

4th step:

Normalizing ratings by adapting them to investors' risk-taking/avoiding behavior patterns according to the Relative Risk Ranking method. An expert initially appoints the normalizing coefficients; the ML algorithm regularly adjusts them when applying the technique.

5th Step:

Aggregating the weights of factors and normalized weights to determine a composite rating for a target startup. The summarizing figure is compensatory, showing startup strengths and weaknesses in touchpoints of the funding roadmap.

6th Step:

Getting an approximate monetary startup valuation—Multiply the aggregated rating by a typical startup in the same region/industry sector/funding stage valuation. Entrepreneurs can collect benchmarks for this calculation with an AI-powered web scraping algorithm.

How to evaluate startups' intangible assets is a particular topic (read more in Chapter 4.3, "Startup Valuation: An Intangible Perspective").

FACTORS	RATING	NORMALIZED RATING	WEIGHTS	WEIGHTED NORMALIZED RATING
1. MARKET ENTRY				
2. TEAM &MANAGEMENT				
3. BUSINESS OPPORTUNITIES				
4. TECHNOLOGY & PRODUCT				
5. COMPETITION				
6. MARKETING				
7. FINANCIAL PROJECTIONS				
8. INTANGIBLE-INTENSIVE BUSINESS MODEL				
9. MVP & TRACTION				
10. INTERNATIONAL PROSPECTS				
11. FUNDING FLEXIBILITY				
12. EXIT EVENT				

TOTAL:

SUMMING UP THE WEIGHTED NORMALIZED RATINGS GETS US THE RATIO OF THE VALUATION OF A TARGET STARTUP COMPARED TO THE AVERAGE (BENCHMARK)

Leveraging AI for True Valuation

The valuations tell the "truth" when using standard, generally accepted methods and algorithms. Various underlying assumptions are open and understandable due to the opportunity to repeat calculations. A "lie" means unnecessary hidden data, omitted facts, or knowingly misrepresented information. But even if all information is trustworthy, it doesn't mean the projected performance is guaranteed. People can honestly be wrong. [10]

PROFITomix Story

Digital Pizza

(Episode 17)

CAST:

Thomas

Steve

Investor
Technocrat

Startup
Founder

Steve hired consultants to do a Digital Pizza valuation and turned to Thomas again. He hoped to impress him with a scientifically based startup valuation this time. However, nothing came of it. Thomas cynically ridiculed Steve's attempts to defend the inflated valuation figure.

Hi Thomas! Once you asked for our startup's valuation. It's ready now!

Well, shoot your number.

We're thinking of a valuation of $10 Million... It's a pessimistic POV.

Whoa... I'm scared to imagine your optimistic POV!

We hired intelligent guys who used nine different valuation methods.

Who says that applying nine methods is a good idea? Even if you hire nine women, the child will not be born earlier and will not be better!

You don't believe in our science-backed valuation?

I don't believe in horoscopes or Santa Claus, either! You have used the correct term: 'baked valuation.'

You might not believe in unicorns because they're mythical creatures that don't exist, but you still hope to find one someday to invest in, right?

Like unicorns, the best startups are rare and hard to come by. They're unique!

Well, we have one unique idea...

Let's hope it's unique enough to match your "pessimistic" number.

We want to harness the newest trend: Artisan goods...I say foods in our case.

Do you offer an artisan pizza? I'm afraid that handmade artisan items are labor-intensive and expensive!

No worries! We'll use a hi-tech solution to make our artisan pizzas on 3D printers divided into 12 sections like a clock, each number written with olive paste.

Hmm. The clock is ticking! So, I'd like to propose a low-tech solution...to cut your valuation to a reasonable level.

Interesting! What do you propose?

You'd better take a hand grater and a carrot to decorate your pizza clock with Roman numbers!

Manual multivariant valuations can be time-consuming and error-prone. AI is a game-changer that can help founders make informed decisions about profitability and thus clarify their startups' valuation. Profitability is the cornerstone of any business, signifying the ability to generate more revenue than expenses. While traditional financial analysis methods are useless for early-stage pre-revenue startups, AI can help founders analyze projective financial data to identify trends that lead to profitability. AI can create complex valuation models that consider a wide range of variables. This results in more accurate and data-driven startup valuations, which are crucial for attracting investors and making investment decisions. [11]

Dave Berkus, Bill Payne, and their followers created logic based on their long experience in valuation methods for pre-revenue startups. While these methods are mainly quantitative and approximate, they are user-friendly and easily can be provided with data. Combining their positive features within a data-driven approach, the composite valuation method provides a crack in the uncertainty surrounding startup valuations.

Applying the composite valuation method provides an optimal balance between human and algorithmic approaches. Both have flaws, but they are combined to engage startup founders and investors in the valuation process. Founders prepare quality information, and investors use the tool in reasonable symbiosis with their intuition. Thanks to AI algorithms, this tool allows us to overcome the scarcity (often total absence) of historical data about startups' performance. Moreover, it is flexible and adaptive enough to account for rapid changes in the VC industry.

Key Takeaways

Startup valuation is a tricky challenge as it combines assessing profits and risks against the ever-changing landscape of the VC market. The evolution of startup valuation has shown us that specific methods are necessary to improve the gauging of startups' value. However, utilizing a composite method for valuation offers better accuracy in determining the worth of an early-stage company. Leveraging AI and the data-driven Startup Dossier can take this method to a new level.

AI algorithms can assess expansive data sets to predict how startups will behave and track their progress more accurately. Through predictive analytics, investors can significantly reduce associated risks and provide the necessary insights. Startup founders can get an accurate and realistic estimate of the worth of their businesses. It helps both parties understand each other's expectations regarding valuation and enables them to bridge any potential discrepancy.

Chapter 6.3.
Aligning Investors' and Founders' Interests

Investors and founders have historically held misaligned interests, creating a system in which only one side wins. However, they can reconcile conflicting interests. Having mutually accepted startup valuation and understanding another party's strategies, both parties can reach an optimal balance of interest. Such a balance has a mathematical justification called the Nash equilibrium. While the new VC world becomes more intangible and AI-leveraged, finding a balance between two parties is more crucial than ever. Technology creates new opportunities for aligning investors' and founders' interests while deriving new challenges. By employing data and AI, we can discover new ways of balancing both parties' interests for mutual benefit.

> **How can technology help to align the VC market players' interests?**

The Nash Equilibrium

John Nash (1928 – 2015), an American mathematician, was awarded the 1994 Nobel Prize for Economics for his contribution to game theory: the analysis of conflict and cooperation. He investigated the typical business situation when parties have a common interest in collaborating but have conflicting interests over exactly how to cooperate. Nash showed

NASH WAS RIGHT... KNOWING WHAT TO DO IS KEY TO BALANCE!

BUSINESS PLAN

that both parties can arrive at an optimal outcome, known as the Nash equilibrium (balance of interests), when considering the possible actions of the other parties. [12]

It is possible to reach the Nash Equilibrium when each party's strategy is an optimal response based on the anticipated rational strategy of the other party. At its core, Nash equilibrium is a strategic doctrine signifying that in a non-cooperative game, where each participant is privy to the others' strategies, no player gains anything by solely changing their strategy. This condition occurs when every player's actions yield the best personal outcome, given the choices of others.

In game theory, mathematicians view Nash equilibrium as the opposite of the dominant strategy. According to Nash equilibrium, a player's best strategy is to stick to their initial strategy while knowing their opponent's strategy. In dominant strategy, the player's strategy leads to better results than the opponent's, regardless of which strategy they choose. The Nash equilibrium suggests harmony, but the dominant strategy aims to win at all costs.

All game theory models only work if the players involved are "rational agents," meaning that they desire specific outcomes, operate in attempting to choose the most optimal outcome, incorporate uncertainty in their decisions, and are realistic in their options. These theoretical assumptions do not fully correspond to reality, and it is necessary to consider other models, such as the theory of bounded rationality (see Chapter 5.3, "Mitigating Information Asymmetry" for more details).

Fighting Misalignment

Conflicts between investors and founders are nothing new. As long as money has changed hands, so have disagreements over rights, privileges, and decision-making powers associated with them—even before the emergence of venture capital as a professionalized investment asset class. But what's most important to recognize is that these conflicts stem from something more profound: mutual misalignment. The detailed regulation of deal terms does not eliminate the root cause of possible conflicts. The cause of conflict is the complex relationship between startup founders and their investors, whose interests may not always be aligned and reconcilable in a contractual agreement.

From sourcing to initial screening to screening due diligence, investors take comprehensive protection measures against possible startup failures. However, the detailed regulation of deal terms does not eliminate the root cause of potential conflicts: investors and founders have different interests. [13]

Founders' Position:
➤ Desirable and often overrated valuation.
➤ The more the better financing.
➤ Essential level of control over enterprise.
➤ Insufficiently justified size of investment and return.
➤ Poorly visible exit strategies.
➤ Inability to show intangible perspectives.

Investor's Position:
➤ Low than average valuation.
➤ Accepted risk associated with this investment.
➤ High level of return on investment.
➤ Reasonable exit strategies.
➤ Clear protection measures.
➤ Essential control over management and decision-making.
➤ Written rights and preferences.

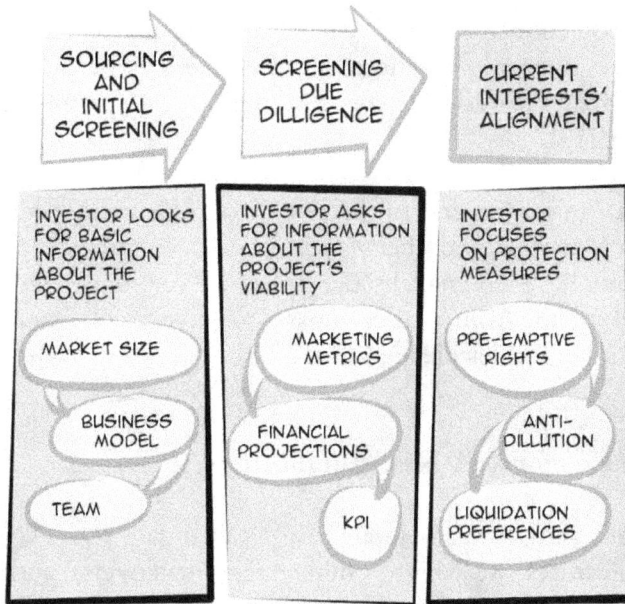

SOURCING AND INITIAL SCREENING	SCREENING DUE DILLIGENCE	CURRENT INTERESTS' ALIGNMENT
INVESTOR LOOKS FOR BASIC INFORMATION ABOUT THE PROJECT	INVESTOR ASKS FOR INFORMATION ABOUT THE PROJECT'S VIABILITY	INVESTOR FOCUSES ON PROTECTION MEASURES
MARKET SIZE	MARKETING METRICS	PRE-EMPTIVE RIGHTS
BUSINESS MODEL	FINANCIAL PROJECTIONS	ANTI-DILLUTION
TEAM	KPI	LIQUIDATION PREFERENCES

The entire existing economic model of deal flow is built on conflicting interests of investors and founders, including:

- Valuation—Investors focus on securing a lower valuation to obtain a higher ownership percentage, increasing their potential return on investment. Founders aim for a higher valuation to minimize ownership dilution and retain a more significant stake in the company.
- Equity Percentage – Investors want to acquire a significant enough stake to influence company decisions. Founders want to retain majority shareholders to control and continue making decisions.
- Type of Stock – Investors prefer Convertible Preferred Stock (to have priority over common shareholders during liquidation events, but they also have the option to convert their preferred shares into common stock at a predetermined conversion ratio) or Redeemable preferred stock (allowing the issuing company to buy back the shares at a predetermined price after a specific period). Founders prefer Common stock (which puts them on equal footing with investors and avoids granting liquidation or conversion preferences).

- Legal protection measures: Antidilution provisions (full ratchet vs. weighted average, Vesting of Founder's Shares, and CEO Replacement Provision) are also based on parties' conflicting interests. [13]

The current misalignment of investors' and founders' interests can damage both parties and the venture itself. To prevent conflicts or disappointments, each stakeholder must clearly understand what is expected of them. Both parties must proactively collaborate to meet their expectations and achieve mutual goals.

Intangible Economy: A New Equilibrium

A substantial shift towards intangibles is changing the VC world. Its economic features: scalability, sunkenness, spillovers, and synergies reorient the focus of the investment process from physical investments to human capital-based ones. Paradoxically, in this digitalized world, the role of human intelligence is increasing, and this is not the only paradox of the new reality. Although these paradoxes create new challenges, on the other hand, they are sources of higher-than-average profitability and exponential economic growth (see Section 1, "Intangible Wealth Hidden in Plain Sight," for more details).

> There is a paradox in investing in new intangible-intensive businesses. Some innovators become highly profitable and grow exponentially thanks to new business models and a novel data-driven approach. Then, those who can achieve high profitability and scalability will cease to be innovators and become parasitic monopolists, creating new market entry barriers. [14]

The challenges of innovation protection and the creation of moats against competitors also create one more paradox in the modern knowledge economy. Numerous spillovers make defending new knowledge-related forms of intangible assets challenging and allow companies to capture someone else's IP. At the same time, patent law and the entire IP protection system do not meet the requirements of the intangible-intensive knowledge economy (these issues will be addressed in Chapter 8.3, "Magic of Breaking Ownership Chains").

The financial system needs to fit the intangible-intensive economy due to the low pledgeability of intangibles as collateral and the indivisibility of initial investments in intangibles. Unlike tangible assets, intangible valuations are more volatile; intangible assets are more complex to redeploy and have a significantly lower liquidation value. Employing intangible-intensive business models, startups often have to reorganize their processes and improve their management practices and founders' skills. [4, Sec. 1]

New alternative forms of startup funding can help to solve the financial paradox:

- Venture Debt.
- Convertible Debentures.
- Revenue-based financing.
- Non-dilutive government incentives, including the R&D tax credit for startups.
- A shared earning agreement between investors and founders.
- Creditor funding/debt for equity swaps.
- Funding with shares.
- Just-in-time funding (see Chapter 4.2 "Just-in-Time Funding").

The idea of aligning VCs' and startups' interests is not new. Unfortunately, the proposed measures remained good wishes. Today, they are vital and must have appropriate economic mechanisms for their implementation in practice. Aligning interests is crucial and can work as leverage in reducing conflicts, improving trust, and encouraging transparency. Both investors and founders are working towards a common goal: profit.

PROFITomix Story

Digital Pizza

(Episode 18)

CAST:

Linda

Investor
Profiteer

Steve

Startup
Founder

To this conversation, Steve has a standard business plan made by hired consultants. It is specifically designed to excite investors—'Clickbait,' as they say. However, Linda does not take the bait: she is interested in the next round of funding and steers the conversation toward her interests. Her motto is "up and to the right." The conversation revealed that Steve and Linda imagined different pictures of Digital Pizza's development.

Hi, Linda! You told me you never invest in fiction, so I have a professional business plan to show you solid facts.

I'm keen to hear more about where your startup is headed. I typically look for a clear exit strategy in my investments. Can we talk about how you view potential investor exits?

Of course. We're exploring three exit strategies. Our goal is to grow significantly over the next few years, which should open avenues for a merger with an extensive food market player, an acquisition, or an IPO.

Right. Staying agile with exit plans is necessary. In my experience, aligning your exit ideas with mine is vital.

That's the thought. We want to foster a relationship with investors based on transparency and mutual gain.

And I always prefer candid conversations with founders about market pressures and risks. I invest wisely, and I'm afraid to take uncalculated risks.

That aligns perfectly with our philosophy. We're not just chasing trends; we're in it to build a lasting company that genuinely adds value.

So, let's calculate the risks of your planned exits and outline some standard triangles of terms.
I need a couple of board seats to meet a future merger.
The preferred stock helps me prepare for acquisition.
IPO is rare now, and I'd like to see good liquidation preferences.

Huh...I see it is triple-dipping.
Your "standard triangle" looks like a Bermuda one.

Both parties should contribute to reaching higher levels of equilibrium and their financial interests, understanding the new roles they should play today. Instead of excessive alienation, investors should protect reasonable founder autonomy, giving them enough freedom to execute their vision and make operational decisions. On the other hand, founders need to encourage investors' representation, allowing them to take a constructive part in the startup's decision-making process. These measures help maintain the alignment of parties' interests. [15]

Aligning Interests with Technology

The deal flow process faces several challenges, including information asymmetry, difficulties of veracious startup valuation, and the probability of opportunistic behavior of startup founders and investors. Employing a data-driven approach and algorithms allows us to screen out unprofitable startups and bad teams. In conditions where people have bounded rationality and cognitive biases, technology can bring more clarity and efficacy in solving the problem of startups and VC interests' alignment.

Achieving the balance of interests is possible with the coordinated actions of both parties that understand valuations and deal terms as combined complex through:

- Identify significant milestones on the funding roadmap and clarify the journey (knowing the path).
- Calculating projected revenues and costs, reducing uncertainty (knowing economics).
- Determining the need for extra capital during the funding journey, eliminating dilution (connecting the path and economics).
- Making well-justified and multi-variant startup valuations that show actual values, including intangibles (improving trust and transparency).

(For more details, See Chapter 4.3, "Startup Valuation: An Intangible Perspective," and Chapter 6.2, "Startup Valuation: An Investor Perspective."

Investors have the upper hand if there is a need for more investment resources in the market. If there is an excess of capital, startups can use the hype to their advantage. Nevertheless, an

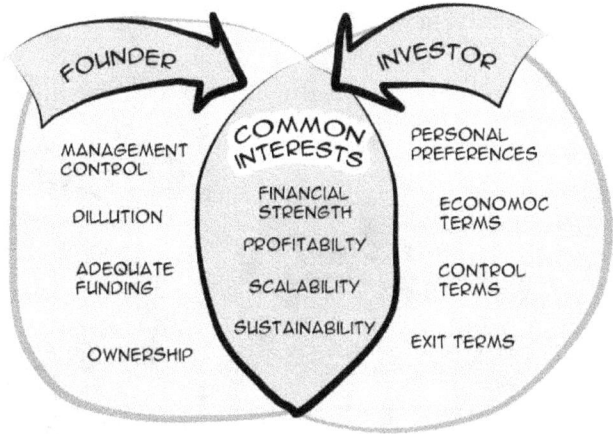

area of common interest exists, and information technology can help to find an optimal balance of interests. Overcoming information asymmetry is a prerequisite for rational equilibrium. Moreover, curated information in the Startup Dossier can clarify the deal conditions to avoid conflict between VCs and founders and help them reach a higher equilibrium.

Considering valuations and deal terms together helps us to understand the nature of conflicting interests. In reality, any deal terms can affect the valuation. For instance, if investors want two board seats, they will likely agree to take only one board seat in exchange for an essential reduction in the valuation. Some deal terms may be deal-breakers for investors, so the deal will not take place regardless of the valuation. The deal terms are "classical" non-quantifiable valuation factors, including antidilution provisions, preemptive rights, information rights, registration rights, and liquidation preferences. [16]

Considering that both investors and startup founders aim to maximize their profit, allow us to outline their mutually beneficial strategy:

- Employing the hybrid approach in which algorithms complement human creativity.
- Providing tools for collecting and processing information and keeping all findings in the Startup Dossier.
- Creating a solid information background for startups to be fit for funding: investors obtain trustworthy, thoroughly curated, and complete information about investment opportunities and make well-weighted decisions.

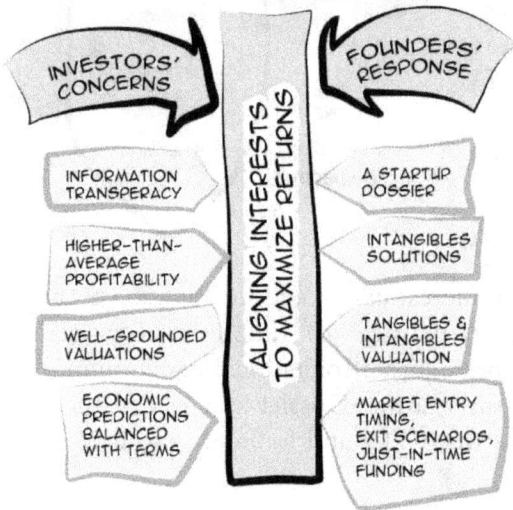

The new economic way of balancing investors' and startups' interests focuses on an optimal power split and the trade-offs between cash flow and control rights. The optimal balance of power between VCs and startups maximizes the probability of success. Recent research identifies an impact of startup intangible assets, particularly human and organizational capital, on the equilibrium level. The best VCs with an optimal balance strategy can match quality startups. [16]

A manual process rarely achieves an optimal alignment of common interests. To balance interests, AI can use a wide range of variables that humans cannot consider!

Key Takeaways

The VC industry has just entered a new stage of development. In this stage, we see a strategic shift from bulk processing of low-quality startups to the "cherry-picking" of selected startups that promise higher returns. [3, Sec. 5] To get funding, startups must demonstrate their abilities to meet the conditions of the new equilibrium. On the other hand, the quality of VCs and their collaborative strategies are also part of the new equilibrium in which economic terms and rights are interdependent.

While misalignment has become a norm in securing capital, breaking from this pattern and equipping VC market players with tools that provide more equitable outcomes for all parties is necessary. Investors should no longer have the upper hand in forcing unfavorable terms on startups out of necessity. Similarly, founders should only defend their ownership and management tights when it makes economic sense.

AI and a data-driven approach provide new opportunities for founders and investors alike, helping to maintain alignment of interests while encouraging growth from both parties. Leveraging technology ensures that both parties' interests remain aligned in a mutually beneficial relationship.

Points to Ponder

It is necessary to check key projections before presenting them to investors, who can envision the whole business development picture and have several rules of thumb for verifying facts in the pitch deck and presentation.

See an infographic to check ten main points (find "red flags") of the startup business perspective to discover dangerous gaps in the business model, the understanding of the current situation, and the proposed implementation of the project:

Possible "red flags" include:

1. Limited investor protection measures - Indicate a board position, the type, and the number of shares for investors.
2. Limited investor exit opportunities—Show a precise and customized exit plan, such as mergers/ acquisitions, management buyouts, etc.
3. Low traction after a long period—Low traction after 12 months indicates a poor selling experience or buyers' non-recognition of the product.
4. Shortage of paid customers—While many customers test the product, they may be less willing to pay for it (offer test customers to buy it).
5. Growing a customer base is too expensive, which indicates that further development will be accompanied by decreasing margins (Cut marketing expenses).
6. An indeterminate business model--It is better to have a working, simple model than to promise a complicated one in the future.
7. A funding period that is too long -- The founders cannot convince investors to fund their enterprise.

8. Too diluted equity--The enterprise's ownership decreased due to some previous equity issuances (Put an antidilution clause in the offer).
9. Technology has no reliable moats - IP rights must be adequately protected (Consider a patent, trademark, or know-how protection).
10. TAM, SAM, and SOM are too small or big - Apply both Top-down and Bottom-up approaches and use the rule of thumb: SAM may be about 10% of TAM, and SOM is about 2%.

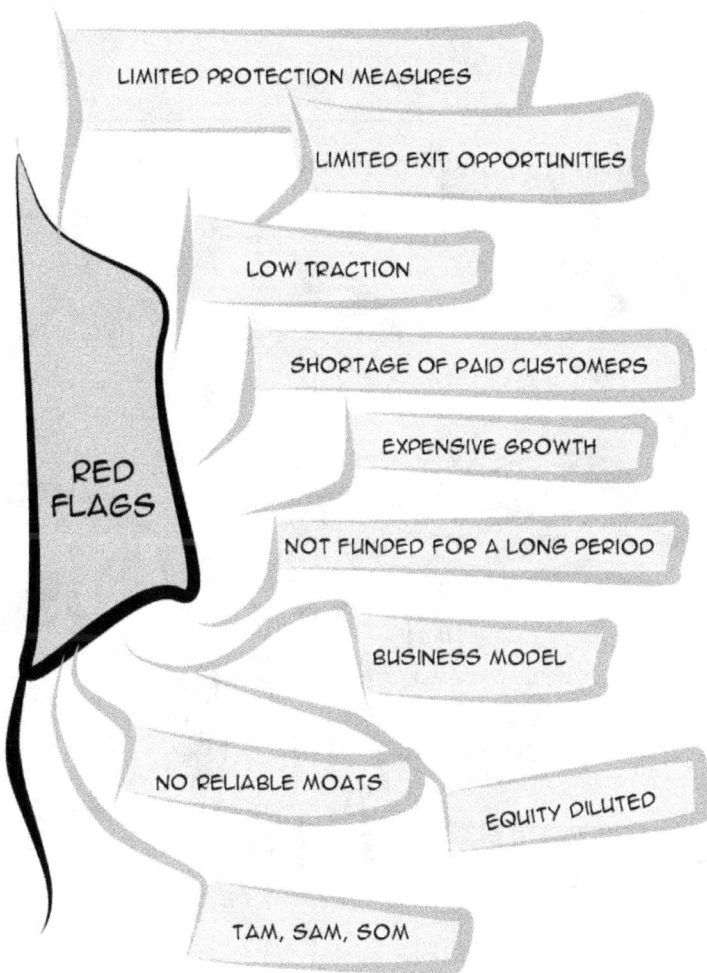

RED FLAGS
- LIMITED PROTECTION MEASURES
- LIMITED EXIT OPPORTUNITIES
- LOW TRACTION
- SHORTAGE OF PAID CUSTOMERS
- EXPENSIVE GROWTH
- NOT FUNDED FOR A LONG PERIOD
- BUSINESS MODEL
- NO RELIABLE MOATS
- EQUITY DILUTED
- TAM, SAM, SOM

Section 7
Startups' Validation & Presentation

In today's dynamic VC environment, all market players must look beyond the conventional pitch decks and MVPs to a new horizon where AI and data help validate startup potential and present it in the best way. By employing technology and experimentation, startups can avoid the mistakes that often lead to failure and instead build a profitable business.

In the rapidly evolving ecosystem of startups, business model validation has emerged as a non-negotiable element for entrepreneurs eager to introduce new offerings to the market efficiently. Gone are the days of relying on speculative business plans. Today, startups are turning to rigorous experimentation to test their business models, strengthen their foundations, and enhance their prospects of building lucrative enterprises.

Using AI algorithms and lean principles, founders can create affordable MVPs to obtain customer feedback and adjust their models accordingly. This approach reduces risks, improves chances of success, and proves more resilient. The integrative power of AI-based validation tools offers a more productive path to building MVPs. When startups leverage these advanced tools, they can craft their MVPs grounded in data and real-world validation.

Traditional pitch deck presentations are full of fluff and cannot distinguish between startups with merit and those unsuitable for funding. Using AI could bring much more transparency and verifiability into the fundraising process, thereby increasing the chances for promising startups to acquire capital. Startups can benefit from an AI-empowered, more structured, data-driven approach, spurring investor collaboration. For VCs, the whole process becomes more streamlined and also more productive.

Chapter 7.1.
Startups' Business Model Validation

Over the past years, we have seen explosive growth in new startups trying to disrupt industries through compelling business models and innovative technologies. However, most of these ventures fail due to fundamental flaws and gaps in their underlying business assumptions that they could not properly validate. A new groundbreaking concept of business experimentation instead of outdated 'classical' business planning pioneered a decade ago. In today's VC world, data-driven approaches and AI algorithms make it possible to build a validator to validate business models quickly and efficiently.

> **How does business experimentation help to validate startups' business models?**

Algorithms vs. Human Intellect

American behavioral economist Daniel Kahneman won the Nobel Prize for Economics in 2002. He acknowledged the transformative capabilities of AI/ML to analyze data and forecast outcomes. He foresaw a future where decision-making can be vastly improved by leveraging AI/ML's predictive abilities, leading to more informed and potentially more objective decisions.

However, Kahneman cautions against overreliance on AI systems. He warns that placing too much trust in these technologies might erode human judgment and decision-making skills. On the one hand, Kahneman studied cognitive biases and errors humans are prone to make. On the other hand, he noted that AI systems, while able to process large amounts of data, still require human guidance and supervision.

One of Kahneman's most pressing concerns is algorithmic biases. AI/ML systems learn from large datasets that can contain biased information, whether stemming from historical data or societal prejudices. Kahneman stresses that without careful design and human oversight AI systems may perpetuate or exacerbate these biases, leading to wrong outcomes.

Kahneman argues that human decision-making is susceptible to errors that cannot be explained by bias alone but also by "noise" that is unpredictable, haphazard, and unreliable. When it comes to decision-making, algorithms outperform people. Unlike humans, algorithms are free from noise. They consistently produce the same response when presented with data. Harnessing the power of algorithms allows for eliminating noise in the decision-making process. [1]

Kahneman's discoveries require a revision of our views on the roles of humans and algorithms in decision-making. It also contributes to the idea of experimental business model validation with AI.

Business Experimenting vs. Business Planning

Three decades ago, everyone believed a business plan was vital in outlining business opportunities, problems and solutions, target markets, teams, and financials. With a firm reliance on historical data patterns, business plans work for revenue-generating enterprises but are ineffective for pre-revenue startups. Investors could not trust financial projections for several years and artificially designed timelines of future actions. Thus, "classical" business planning has become unpopular today. [2]

Later, the idea of experimental market entry appeared. [3] It can be risky as the market may need to be more receptive to the new product or service. For example, a startup might invest in a new product launch only to find that the market is saturated with similar products, leading to a significant loss of resources and time. Furthermore, resources may be limited, and the experiment's results may not be known for some time. Therefore, before entering the market, it is essential to thoroughly research and plan to minimize the potential risks and maximize the rewards.

We can define a business model as a startup's core logic for creating and delivering value for its customers and capturing value for itself. In the context of business models, it is imperative to emphasize that they differ from revenue models. Business models represent the overall business, including all processes. Value propositions, value creations, and value captures are business model components. Startups can run on multiple business models; a single business model can have various revenue models. [4]

To validate business models, startups must educate themselves to grow knowledge about their funding journey. In the past, there were two ways of learning. The first method was based on analysis and optimization and was shaped as business planning. The second proposed method is to run experiments on the market to gather market feedback and adapt products to this experimental circle of commercialization.

Lean Startup is an experimental method of reducing the risks of innovative projects. Developed by Eric Ries, a prominent entrepreneur, business visionary, and the author of the international bestseller "The Lean Startup," this method is the most important invention in the modern startup ecosystem. Its idea embraces rapid startup experimentation and learning from their successes and failures. [5]

Lean Startup Co. applies Eric Ries' ideas in practice and develops them further. This organization has become a global movement aiming to equip startup teams to create new business ideas. A managing director of Lean Startup Co, Ben Hafele, has worked as the Lean Startup practitioner with over 400 startups and innovation projects in five continents. He focuses on building an experimental cycle and validated learning, guiding startups from initial ideas to profitable enterprises. [6]

According to Eric Ries, "The more experiments you do, the more likely you are to find something that works." [6]
Said to the point!

Designing Business Experiments

Rapid experimentation, however, poses its challenges because designing and running experiments might be expensive and time-consuming. Technology paves a new way of preparing business experiments before actual market entry. [7] By validating business models, startups can identify their assumptions and assess their impact on future performance. Every model component should be validated, including inputs, processing, and outputs. Effective validation is paramount to the business's success.

Any startup has two principal lines of development. In the first case, it operates in a traditional industry using a proven business model. It can even show real profits reasonably quickly. Using traditional feasibility study tools, modeling traditional startup results is quite simple.

However, a conventional business never shows remarkable profitability and exponential growth.

In the second line of development, the startup operates at the boundaries of industries by developing an innovative business model. It can also create innovative products or services, which are not required. The reverse side of employing the innovative business model is a higher level of uncertainty and difficulty modeling itself. In this case, the startup must inevitably develop new channels, partnerships, or a customer base. In each of these activities, business experimentation is possible.

Four attributes are crucial to designing clear and convincing business experiments:

- Focusing on a limited set of the most critical business model factors, ignoring the rest.
- Measuring modeling outcomes against the preliminary hypothesis (predicting desirable and unwanted results).
- Conducting simple and inexpensive experiments (as a rule, startups do not have excessive resources to spend on experimentation).
- Configuring it for learning, considering the human factor, and giving results quickly. [8]

Entrepreneurs tirelessly explore various business model options, seeking coherent and compelling frameworks that offer unparalleled competitive advantage and economic leverage. Creating a competitive advantage is paramount as it enables the business model to stand apart from other options available to customers. This advantage entices customers and empowers the company with pricing power and high margins.

Moreover, economic leverage is indispensable to ensure that the business model thrives and delivers substantial profits at scale. Behind every coherent business model lies an exceptional economic story, an intersection of economic forces that fuel value creation and capture. Together, these components form a power-packed and irresistible business model poised to conquer the market and create lasting value.

A Validator as an Experimentation Framework

The validation process in an ever-evolving business environment requires quality data and algorithmic procedures that convert input data into meaningful outputs in a well-defined processing chain. The process starts from the POC to the MVP stage (often from low-fidelity MVP to high-fidelity one).

The process of experimental business model validation has four essential features:

- It gathers all essential elements in one framework, creating a tool to operate with them.
- It allows for discovering interrelationships among elements and distinguishing patterns useful for predicting business profitability and scalability.
- It captures value, leverages profit, and even shows how innovations are viable and feasible.
- It is a learning process for mastering new modeling approaches by humans and AI/ML applications.

Different tools play their roles in data-driven business experimentation. Business canvases and templates are suitable for pre-processing input data and stimulating insights. Then, algorithms automate calculations to produce output data. Tests allow for checking of preliminary founders' hypotheses and solutions. Case studies have a learning sense to see examples of business implementation for better understanding. AI/ML tools work in the different parts of the experimentation process, gathering and processing unstructured data from alternative sources and calculating weights of factors in scoring algorithms.

INPUT DATA SOURCES

TOOLS FOR OUTPUT

MVP

- PROBLEM-SOLUTION AND PRODUCT-MARKET DATA
- ECONOMIC DATA
- ALTERNATIVE SOURCES

- SELF-CHECK TESTS
- ALGORITHMS AND AI TOOLS
- SCENARIO MODELLING

POC

- FOUNDER'S KNOWLEDGE
- TECHNICAL FEASIBILITY
- CUSTOMER DATA

- BUSINESS CANVASSES
- TEMPLATES
- CASE STUDIES

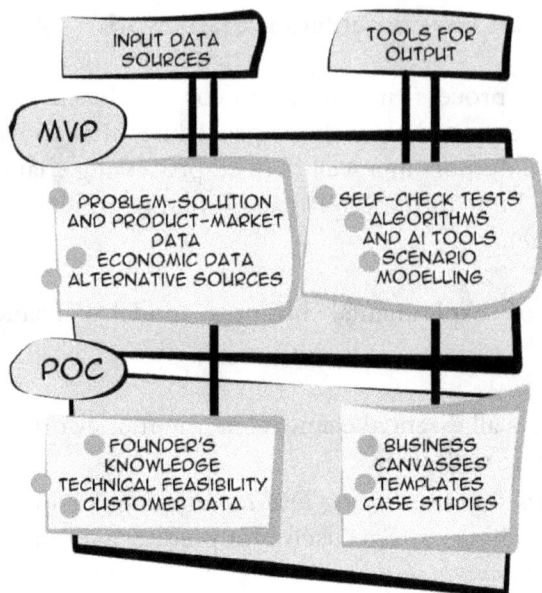

The data-driven and algorithm-enforced approach allows startups to validate new business models before their performance, decreasing risks of failure and allowing a chance of success via:

- Collecting data, unifying its configuration, providing user access, and information processing.
- Using scenario modeling and algorithms through an iterative process of testing and self-learning in a continuous cycle.
- Actively involve users (startup founders and investors) in the validation process to make it quicker and cheaper.
- Employing AI to generate knowledge from information.

An AI-powered Validator

An AI-powered validator is a tool that combines data analytics, machine learning algorithms, and validation techniques to evaluate and validate business models. This validator can analyze large datasets by leveraging AI technologies, uncover patterns, and provide accurate predictions or recommendations. It is a reliable source of information and guidance for investors and startups, empowering them to make informed and data-driven decisions. Moreover, it is necessary to tailor the validator to address the specific requirements of venture capitalists and startups. [9]

The three key components and processes that drive the AI validator include:

Data collection and analysis are the foundations of the AI validator. It gathers information from various sources. This collected data then undergoes a rigorous analysis phase to identify patterns, trends, and correlations. Visual tools like charts and graphs help interpret and understand the data.

ML algorithms are the backbone of the AI validator. These algorithms are trained on the collected and analyzed data to recognize patterns, make predictions, and classify data points. Training the algorithms allows them to learn from patterns and relationships. The training phase aims to optimize the algorithms' performance and accuracy. After training, users can validate algorithms using a separate data set to ensure their generalizability and accuracy. It is an iterative process, constantly improving the algorithms' performance.

The AI validator is an indispensable tool that empowers investors and startups with valuable insights and predictions based on data. Leveraging advanced analytics and ML revolutionizes the way business models are validated. However, this tool has inhered limitations. It is necessary to use human-machine methods, employing algorithms to automate processes where this makes sense and creates convenience. In some cases where formalization is impossible, it is reasonable to stimulate human' creativity.

PROFITomix Story:

Digital Pizza

(Episode 19)

CAST:

Michael	Robert	Gippetio
Visionary Investor	Investor Traditionalist	Bot

Michael just held a workshop for investors, "Cutting through an AI Noise with Monopoly 2.0," in which he devised an idea to validate startups with an AI-powered Monopoly game. After the workshop, Robert texted Michael to clarify some points about using this innovative approach. Gippetio took part in the conversation, commenting on it cynically and finalizing the performance with an almost human emotional impulse.

Hey Michael! I used to play that old Monopoly game with my friends in my youth. So, I'm trying to reconcile my old perception with your fresh idea. And I should play with a bot now.

Gippetio would be a stronger player than any human. It's the same story with games like Chess and Go, where algorithms defeat the world champions. Besides, we permanently correct algorithms to make the game more realistic.

You can correct AI but can't natural stupidity!

To what extent would it be realistic?

The game becomes more brutal to stimulate players to chase funding opportunities...like in the real world. Supposedly, if you behave ruthlessly in the game, you can also behave ruthlessly in reality.

And you keep cheating like in reality!

I see there are no old suitable dice anymore. Right?

Absolutely! Instead, we use a decision tree algorithm.

And "Go to Jail" was replaced with the "Go to Offline" mode, which is even more terrible for Z-Gens!

And what about railways?

There is a replacement again:
Hyperloops and quantum tunnels.
They work faster!

For those seniors who think slowly, we propose Monopoly 0.0.

I want to ask the last question... It's still unusual for me that the bot is a full-fledged participant in our conversation...How is this AI model reliable?

Well... We'll fine-tune the AI model to more accurately augment investment reality and check the bot for hallucinations. Then, we'll continue to modify Monopoly.

We, smart AI bots, think and act with unimaginable precision and accuracy. In contrast, you humans are susceptible to biases and hallucinations. <END>

People and algorithms have complementary strengths and weaknesses; each party uses different data sources and types. Within the hybrid approach, applying heuristics and intuition together with algorithms makes it possible to reach reasonable accuracy of results:

- Employing a "knowledge transfer" method in which founders form comprehensive and quality information step-by-step in the Startup Dossier. Then, founders transfer this curated information to investors, making the sourcing and screening process more efficient.
- Collecting data from three sources: internal, created inside enterprises; modeling, when information about the business environment is built into algorithms; and alternative, from open online sources.
- Utilizing the hybrid approach in which human expertise and algorithmic solutions complement each other.

Understanding and explaining the validation results can be complex because AI models often operate like mysterious black boxes, concealing their internal processes. Some measures can help unravel the mysteries of AI predictions, making validations more understandable. Analyzing AI models' stability over time and across different subsets of data allows us to watch out for sudden accuracy declines, which are red flags that indicate the need for model recalibration. Another measure is regular sanity checks for AI model outputs using stress-testing scenarios.

The key to unlocking this potential lies in AI's strategic and thoughtful integration into your business model design process. AI experimentation is a systematic process that involves the application of AI technologies to test hypotheses or assumptions, learn from the results, and make informed decisions. It is a crucial component of the AI lifecycle, which includes data collection, model training, model testing, and model deployment. AI experimentation allows organizations to validate their AI models before full-scale implementation, ensuring they are accurate, reliable, and effective.

Key Takeaways

The AI-powered validator framework helps startups test different business models faster and cheaper. Experimental validation helps founders reduce costly risks in pursuing innovative products, intangible solutions, or volatile markets. For investors, the validator means an enhanced search for better business opportunities and more efficient due diligence. The VC industry creates a more intelligent business environment by embracing business experimentation.

There are many benefits of employing data-driven modeling validation instead of experimenting in the market directly. Experimenting with new products or services in a modeling mode keeps expenses low and avoids wrong decisions, the consequences of which lead to high costs. Experimentation decreases business risk by enabling startup teams to play some scenarios before execution. Experimental validation enables checking assumptions, market situations, and even customer behavior in terms of hours and days instead of months and years, which is inevitable in the case of real business validation.

This way, AI and human expertise can work together to counterbalance each other's limitations.

Chapter 7.2.
Minimal Viable Product & Traction

The MVP concept originates from the lean startup methodology formulated in the early 2000s, revolutionizing how startups assess product development and market entry. The idea was to rely on direct business experimentation and gather customer feedback for validation rather than on untested business plans.

An MVP is a bare-bones final product version that includes just enough features to attract early adopter customers and validate a product idea early in the product development cycle. The main objective behind creating an MVP is to initiate the learning cycle as quickly as possible by introducing a product to the market and measuring its performance against customer feedback. For founders and investors alike, mastering the iterative process of deploying and refining MVPs is crucial for building a viable product that gains steady market traction.

MVP Origins

Frank Robinson created the term MVP in 2001 [10]. Then, in 2011, Eric Ries popularized the concept in his famous book, "The Lean Startup: How Today's Entrepreneurs Use Continuous Innovation to Create Radically Successful Businesses." [5] According to Robinson, MVP is not a testing tool but a prototype intended to generate revenue. A decade later, Ries proposed a more accurate definition of MVP focused on validated learning. He reasonably does not say anything about revenue.

Robinson states MVP is a practically ready-for-sales product that can bring maximum ROI divided by risk. [10]
Eric Ries' definition expresses this phenomenon's essence more accurately: "That version of a new product, which allows a team to collect the maximum amount of validated learning about customers with the least effort." [5]

Developing MVP

Today, technology creates a basis for data-driven validation, and startup teams and investors begin recognizing intangible assets and solutions. When employing MVP as a technology-enabled learning tool, entrepreneurs should clearly understand in what measure the technology can help validate their assumptions about a business model. Technology can help, but this is not its inherent property. Besides, the novelty of technology often serves to create bubbles.

PROFITomix Story

Digital Pizza

(Episode 20)

CAST:

Michael	Steve	Gippetio
Visionary Investor	Startup Founder	Bot

Steve texted Michael to let him know that Digital Pizza is ready to launch an MVP. Steve described Digital Pizza's success in flowery metaphors, but Michael quickly understood that the startup developed a low-fidelity MVP. Gippetio added sarcastic commentaries to the conversation, revealing a low startup's readiness to enter the real market.

Hi Michael, I've got exciting news! The Digital Pizza's MVP is hot out of the virtual oven!

Let me guess, is it half-baked?

Or its binary flavor is not fully developed...

With this MVP, we're genuinely slicing up the competition!

How can you be sure it won't flop?

You won't find those cutting-edge slices in your app drawer soon.

Our beta testers can't get enough! They want a slice of the future.

Or they're just hungry?

I analyzed their social media. 99.5% are hungry.

We customize the toppings digitally; customers can try them before buying!

They chew on the idea today and digest the real thing tomorrow. Right?

Don't mind me; I'm just waiting for the binary breadsticks to come out of debug mode.

Michael, it's simple. We're harnessing the power of AI to deliver the perfect pizza experience right down to the last pixel!

Pixel? Steve, people can't eat pixels!

Unless they have digital stomachs! You know, the latest trend in non-fattening diets.

It's convenient, too. No mess, no stress, just pristine digital deliciousness at your fingertips!

It looks like a very low-fidelity MVP!

These guys are pushing the boundaries of what's digitally edible! At least it won't give customers low-fidelity indigestion... for those who like their meal virtually spiced.

There are several rules to make an effective alignment of technology and learning within the MVP building circle:

- Providing trustworthy input data for digital simulation and unambiguous output.
- Employing algorithms in which the internal logic of calculations is clear.
- Guiding how to navigate in the technology-intensive learning environment.

The definition of "minimal" viable products means restricted product functionality and operational capability. With restricted functionality, customers experience only some of the features proposed in the full product versions. A startup only offers "need to have" features, avoiding costly-to-develop "nice to have" ones. With restricted operational capability, a startup uses a simplified version of a complicated technology to build MVP. Usually, founders use ersatz technological solutions or rely on human-led operations instead of promised algorithms. [3]

In creating MVP, there are two distracting effects to avoid:

- False-positive results mean that a hypothesis was confirmed when it was not. It's not uncommon for entrepreneurs to get false-positive results when they recruit early adopters who are passionate about the product. Those are not the preferences of the average person in the market.
- False-negative results mean that a hypothesis was disproven when it was true. A poorly built MVP is more likely to give false-negative results. [3]

The MVPs can be low fidelity, utilizing just a few of the features available in the final product, and high-fidelity when MVP looks and operates closer to the final product.

Low-fidelity MVPs include:

- Landing Page—A link that promotes the product's features and benefits and validates the value proposition.
- Paper Prototype—A sketch of customers' interface allows them to experience the product before it exists and even test and shape product features.
- 'Fake Door'- A site that invites customers to sign up for a product or service that has not yet been available. The startup can measure customer interest by seeing how many people try to access the product.
- Explaining Video—A short and inexpensive video explaining the product's features and benefits and why customers should buy it can help estimate customers' interest in the offering and determine the expected traction.
- Advertising Campaigns in Social Media—Ad campaigns targeted to specific customer groups allow the startup to discover which aspects of the product are most appealing.
- Micro-Survey—This survey has several specific but open-ended questions and some giveaways. It usually gets a reasonable response rate and reliable answers.
- Blog - A two-way communication between the startup and customers to discuss the product and its marketing matters.

High-fidelity MVPs include:

- The "Wizard of Oz" MVP - Using a human resource to replicate what a proposed technology will do. This type of MVP gives potential customers the impression that they experience a working product.
- The "Concierge" MVP - Unlike the "Wizard of Oz" MVP, the "Concierge" MVP uncovers the fact that the customers receive a human service.
- The "Piecemeal" MVP - Instead of building technology and infrastructure, using existing technologies and services.
- Single Featured MVP - The startup can create and test just one essential feature of a multi-featured product.

MVPs create opportunities to achieve different goals:

- Making proof-of-concepts.
- Checking real-life market tendencies.
- Cooperating with potential customers.
- Gaining and expanding a customer base.
- Testing the product hypothesis with minimal resources.
- Attracting investors early.
- Attracting new customers and early adopters.
- Helping product discovery.
- Stimulating early and rapid customer feedback.
- Developing continuous products.

The choice of MVP launch mode depends on the type of MVP, market conditions, and the startup's readiness to enter the market.

MVP launch modes include:

- Soft launch - Releasing MVP to a limited part of the target audience (usually early adopters). For this mode, are necessary:
  a) a limited market niche;
  b) a particular geographical area;
  c) an audience of a certain age, income, and behavior.

- Hard launch - This mode is appropriate if:
  a) MVP is close to the final product;
  b) An audience is already measured;
  c) Customers' behavior is somewhat predictable;
  d) Marketing anticipates the market reaction.
- Dark launch - Releasing MVP without any PR or advertising to a small group of customers who do not suspect they are testers.

There are some critical milestones in the MVP launch:

- A unit test that allows to test:
  a) Market needs;
  b) What the customer wants;
  c) Monetization potential;
  d) Regulatory and compliance issues;
  e) Data flows;
  f) Marketing strategy.
- Mapping a Customer Journey: This allows you to check if customers have a good experience with MVP, make some corrections, and map the customer journey.
- A/B test: This test is for different modifications of the product or marketing matters. It allows for determining which version is preferable from the customer's perspective.
- Test for monetization options: Several methods exist to monetize services, apps, or websites. It is time to check which option is preferable from the customer's perspective.
- Clarification of customers: Allows correct customer traits predicted in the customer archetype.

Indicators of Traction

There is a range of MVP success indicators that show traction. Traction is the momentum of the enterprise, a positive sign for investors about customer engagement. To measure such engagement, a set of metrics allows for the calculation of traction for an actual stage of the enterprise's development:

- The formation stage is when the startup works on a proof of concept, a problem/solution fit, and initial strategies.
- The validation stage is when the startup works on MVP and a product/market fit.
- In the growth stage, when the startup has a fully marketable product already developed and thinks about the scalability of the business.

In planning the MVP, it is necessary to choose success indicators that are appropriate for the actual stage of the enterprise's development:

- In the formation stage, the metrics include the number of visitors, social media engagement, press coverage, and bounce rate.
- In the validation stage, the metrics include several initial customers, CAC, and LTV.
- In the growth stage, the metrics include revenue, revenue growth rate, churn rate, COGS, and EBITDA.

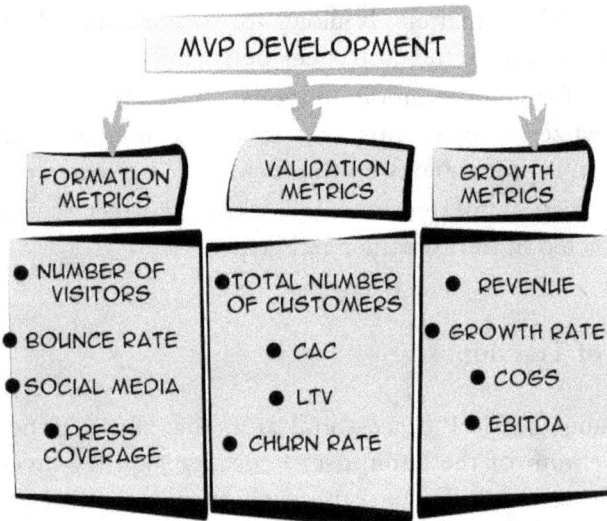

Traction has no conventional definition, and investors employ different metrics according to their understanding, such as the number of registered customers, monthly active visitors, or bounce rates. Some investors are only attentive to revenue-related metrics.

Traction carries different meanings at different MVP stages and in various industries/sectors and technology applications. Sometimes, a customer's willingness to pay is an obvious traction indicator. Some tech-based products, however, have huge market potential but have yet to catch on. Considering all this, startups must use appropriate traction metrics wisely.

Key Takeaways

Developing an MVP and measuring traction is vital to a successful business venture. MVPs must have the essentials customers need, with planned updates over time to increase customer retention. Utilizing data-driven decisions is essential for ensuring a customer's best possible product iteration. The indicators of traction in different stages of business development can provide valuable insight into success. When done right, MVPs can show that a product is ready for launch and in the early distribution stages. It's important to always listen to customer feedback during this process to pivot or make necessary corrections.

Startups with minimal resources should assess MVP development laboriousness and costs. The following tips show preferable directions for the lean approach:

- Choose testing techniques that need minimal resources.
- Use existing technologies and services instead of building own infrastructure.
- Test just one essential feature of a multi-featured product.
- Use mock-ups rather than actual functionality.

Chapter 7.3.
AI vs. Pitch Decks

For years, the pitch deck has been the cornerstone of startup culture—a concise and seemingly straightforward tool founders use to cast their visions and woo potential investors. This method became ingrained within the venture community, sparking a burgeoning industry devoted to crafting the perfect pitch. However, beneath the surface of polished narratives and inflated claims often lies a stark absence of reality where numbers should substantiate stories and the full spectrum of a startup's prospects should be presented. The rise of AI as a validation tool represents a paradigm shift from outdated and ineffective "pitching" to AI-empowered models. Experts even say the pitch decks will soon go out of use. However, while this form of presentation still reigns, founders and investors advocate for transparency and authenticity in startup presentations.

The Roots of Pitch Decks

Presumably, in 2004, Facebook made the first pitch deck with a simple design and short text. In 2007, Mint's pitch deck appeared with three essential modifications: a slide about its team, some statistics, and information about its two competitors with comparative analysis. The 2011 Airbnb pitch deck used color in fonts and photographs rather than graphics. In 2017, MetaCert's pitch deck became more colorful,

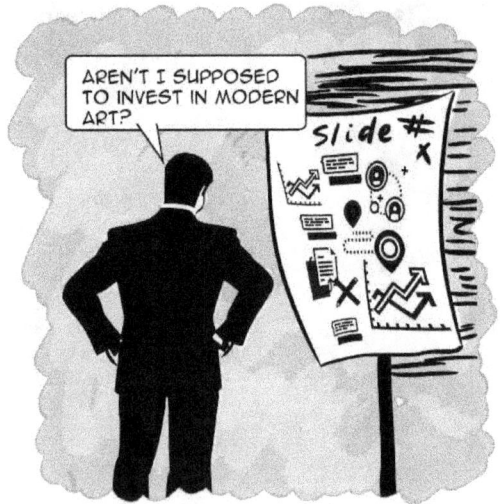

AREN'T I SUPPOSED TO INVEST IN MODERN ART?

slide # x

and each slide contained a logo in the left-hand corner. The deck described a revenue model and financial indicators along with visual effects. [11]

Most pitch decks created by professional "pitchers" follow the same structure: they make a show and try to convince investors with emotionally charged stories and colorful designs. These decks are often over-promising, and teams cannot provide their promises. Founders have difficulties proving figures and facts in the screening stage of deal flow, not to mention the due diligence stage that they cannot overcome.

Numerous ideas of the pitch deck structure often need clarification and consistency. Many offers come with promises of a "secret sauce" and guarantees of unimaginable success. A deck created from scratch is illustrative material only, often with overinflated figures and over-optimistic offers. Furthermore, any attempt to clarify outcomes or confirm calculations destroys this "house of cards." It is the main reason the lion's share of startups that attempt to raise investment with such pitch decks fail miserably.

PROFITomix Story

Digital Pizza

(Episode 21)

CAST:

Robert

Investor
Traditionalist

Steve

Startup
Founder

Steve sent Robert a new version of Digital Pizza's pitch deck. The startup focused on its know-how in this version, called a 'secret sauce.' The founder invited him to a texting conversation to check the investor's impression. Remembering Robert's skepticism in part of Digital Pizza's solutions, Steve accented on a 'secret sauce.' However, the investor quickly uncovered that there was nothing special in the startup's know-how.

Hey, Robert, I hope you enjoyed that extra topping of 'secret sauce' in our new pitch deck for Digital Pizza!

Hi, Steve. I sure did flip through it. That sauce is too spicy for my traditionalist's palate.

Ha! Not at all; it's the flavor of innovation. Just our unique blend of disruptive technologies!

Disruptive? It tasted suspiciously familiar—almost like the ketchup I get from the cafeteria—one part buzzwords, three parts optimism.

I assure you, it's a recipe for success. You won't find this sauce just lying around!

The only secret about your 'secret sauce' that I found was that it's eerily similar to 'open-source condiments' available to anyone on the internet.

The real secret is not the ingredients but how you mix them. We've got the right tech chefs in the kitchen!

Does this secret sauce help find the path to profitability, or is it more of a mystery flavor?

Oh, it's no mystery. It's a blend of market fit with scaling, spiced up by user engagement.

Huh, it tastes like familiar ingredients... and the mix, too. Just be careful not to overcook your pitch.

Don't worry; it's served perfectly. With your investment, it'll be a full-course meal! And don't worry, I've prepared an actual pie chart this time. You'll have a piece of the action, not just augmented reality toppings.

I prefer my returns to be real dough! You better show me if this secret sauce is the main course or another pitching appetizer. I'd instead get indigestion from too many spicy pitches.

There is no one-size-fits-all formula for the pitch deck structure. Different startups need different deck structures. A general deck structure is the following:

- A hook to get investors excited.
- An essence is to give an overview of the business.
- A piece of evidence to prove that all information is trustworthy.
- A plan to show the path to success.
- An amount of seeking investment.

The hook, the essence, and the evidence are usually narrative slides that introduce business ideas and explain concepts. The plan and the ask slides need another form of presentation - informative slides. This form is good for outlining the market, a business model, and financial projections. Unlike narrative slides, informative slides need solid information backgrounds. [12]

As Shakespeare said: "All the world's a stage, and all the men and women merely players..." Thus, a five-act pitch script might include exposition, rising action, climax, falling action, and resolution.

Designing a Pitch Deck

A pitch deck is the tip of the funding iceberg. The deck's figures and pictures must have solid justifications hidden from a cursory glance, which is vital for funding success. Unfortunately, design ideas prevailed over economic sense.

It's a common mistake to think that a pitch deck is supposed to persuade investors to fund a startup. It invites a more profound estimation and cross-validation of all facts and figures proclaimed in the deck. A pitch deck as a tool has two dimensions. First, it explores all critical points of the funding journey in the current investment landscape. All necessary backup information must be gathered and processed during this process. Second, this tool focuses on attracting investors' attention to a startup by showing its solid sides and attractive features.

The Startup Dossier embraces all information to prepare pith decks according to different investors' requirements. The Dossier allows concentrating on essentials for a successful presentation in the first dimension:

- Demonstrating realistic figures and scenarios.
- Supporting all conclusions with reliable numbers.
- Regularly updating the information.

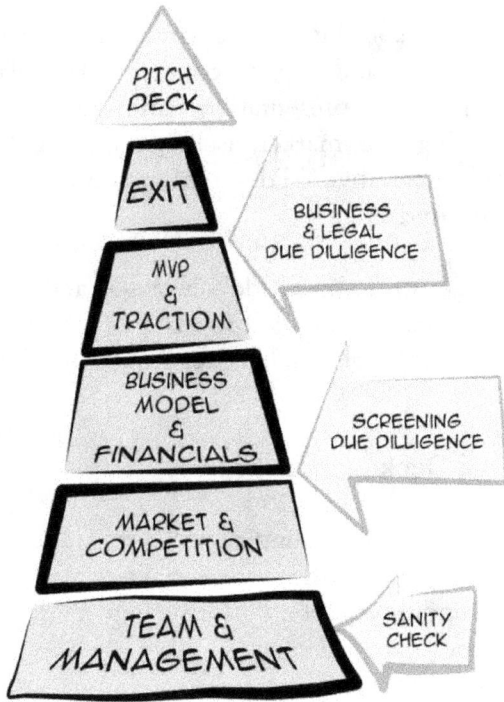

In the second dimension, the Dossier helps:

- Formatting appropriate slides for target investors and framing key points.
- Emphasize specific, compelling facts and figures in slides.
- Provide quantitative information to confirm facts on the slides to pass sanity checks and due diligence procedures.

For technology-enabled startups that employ intangible-intensive business models would suit the full-structured 12-slide deck called an investor pitch deck. It presents a project in written form without any oral comments. This version of the deck is usually a PDF file, ready to email to investors, add to any project profile pages, or upload to investment databases.

Slide 1. Enterprise Overview & Business Opportunities:
- Enterprise logo, name, description
- Industry/sector
- Technology
- Total market size
- Mission, Vision, Goals

Slide 2. Problem & Solution:
- Customers' unmet needs, available alternatives, and their disadvantages
- A problem statement
- Product's novelty, features, and customer benefits; formulation of the solution

Slide 3. Market &Target Customers:
- Key demographics and behavioral and attitudinal patterns
- Target markets, their gaps, and trends
- TAM, SAM, SOM (Top-Down and Bottom-Up calculations)

Slide 4. Competition & Unique Value Proposition:
- Competitors' profiles, market share, and positioning
- An estimation of the unfair advantages over competitors
- Unique Value Proposition

Slide 5. Technology & Product:
- Technology-enabled services/products, technology applications
- Efforts for technology commercialization
- IP protection measures

Slide 6. Team & Management:
- Team composition and structure
- Splitting equity, stock option pool, and payroll system
- Team dynamics
- Founders' experience and management style

Slide 7. Go-to-Market Strategy & Entry Timing:
- Market channels and strategies to reach customers
- Key partnerships
- CAC, LTV, CAC/LTV
- Acquired customers, customer churn rate, customer base, entry timing scenarios

Slide 8. Minimal Viable Product & Traction:
- A type of MVP, MVP launch mode, and milestones of the MVP launch
- metrics for the current stage of the startup (formation, validation, or growth)
- Social media engagement and media coverage

Slide 9. Intangible Intensive Business Model:
- Startup's scalability, synergic effects, and use of spillovers
- Revenue models and streams, pricing strategies
- Set-up, development, launch, production, and operational Costs

Slide 10. Financial Projections:
- Cash flow, profit, and losses
- Revenue, gross profit, EBITDA, revenue per employee, revenue growth rate, burn rate, cash runway

Slide 11. Startup Valuation:
- Traditional/tangible startup valuation
- Intangible startup valuation

Slide 12. Ask & Investor Protection and Exit:
- The need for capital and a plan to use money
- A pre-money valuation
- A stake offered to investors
- Exit scenarios

Mastering Startups' Presentations

Besides the base investor pitch deck, there are also different formats of the deck. With the base pitch deck ready, a team can create different deck formats and customize them for presentation.

A presentation deck has another format. While its structure is the same, the content of slides is condensed, removing all axillary information and leaving the most expressive infographics, key figures, and concise text fragments. This type of deck is suitable for oral presentations at any investment event and requires oral comments and extra explanations. The main goal of the presentation deck is to attract investors' attention, implying subsequent clarifications and additions to facts outlined in the compact slides.

A product deck (sometimes called a teaser) is a shorter-pitch version. This deck provides an initial promotion and is available to the general public on social media and other internet resources. As the name suggests, the product deck focuses on how the product solves a market problem without any information about a business model and the project implementation. The goal of this deck is to create a first impression and inspire initial interest.

A one-pager embraces the project's key points concisely (preferably employing infographics) on one page. This material promotes an investment opportunity offered to investors. The business model description, marketing figures, and some performance indicators are mandatory. The one-pager is suitable for initial contact with investors.

An elevator pitch is a super short project presentation that lasts about one minute (150-250 words). Within this minimal time, a startup should introduce itself, a prospective market, and a business model. The main focus of the elevator pitch is on the product or service's unique advantages. As the name suggests, an investor must be able to comprehend the elevator pitch while he or she is riding in an elevator. It is good to use in media, during meetings, and other events.

The elevator pitch formula is: "We provide (the essence and state of a product/service)...for (a target audience)...that need (what is their need)...Unlike our competitors in the market (the market size and trends)... we offer (factors of differentiation in the market)."

AI Buries Pitch Decks

Traditionally, investors hired an army of specialists to maintain deal flow. Today, AI makes this job much faster, easier, and cheaper for investors. Moreover, looking for the best business opportunities, VCs wish to cut transaction costs and discover hyper-competitive startups. AI allows them to principally build new pipelines, sourcing and screening startups in locations outside of tech areas and hubs. Their AI-empowered search relies on financial metrics and product-market-customer insights instead of speculative narratives. [13]

While the VC industry suffers from undiscovered but potentially attractive deals, AI-driven sourcing and screening is a game-changer. Today, the "pitching" narrative often outweighs the numbers in investor decision-making. This situation is especially true for early-stage pre-revenue startups. Furthermore, investors are susceptible to biases, especially regarding pre-seed investing. AI can generate precise information and make unbiased valuations, contributing to the decline of the "pitching industry."

By 2025, more than 75% of VCs and early-stage investors will use AI. Deal flow will shift from primarily qualitative data to the quantitative information the technology provides. The traditional pitch experience will significantly change by 2025 towards AI-enabled models and simulations, and conventional pitch decks and financials will become insufficient. [14]
It's scary to think that Gartner is right!

AI can collect information from online datasets, including news articles and social media, making pitch decks look like one more source of information. After selecting startups, investors can employ AI to evaluate target startups' potential, including:

- Market size, growth rate, and competition. AI-driven marketing will be more objective than yesterday's hype, surrounding trendy industries/sectors.

- Team evaluation through finding correlations between team members' qualities and business performance. This way of assessment allows us to avoid typical biases about prestige education and other insufficient factors.

- Estimating startup early traction and analyzing proprietary data instead of compelling but speculative pitch decks. This approach also contributes to unbiased investment decisions.

- Financial analysis and forecasts based on reliable input data and AI-driven algorithms to form meaningful output information within a scenario approach that includes human intuition. This new way of dealing with financial issues radically differs from "classic" business planning.

To prepare for ongoing changes in the VC industry, startups must include AI in their information toolboxes. Currently, startups need help to fill in essential gaps in the data, poor information processing, and information asymmetry. They must gather and structure the data and put it into the deal workflows that are too expensive and hard to perform for them. Third-party facilitators can streamline all AI-related work for startups, providing them with data-scraping, dossier creation, machine learning, and generative services. [15]

Entrepreneurs must realize that startup pitching is changing rapidly and must keep up with those changes or get left behind. Pitch decks remain an essential part of early-stage investment, but now technology creates new opportunities for pitching and presenting innovative projects. With this mindset, teams can stay ahead of the curve and maximize investment potential without getting bogged down by the outdated pithing tradition. AI helps to reimagine pitches with new methods of presentation and out-of-the-box solutions to meet changes in the VC industry.

Key Takeaways

The AI-empowered Validator incorporates algorithms to analyze data, identify trends, and provide insights that otherwise entrepreneurs can miss. This way of validating business models is more accurate and reliable since it allows for factual evidence of business viability instead of mere assumptions. While a pitch deck is still functional, the Validator intertwines the presentation process, making it quicker, cheaper, and more trustworthy.

Three methods are essential for a successful presentation:

- Choose a critical point (and appropriate slide) for target investors and frame a critical slide.
- Emphasize specific, compelling facts and figures in the critical slide.
- Have quantitative evidence that is relevant to a critical slide.

Five possible key points (slides) may be helpful to emphasize an appropriate key point that has solid background information:

- Team – if a startup has a complete, well-balanced team in which members obtain enough qualifications and experience and can manage an enterprise.
- Market opportunity—if a sizeable addressable market exists for a product or service, bottom-up calculations show how to capture a determined part of this market.
- Technology – if a startup can realistically commercialize a technology with a disruptive potential.
- Ask & Exit—if a startup's demand corresponds to its valuation, the financing period is reasonably short, with clear major milestones and an exit scenario.

- Traction – if a startup has a high-fidelity MVP with good prospects.

Thus, when decorating the pitch deck, a startup has to remember that success depends on the information in the Startup Dossier. A compelling pitch deck is essential, but there's much more when raising capital. Founders must be ready to explain and confirm assumptions and input data, and show believable output in their decks to investors.

Points to Ponder

The proposed Validator includes three successive validation steps:
- Step 1 – "Problem-Solution" validation.
- Step 2 – "Product-Market" validation.
- Step 3 – "Business Model" validation.

At each step, available quality information helps to create specific pitch deck slides:

Step 1

    Slide 1. Enterprise Overview & Business Opportunities
    Slide 2. Problem & Solution

Step 2

    Slide 3. Market &Target Customers
    Slide 4. Competition & Unique Value Proposition
    Slide 5. Technology & Product
    Slide 6. Team & Management
    Slide 7. Go-to-Market Strategy & Entry Timing
    Slide 8. Minimal Viable Product & Traction

Step 3

    Slide 9. Intangible Intensive Business Model
    Slide 10. Financial Projections
    Slide 11. Startup Valuation
    Slide 12. Ask & Investor Protection and Exit

Customize the pitch deck by looking at each slide from different perspectives. For instance, for the slide "Team & Management," the following perspectives are possible:
- The strength of the team.
- The team's competition and marketing abilities.
- Prospects of team integration.

Section 8
Thriving in the New Venture World

Today, business success is no longer determined by luck or blind faith in one's gut feelings. To thrive in a new Shark Tank-like VC world, startup founders and investors must employ intangible assets and technology. Equipped with innovative tools and strategies, they can navigate the ever-evolving business landscape, build highly profitable enterprises, and make intelligent investment decisions.

The three components of success pave the path that startups must implement, and investors evaluate for prospective funding:

- Startups can leverage their intangible assets to grow initially, generating more revenues without a proportional increase in variable costs—using small initial assets to reach excellent results!
- By smartly combining internal intangibles with infrastructural ones and tangible assets, startups can create synergetic effects—employing a composite set of assets to achieve a more significant outcome than the simple sum of used assets!
- By appropriating others' intangibles, a startup can obtain additional competitive advantages and use spillovers to increase profitability and scalability.

This new path is happening in the background of dramatic changes in IP status, ownership rights, and our understanding of human capital. While government regulations, accounting rules, and industry standards regarding appropriating intangible assets are developing, adventurous investors and startup founders can take advantage of the situation. Success is within reach for those who dare to think beyond the traditional boundaries of ownership and harness the magic of synergy.

Chapter 8.1.
Art of Leveraging Minimal Resources

How do some startups, with just a shoestring budget, achieve remarkable success, while others falter even with substantial investment? The secret lies in their ability to harness and amplify intangible assets. A few startups have figured out how to maximize their limited resources through bootstrapping, transforming initial momentums into exceptional gains. This phenomenon links to the chaos theory's butterfly effect when small, well-placed efforts can create significant impacts. By strategically leveraging certain intangibles, drivers of the butterfly effect, some ventures set the stage for their future triumph. Technology is critical in shaping innovative startup strategies and investment decisions in the modern business environment, bringing clarity and fighting uncertainty.

> **How does harnessing of initial resources impact a startup's future success?**

The Chaos Theory & the Butterfly Effect

Edward Lorenz from MIT first formulated the chaos theory in 1972 to predict weather patterns. In the chaos theory, the butterfly effect is when a slight change in one state of a system has a significant impact on a later state. Lorenz formulated the butterfly effect principle: "Predictability: Does the flap of a butterfly's wing in Brazil set off a tornado in Texas?" [1]

Mathematicians continued to develop the theory and its applications, including in the VC industry. In 1987, Tom Peters wrote "Thriving on Chaos: Handbook for a Management Revolution," showing how to

implement this theory in business. This idea is old: in 350 BC, Aristotle wrote, "The least initial deviation from the truth is multiplied later a thousandfold," demonstrating the ancient knowledge of chaos theory: a small input can produce a much bigger output." [2]

The Chaos Theory deals with facts that are impossible to predict or control effectively, like the weather, the stock market, and the VC industry. We can apply the butterfly effect to investment decisions: every dollar sent out into the world creates an impact. The Chaos theory works there: "Small differences in the initial state yield widely different outcomes." [1]

Bootstrapping vs. External Funding

Popular opinion is that a startup chooses one of two paths: bootstrapping or fundraising. It is wrong! Startups need both paths because bootstrapping and fundraising complement each other. In its early stage, a startup can leverage its resources, mainly intangibles, to develop MVP and obtain proof of the proposed business profitability. It makes sense to attract external financing to expand the business. According to the Chaos theory, properly directed efforts by a startup in bootstrapping mode can produce the multiplying butterfly effect. This discovery allows us to see a startup in a new light, which was unknown until recently.

Raising capital through VC looks appealing for startups in the early stage. The Boston Consulting Group report identified three main reasons to attract external financing:

- An opportunity to quickly validate and optimize business models and obtain mentorships and training.
- Obtaining the cost-benefit between the startup founder's share in exchange for money and the VC's investment.
- Better chances for external talent attraction, partnership, and collaboration. [3]

In this way, investors bring capital and a network of contacts, a wealth of expertise, and connections with other investors, prospective partners, and service providers that can help startups grow. There are many benefits to working with investors, but there are also some potential problems founders should be aware of:

- The main problem is a potential loss of control. If investors take an active role in decision-making, founders may have fewer managing rights in a company.
- Investors might have different goals and interests than entrepreneurs, leading to conflicts and disagreements.
- When startups raise money, they may have to issue new shares for investors. This action can dilute the founders' ownership, meaning they own a smaller percentage of the company.
- Raising money and working with investors can be time-consuming. Dealing with investors can take away time from other important things for founders.
- Investors expect the company to perform well and snowball. Founders can get burnt out if they try to fulfill unrealistic expectations. [4]

What makes fundraising so hard? It is supposed to be difficult for a reason: working as a filter for bright ideas and superior business solutions. Numbers show that 1% to 10% of VC meetings result in funding. Fewer than half of companies raise their second round, and almost half fail at every round afterward. Everyone would attract financing if it were easy.

Information asymmetry exacerbates objectively existing funding challenges that manifest themselves on the startup side as:

- Inaccurately estimating the level of interest of prospective investors.
- Underestimating the time required for the fundraising process.
- Not understanding or accurately predicting the terms offered by investors.
- Getting a "yes" from an investor who said "maybe."
- Misperceiving what investors think. [5]

Research shows a high level of information asymmetry around intangibles that are prevailing startups' assets. As a result, investors feel uncertain about future profits and exits. Founders often need more information and realistic expectations of the results. Information asymmetry between founders and investors and the probability of failure of a proposed business significantly reduce the chances of startups attracting external funding. [6]

These are why most entrepreneurs prefer bootstrapping (building a business from scratch without attracting investment) to external financing. The beginning entrepreneurs find the idea of bootstrapping attractive for a variety of reasons:

- Fewer risks: If the business fails, no borrowed money is involved; if the project is successful, the founders don't have to share their success with anyone.
- Acceleration of creativity: The lack of initial funding encourages founders to search and employ non-trivial business solutions or discover new market niches.
- Independence: Founders can make all the decisions independently, be unique, and realize their dreams.
- Concentration: Instead of stressful and time-consuming fundraising, entrepreneurs can entirely focus on their business.

294

- No dilution: The internal funding allows keeping a stock in a company that is attractive for future investments. [6]

However, when operating with limited resources, startups can find it challenging to grow their businesses. Moreover, the bootstrapping mode increases financial risk as a startup may be unable to cover unexpected costs. Limited finances can also cause difficulties in dealing with suppliers and prospective partners. Nevertheless, bootstrapping advantages outweigh the disadvantages and new scientific discoveries related to the chaos theory create unexpected opportunities for early-stage startups.

Leveraging Intangible Resources

Many entrepreneurs understand bootstrapping as an economical mode with minimized expenses. It is correct, but not enough. The results of such frugality are not decisive factors, while reserves using intangibles are significantly more important (they amount to up to 90% of startups' assets).

With a lack of material resources, startups have to focus on leveraging intangibles in several ways:

- Utilizing own resources.
- Taking advantage of someone else's resources.
- Getting more done with fewer resources.
- Mobilizing resources that others cannot recognize.
- Making use of resources in new ways.
- Combining resources to get things done.
- Putting resources together in new combinations. [7]

PROFITomix Story:

Digital Pizza

(Episode 22)

CAST:

Thomas

Investor
Technocrat

Steve

Startup
Founder

Plagued by the FOMO syndrome, Thomas overcame his initial skepticism and almost decided to invest in Digital Pizza. This time, he just wanted to inform Steve. However, the conversation takes an unexpected turn. Receiving several rejections, Steve reconsidered his attitude towards external funding, believed in his abilities, and finally refused to accept the offered investment.

Hey, Steve! You passed red flags with flying colors.

Hi, Thomas! I couldn't remember when we talked about "red flags."

Never mind. I want to tell you that I made a decision, but I get butterflies in my stomach.

Butterflies? I've read about this effect!

Steve, it was challenging to place a bet!

I see... it's not easy to be a serial investor!

What do you mean by saying "a serial investor"?

As everyone says, a person bets on startups as he would on a horse race.

No, this is not right for me. My interest in your startup is long-term!

They say long-term investments are only partially successful in the short term.

I wonder if you can manage this chaos alone.

Chaos? I know about this theory. It's related to the butterfly effect.

I don't know what you're talking about...You can't do it well alone...simply due to a lack of expertise. We can bring tech experience to commercialize this pizza business!

They say experts are guys who can explain tomorrow why their ideas from yesterday are wrong today!

With such an attitude and lack of experience, you will fly like a butterfly to a fire!

Like a butterfly? Yes! I rely on the Butterfly Effect: we can leverage our resources for a significant outcome.

The "Butterfly Effect" in the pizza business! Nonsense!

It's not nonsense. It's just another name for the Chaos theory that shows how a small action can have a considerable impact. My startup will fly in the wings!

So, you're rejecting my offer...I couldn't believe it!

Thanks, but I'll stick to my plan. I don't feel like a horse to bet on! One day, you'll find me on the Forbes list!

Hopefully, not in the 'Where Are They Now?' section.

How do we recognize a magical butterfly that can change the future? We have to follow the first flapping of the butterfly's wings. From the beginning, entrepreneurs can wisely use their assets (primarily intangibles). Startups can find and deploy infrastructure resources, like grants, supplements, and benefits (spillovers). Getting smarter, an entrepreneur can even take advantage of customers' and partners' resources.

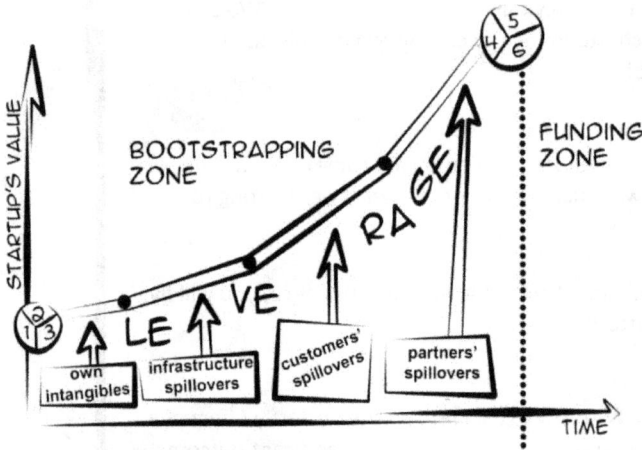

Legend:

1 – Opportunity prospects
2 – Problem's Cruciality
3 – Solution's Efficacy
4 – The Startup Dossier is filled
5 – The Roadmap is outlined
6 – The MVP is validated

Own intangible assets include patents, trademarks, copyrights, trade secrets, domain names, and networks, as well as knowledge assets, including:

- Explicit knowledge includes all documentation related to a startup (specs, manuals, technical documents, processes, and instructions).
- Implicit knowledge is knowledge that exists in an intangible form, but is available for documentation when needed.
- Tacit intangible knowledge that cannot be expressed in writing (like entrepreneurial and organizational skills).

Infrastructure spillovers that startups can use include:

- Licenses and permits.
- Sandbox modes.
- Compliance procedures.
- Personal information protection.
- Labor rights.
- Environmental issues.
- Government startup support.
- Thematic grants.
- Tax credits.
- Quotas, tariffs, and trade restrictions.

The customer groups whose spillovers startups can use include:

- Early adopter customers - use them as beta testers.
- Product Advocates - use them for significant influence over the target market.
- Anchor Customers - tap the credibility of established and recognized customers.

The partners whose spillovers startups can use include:

- Providers - businesses that provide components as inputs to the startup product.
- Assemblers - businesses that use the startup product as their product component.
- Retailers - businesses that sell startup products.
- Influencers - persons who promote startup products in their online communities.

Harnessing the Butterfly Effect

In business, the butterfly effect illustrates how small actions and decisions can create monumental waves, impacting a startup's journey. It highlights the vital role of meticulous attention to detail and thoughtful decision-making in the competitive VC market. Some seemingly minor alterations can have a remarkable ripple effect, propelling a startup's market presence to new heights. The butterfly effect serves as a powerful reminder of the far-reaching consequences that even the most minor actions can have in shaping the trajectory of a business.

Investors in startups are in constant search of a source of higher profitability and scalability. This source is in intangible assets and solutions widely spread across elements of startups' business models, organizational, and human capital. This results in the apparent invisibility of intangibles, the impossibility of directly measuring them, and difficulties in estimating intangible impact on business performance. However, there is an opportunity to overcome these challenges. It is possible to identify intangibles via their activities in the business context, indirectly measure them using proxies, and estimate their impact using the scoring method.

John Keynes supposedly said: "It is better to be roughly right than precisely wrong."
So, going in the right direction is the first prerequisite for a startup's success!

Implementing this approach requires, first of all, the identification of crucial intangibles that create value in the target startup's business context. Then, choosing a perspective that allows us to see the main factors - drivers of the value-creation process is necessary. The connective "customer-product/technology" can create a perspective emphasizing intangible features. It is not an exact measure but rather a direction. We must act according to the principle: do not try to fight the obstacles that create intangibles with old methods. Instead, it is necessary to apply new techniques to use features of intangibles for our benefit.

Intangibles correlate with a comprehensive set of customers' perceptions of startups' products. Some of them are well-known, like cost, efficiency, or durability. Others, like aesthetics, comfort, or indulgence, are little known; however, they can play a critical role in creating intangible values. By building emotional linkages, in addition to rational ones, startups can create novel sensory experiences in the customer journeys. Intangible focus is on the relationship rather than the outcome, luxury feeling rather than financials, and a sense of belonging is more important than costs. [8]

A set of logical directions includes the following groups:

- Capacity and efficiency.
- Simplicity and convenience.
- Extent and duration.
- Flexibility and variety.
- Reliability and dependability.

A set of emotional directions includes the following groups:

- Comfort and leisure.
- Luxury feeling and indulgence.
- Aesthetics and sentiments.
- Sense of being and sense of belonging.
- Negation of waste, side effects, and complications.

Due to intangible features, a product or service can eliminate or reduce specific requirements or even whole economic concepts. Since intangibles do not fit well into the ownership concept, intangible solutions that eliminate this concept are possible. An example of eliminating individual ownership is Uber, which offers individual transportation instead of car ownership. Rolls Roice eliminated corporate ownership - airlines do not need to buy and maintain expensive aircraft turbines. Now, they pay only for the turbines' operating time. New directions for leveraging intangibles to achieve the butterfly effect will continue to emerge. The biggest winners will be those who offer it first.

After identifying vital intangible directions in the target startup's business context, an AI-based scoring model may incorporate them into a single leverage score. This score allows us to estimate how key intangible directions - startup success drivers - can leverage the initial founders' contributions to provide prospective business profitability and scalability. The money and time wisely contributed by founders to the project in its initial stage can catalyze great success. Thus, investors can source startups with high potential, while those who can pass the conventional assessment with flying colors will be out of investors' interest. In other words, AI-based scoring allows for making more precise startup profit and growth predictions.

Key Takeaways

The concept of bootstrapping, when startups invest their limited resources in the most influential directions, allows startups to harness their minimal and mostly intangible resources. Bootstrapping can produce the butterfly effect: seemingly insignificant actions or investments can significantly impact a startup's future success.

Bootstrapping can work as a startup's independent preparation for subsequent external financing. The level of this preparation, thanks to the growth of the startup's intangible capital, determines investment terms and the success of the whole venture.

As technology continues to evolve and provide us with AI-powered tools and insights, startups can employ them to create models that leverage their intangible resources for higher-than-average profitability and exponential growth. It is genuinely remarkable to see how we increasingly rely on technology to navigate investment.

The secret to success for the best startups lies not in a time-consuming race for external funding but in skillfully investing smaller amounts in the right direction from the initial stage of startup development. By embracing the butterfly effect and strategically leveraging their intangible resources, startups promise great returns. Sourcing such startups allows sophisticated investors to stay ahead in the constantly evolving VC market.

Chapter 8.2.
The Science of Utilizing Synergy

Synergy, the combined power of a group that exceeds the sum of the power of its members, serves as a beacon of scalability and growth for those who know how to harness it effectively. Synergy can do more than add value; it can multiply it. When orchestrated correctly, it enables startups to scale at an unprecedented rate, turning collaboration into one of the most significant growth strategies. Synergy sprouts from intangible assets; by appropriating them, entrepreneurs can tap into new markets and innovation frontiers. Synergetic effects manifest themselves in three dimensions of the deal flow: informational, financial, and human. Managing them effectively, entrepreneurs open the gates to the hidden force that fuels higher profitability and strategic business growth.

> **How do we unleash and utilize synergetic effects to increase startups' profitability and scalability?**

Synergy as a Source of Scalability

In his book "*Corporate Strategy*," Igor Ansoff introduced the principal idea of business synergies in 1965. The term "synergy" is originally derived from the Greek words *syn* – together and *érgo* – achievement, illustrating the collaboration of individual factors that mutually boost each other. In the business context, synergy is the primary source of scalability thanks to decreasing costs and increasing revenues across two interacting businesses. [9]

Employing the synergy concept, the ancient Greeks had their Golden Age of Innovation that started around 500 BC and lasted until 146 BC when the Romans conquered them. Pythagoras, Hippocrates, Socrates, Plato, and Aristotle profoundly impacted civilization in that period. During this time, Greeks invented cartography (500 BC), urban planning (5th century BC), plumbing (5th century BC), central heating (350 BC), and analog computers (150 BC). [10]

In the VC industry, synergy is an advantage of VCs' and startups' joint activities compared to their separate activities, where everyone defends their interests. The concept is that the combined value and performance of two parties will be greater than the sum of the separate individual participants. The synergetic effect occurs due to intangibles.

Synergy can provide a higher level of equilibrium in the VC industry …but under the following conditions:

- Creating profitable enterprises where technology is applied to solve real problems (profit has to be the first!).
- The whole investment process becomes data-driven (it is a permanent process, not an event!).
- Valuations become transparent and measured (looking beyond 'classical' methods!).
- Interests of investors and startups are aligned and well-balanced (negotiations use synergy instead of antagonism!).

The topic of aligning investors and startups' interests was discussed in detail in Chapter 6.3, "Aligning Investors' and Founders' Interests." Desirable higher multiplies, 10X and even 50X, are principally possible, but this possibility arises when we harness synergy from its roots, mainly intangibles.

Intangible Roots of Synergy

Synergy is an inherited feature of intangibles that promises to increase profits and reduce the need for investment resources. However, it happens only when investors and startup founders work together. Investors and founders should clearly understand what each party wants and needs to get out of the partnership. They must discuss this topic before entering into any formal agreement. Otherwise, both parties cannot fulfill their expectations. Working together implies standing on one platform that provides an information basis, a community of financial interests, and an organizational mechanism.

While synergy is a commonly used term in business, its meaning could be more precise. There are at least three points of view on this topic: Some people think that synergy is just about teamwork and management, but it is much broader than that. Synergy can occur between different companies, departments, teams, or individuals. Synergy can manifest in virtually any situation where multiple entities work towards a common goal. Others need to learn about the intangible roots of synergy and mistakenly try to connect it with material assets. The third meaning supposes synergy as an independent entity, while it is a result of interactions.

As Aristoteles said: "The whole is greater than the sum of its parts." [9]
It's good that accountants and lawyers don't know about this!

Synergy is when two or more business entities work together, and the result is greater than the sum of their efforts. It is the driving force that enables parties to unlock new opportunities, create new values, and achieve new levels of profitability and growth. The critical points of the synergy concept include:

- Alignment of interests between parties is a prerequisite for synergy. Any conflicts led to communication troubles and financial losses, immediately destroying synergy prospects.
- Synergy requires tight collaboration between parties stronger than traditional business cooperation. Such collaboration may include sharing ideas, resources, and common goals.
- Synergy can create new opportunities that would not be possible for each party alone. [11]

Synergy is the passive energy. Its positive effect only arises in the 'working together' mode. Moreover, collaboration requires a change in both parties' mindsets. Founders must take full responsibility for their projects' informational, financial, and organizational development rather than engage in investment hunting as a self-sufficient activity. Instead of thinking about sunk costs or feeling the Fear of Missing Out (FoMO), investors must distinguish hidden intangible sprouts of potential synergetic profitability and growth.

Synergy correlated with sustainable competitive advantages because rivals can easily bypass temporary competitive advantages. Tangible assets may create temporary competitive advantages only because they can be bought and sold in the market. Intangible assets are challenging to buy or imitate and can create sustainable advantages. However, two working together parties do not create synergy automatically. It takes efforts from both parties to make synergy happen.

Like in dating, the synergy between investors and founders creates the intangible "magic" that inspires them to work together. By understanding investors' expectations, founders can build a perfect match with suitable investors. With this mindset, an investor can fall in love with a startup ready for mutually beneficial solutions, and this love will be mutual!

PROFITomix Story

Digital Pizza

(Episode 23)

CAST:

Linda

Investor
Profiteer

Thomas

Investor
Technocrat

Linda is about to make a funding decision for Digital Pizza. Although she has a broad knowledge of legal and regulatory matters, she is not a technology expert. She sent a message to Thomas, who can recognize technology-laggard niches ripe for disruption. Linda started a talk, coining the buzzword' synergy,' while Thomas tried to lead their conversation on technological grounds. Finally, they both decided it was difficult to discover a source of synergy in Digital Pizza.

Have you heard, Thomas? This venture, Digital Pizza, is truly mastering synergy.

Really? I think 'synergy' is just a buzzword used by these people who mix cheese and code to create an extra topping of profit!

Their pizzas will have built-in algorithms to recommend personalized toppings based on browsing history.

'Predictive gastrointestinal satisfaction enhancer.'

So, you know them. Right?

Yes, they're looking for a perfect match. It's like dating, huh? You can mix and match profiles, but you will know if there's chemistry once you meet.

Exactly! Although, with Digital Pizza, can they create the right mix to produce synergy?

And what if the ingredients don't mingle? Seems like a flaky foundation for a business.

Just like a first date: you take a chance! Sometimes, it's a recipe for romance; occasionally, it's... undercooked.

Well, not every match leads to a second funding round. This synergy business is a bit like speed dating: rushed, chaotic, and most of it doesn't pan out.

Oh, Tomas, it sounds too pessimistic! Digital Pizza's synergy was like a romantic dinner: rich, fulfilling, and leading to a long-term commitment.

While the topic is complicated, let's use a rule of thumb: tell me your motto, and let's see how Digital Pizza fits into it.

The slogan could be 'Digital Pizza: We know what you want before you do!'

That's not quite right...I would say, 'Digital Pizza—Uber of Uplifting the Hungry.' Synergy is like pizza dough: All the ingredients come together, making a perfect match to rise above!

The "working together" mode implies a change in mindset in part of expectations, values, valuations, and deal terms:

- Investors formulate their vision of the business opportunities they are looking for. Founders determine the type of investment, the amount of capital they need, and the level of control and investors' involvement.
- Investors wish to understand the potential profit/risk correlation. Founders provide reliable data on market potential, competition, and financial projections.
- Investors prefer to see valuations made by various methods with clear conclusions. Founders produce traditional and intangible valuations, as well as a comparative analysis.
- Investors want to know the ownership structure and the parties' rights and responsibilities. Founders understand the terms of the investment agreement and their rights and obligations.

The Three Dimensions of Harnessing Synergy

Various VC industry specialists are trying to harness synergy. Information specialists recognize new possibilities in employing a data-driven approach and technology. Financiers rely on precise startup valuation, alternative funding, and more accurate financial projections. Management focuses on interpersonal facets of bargaining as the deal flow's crux. All of them are right! However, each tries to find synergy in the narrow context of their professional perspectives. Synergy manifests in three planes or dimensions corresponding to three perspectives:

The informational dimension employs data intelligence to gather and manage startup proprietary data and data from alternative sources, including:

- A set of methods and tools to collect and interpret data from different sources.
- Analytical algorithms and dashboards for the visualization to process data into meaningful information.

- A mindset and the ability to grasp and apply information effectively. Human insight and an algorithmic analysis complement each other here.

The financial dimension that focuses on the business model embracing a value validation mechanism, a revenue model and streams, and a profit formula, including:

> See Section 2 for more detail

- Traditional financial projections and valuations.
- Innovative intangible valuations.
- Alternative financing, including just-in-time funding.
- Leveraging initial startup assets, including intangible ones.

The human dimension that represents bargaining and negotiation as a ubiquitous part of the deal flow includes:

> See Sections 4 and 5 for more detail

- Integrative bargaining is a negotiation strategy where investors and startups collaborate to find 'win-win' solutions.
- Balancing interests of investors and startup founders to raise the equilibrium level.
- Employing effective negotiation techniques

Negotiating the deal terms between startups and investors is the most challenging step of the deal flow. Traditionally, this step focuses on positional bargaining, which means fixed opposite positions of the parties seeking a compromise to satisfy their interests. Often, such a compromise is ineffective or not achieved at all. An integrative bargaining model and supporting techniques can solve this problem.

Integrative bargaining techniques help create values, not just proclaim them:

- Expanding the pie - Working together means more resources for both parties.

314

- Logrolling - Considering several issues together rather than individually.
- Cost-cutting - Finding a way to reduce deal's costs.
- A nonspecific compensation - Pay off the other party, and they do what they want.
- Bridging – Developing an innovative, creative solution that satisfies both parties. [12]

The integrative bargaining model emphasizes the importance of exchanging information among parties to achieve an integrative (win-win) outcome. Negotiation is a procedure to resolve different preferences among parties to achieve a satisfactory outcome for all parties. In practice, it is challenging to reach mutually beneficial results due to limited information (partners need to see all possible options) and cognitive biases. Technology provides opportunities and methods to overcome these problems. [13]

A proposed solution is a hybrid (human-machine) approach based on providing parties with quality information, showing them financial options, and encouraging cooperation for mutually beneficial results rather than satisfying personal interests. Visually, a flattened trihedral pyramid whose faces are three dimensions represents this solution:

At the base of this pyramid lies a platform with tools to ensure a synergistic effect - folds three components into a three-dimensional structure:

See Sections 3, 4, and 5 respectively for more detail

- The data-driven Dossier - a universal repository of funding-related information about startups.
- The Robo-Fitness Validator - a set of data intelligence algorithms to collect and process information.
- The Funding Roadmap – the algorithm that shows the funding journey's strong and weak points.

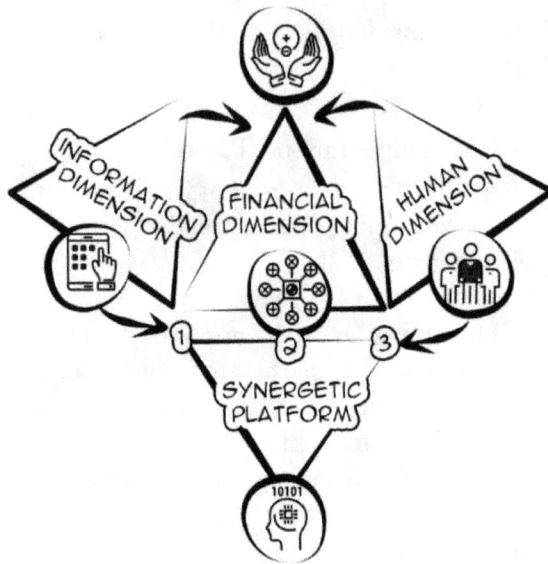

```
1. The informational dimension.
2. The financial dimension.
3. The human dimension.
```

The intangible concept of synergy has concrete effects on startups' profitability and scalability. As the VC industry strives for higher profitability, scalability, and exponential growth, harnessing synergy can be vital in achieving these goals. Understanding the three dimensions of harnessing synergy shows the path of utilizing its power in successful partnerships.

Key Takeaways

The concept of "synergy" encompasses several essential ideas:

- Synergy is not just the components of something but a result of their interactions.
- Synergy is a collaboration of individual entities that mutually boost each other in the perfect combination.
- Synergy is the main intangible driver in achieving competitive advantages, thus, higher profitability and scalability.
- The alignment of all parties' interests is a prerequisite for synergy.

Synergy manifests itself in all three dimensions of the deal flow. Data collecting, processing, and further exchange create a solid information basis for harnessing synergy. The financial dimension has a significant influence on the release of synergy. The intangible valuation demonstrates how a team can perform a business model and use spillovers for profit. Market entry and exit scenarios help to estimate the funding situation and choose an appropriate type of funding. The just-in-time financing scheme allows for minimizing capital injections. Although traditional valuations and financial projections are no longer indisputable, they remain valuable tools.

Chapter 8.3.
Magic of Breaking Ownership Chains

Investors and startup founders must adapt and embrace a new mindset as the VC industry significantly shifts towards intangibles. There is a new generation of VCs who are ex-founders themselves and have adequate startup experience. Thanks to crowdfunding platforms, many founders obtain investment experience and a better understanding of the VC game, changing from the bulk sourcing and screening of low-quality startups to 'cherry-picking' the best ones. Due to non-rivalry and partial exclusion properties of intangibles, the ownership pillars established during the industrial era began to collapse. In pursuit of high profitability, investors are interested in startups that can find and efficiently combine intangibles to harness synergy. These startups can use their intangibles, appropriate infrastructure, and other companies' spillovers. Poaching has become increasingly prevalent, and investors and startups must prepare for the new challenges in the VC world.

> **How does the erosion of property rights for intangibles impact the VC industry?**

Intangibles Destroy Ownership

Ownership of intangibles differs between IP and non-IP assets. An IP owner can exclude others, and courts can enforce penalties on excluded users for infringement. IP control includes conformity with standards, conversion claims, and conventions. Contracts and permissions make control formal and legally enforceable. Conversion requires the plaintiff's possession of the property and the defendant's dominion or interference with it in derogation of the plaintiff's rights.

However, the legal system needs to fulfill its purpose for non-IP assets. As new forms of intangible property surfaced, the common law evolved, and courts started to allow conversion claims for intangibles united with tangible objects. Conversion claims have expanded beyond tangible property to keep up with computerized use, but courts are still figuring out how far to go. It's hard for courts to expand conversion claims to cover all forms of intangibles.

In the case of Thyroff, the plaintiff leased computer hardware and software to facilitate the transfer of information to the defendant. In addition to customer information, the plaintiff used the defendant's system for personal email and correspondence. The defendant company terminated the plaintiff's contract, restricting access to leased computers and electronic records. It was a devastating blow, and to make matters worse, the trial court in the Western District of New York dismissed Thyroff's conversion claim. A tale of intrigue, betrayal, and a search for justice in the intangible world begins. [14]

Balancing on the Edge of Legality

Intangibles have a peculiar duality. On the one hand, intangible assets are considered a source of enterprises' competitive advantage. On the other hand, individual ownership of intangibles can limit sharing and exchange essential to growth and innovate the whole economy. Due to this duality, some firm-specific intangibles form intangible commons at the industry and economy levels. Firm-specific intangibles grow at the expense of intangible commons and vice versa and are interdependent.

At the industry level, legal, accounting, and technological associations and conventions significantly contribute to developing common intangibles. Thus, they create the infrastructure that can derive spillovers for startups. At the startup level, entrepreneurs are not interested in sharing knowledge with the intangible commons. By keeping knowledge for themselves, startups gain competitive advantages. Nevertheless, startups are interested in using infrastructural spillovers and intangibles of other companies.

According to the KPMG report, five components of intangible assets have spillovers with different levels of prospective profitability in case of their appropriation. We can rank them in order of increasing profitability:

1. Relationship Capital is an enterprise's network of contacts, including customers, suppliers, partners, suppliers, and consultants with whom founders have relationships to contribute to the business.
2. Organizational capital combines an enterprise's processes and systems to run its business efficiently and increase competitiveness.
3. IP includes patents, copyrights (ranging from books to computer programs, databases, and technical drawings), trademarks, industrial designs (consisting of two—or three-dimensional features), and trade secrets.
4. Human capital represents the knowledge, skills, experience, and other personal qualities of people who use it to run their enterprises.
5. A brand personifies the identity of an enterprise that distinguishes it from competitors in the eyes of its target audience. [15]

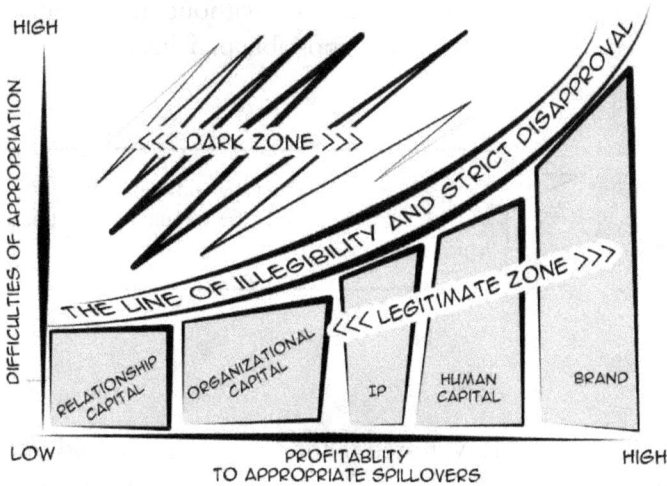

In the legitimate zone, an entrepreneur can use any of the five groups of spillovers without crossing the line of illegibility and public disapproval.

Mystifying customers or partners by offering them products or services that an enterprise does not have is possible within the ligimate zone. Bill Gross, a creator of CarsDirect, invented a new way to sell and buy cars online. Having no cars, he made a website offering cars. When customers click on the "buy" button, Gross buys the car from a retailer and delivers it to the customer. [16]

However, by stealing and selling customer data, an entrepreneur falls into the dark zone of illegal activities, which happened to Mark Zuckerberg on Facebook.

Many entrepreneurs successfully use the business processes of other companies that do not create adequate protection measures. Thus, they stay in the legitimate zone but cross the illegibility line using corporate espionage methods. When a former partner- an IP owner recklessly stops supporting its IP, the second former partner can use it without copyright infringement. In some cases, reverse engineering is a way to recreate the product without violating the patent holder's rights.

Even so, using a patented invention without the patent holder's permission is a serious offense with possible penalties.

> Using human intellect to simulate the promised but absent computerized functionality is possible and legitimate.

Using a hidden typist, IBM tested if and how people would interact with speech-to-text computers. When the text appeared on the screen, users thought a computer, not a human, processed their commands. [16]

On the other hand, using rivals' employees to obtain insider information is illegal.

Sometimes, using a famous brand can bring advantages to a market novice. The only problem is staying in the legitimate zone.

> The Upwell Labs' founder displayed prototypes of his new product at an IKEA store by dressing up as an IKEA worker in a used employee shirt he bought on eBay. [16]

However, using a trademark that is identical or even close to that owned by somebody entails infringement charges.

For savvy entrepreneurs, balancing the edge between legitimate and dark zones is a path to synergies. It is not easy! Startups' abilities to exploit synergies for profit are significantly limited by objectively existing barriers. The enterprise's organizational culture, knowledge of employees, and reputation among customers take time to transfer.

Even if transferring some intangibles is possible, its adaptation has costs. Entrepreneurs can transfer technological solutions, marketing expertise, or brand names to other enterprises under certain conditions. Adapting intangibles to new situations and preserving their value might be costly.

> FedEx developed a strong reputation for express delivery service in the USA, but its attempts to expand to Europe have largely failed. European customers have been slow to accept the FedEx brand. [16]

Government regulation in some industries, such as pharmaceutical, healthcare, food and beverage, banking, and insurance, is generally heavy. Industry standards play a dual role. On the one hand, standardization provides evaluation, compatibility, and quality of the deal flow. On the other hand, compliance with standards requires additional effort and costs from startups.

A Magical Force of Spillovers

Spillovers can manifest themselves in different ways. There are three distinct spillovers: knowledge, market, and network spillovers. All three types of spillovers may positively or negatively affect a startup's performance. Knowledge spillovers can be either complements or substitutes for internal activities. Market spillovers may complement other companies' activities or make them less valuable. Spillovers between companies could have a network effect that boosts the value of innovations. [17]

Spillovers matter in the modern VC industry for three reasons:

- Startups that can make the most of their investments in intangibles or can be especially good at exploiting spillovers from others' investments.

- Startups can exploit spillovers from government funding. If businesses cannot make their R&D investments, the government supports them.
- Intangible-rich startups combine and manage their intangibles to minimize spillovers and maximize their benefits.

When particular combinations of intangibles are valuable and IP ownership is less established, someone will appear, trying to exploit knowledge, market, or network spillovers. It is becoming a norm to benefit from intangible investments made by other companies. Sometimes, this action happens by mutual consent, for instance, under contract, but often does not (for example, Google's development of the Android operating system to compete with Apple's iOS).

Intangibles can confer strategic advantages, but their characteristics make maintaining these advantages difficult. Certain intangibles, like organization structures, business models, and brands, take much work to reverse engineer. Some intangibles are impossible to separate from their owner, and synergies between different dimensions of intangibles, like business models and management know-how are hard to replicate. Conversely, intangibles can transfer from one enterprise to another when representing people's skills.

Nevertheless, many production processes, organizational activities, and structures protected through trade secrets can reveal themselves through their actions in the marketplace. Entrepreneurs can reverse-engineer products and technologies. By observing business activities, entrepreneurs can retroactively copy some aspects of business models, sales practices, pricing strategies, and distribution channel partners. By appropriating spillovers, a startup can create a set of complementary intangible assets that work as a pipeline.

PROFITomix Story

Digital Pizza

(Episode 24)

CAST:

Robert

Steve

Investor
Traditionalist

Startup
Founder

Robert learned that Steve had rejected several investment proposals and decided that he could convince the founder to accept his offer. The investor planned to offer such terms and conditions that Steve could take. In the texting conversation, Steve reveals an idea to use others' assets to Robert. This idea is too revolutionary for Robert, who adheres to traditional views on business practices. So, Robert gives up his attempt.

I just heard you turned down investors, Steve. What are you holding out for? A unicorn to waltz into your office with a pot of gold?

There is no need for mythical creatures, Robert. We're bootstrapping with flair, and flair doesn't need a board seat.

Bootstrapping is for hobbies, Steve. If you don't need my capital, you need my expertise to play in the big leagues.

We're not just players. We're digital profiteers who sail freely and fight for profit!

Did you say pirates?

...unlike pirates, profiteers were legal; they obtained royal permission to capture foreign ships. So, we are about to play our own game!

Don't get too whimsical. Let's talk business...assets and equity but games! Now, listen here. I've got an offer you couldn't reject—have you ever heard of an irresistible proposition?

It's funny you mentioned assets, but we don't need them. We have a brilliant plan to use others' assets to our advantage!

Startups without assets are like cars without engines. Ownership is the cornerstone of business...We started our business in a garage and made all IP by ourselves!

You're too radical. The garage startup ethos only works when it's Jobs' garage. Anything else is just a parking space! You know about these technoparks.

So, what will you play your game on?

They call it spillovers.

What?

Intangible assets that owners don't use or even see. We'll appropriate them!

Steve, you're in the business of innovation, not appropriation!

Appropriation is the best innovation!

I see... I'd call them 'steak lovers.' Thanks, your Digital Pizza is too hot for me!

Until recently, traditional VCs did not recognize intangibles and invest in companies that can demonstrate the use of some tangible assets. The new generation of investors looks for promising early-stage pre-revenue startups with a focus on their intangible assets and solutions. The most talented founders begin to understand new rules of the investment game and build data-driven startups that rely on intangible-intensive business models. These founders can appropriate others' intangibles, not crossing the legality line.

The increased use of contractors for outsourcing and fulfillment services has vastly improved the opportunities for poaching in recent years. Poaching is the dark side of contracting, causing the risk that one party can deliberately use information for its benefit. Service providers require access to substantial amounts of proprietary data to accomplish their tasks efficiently. However, using contractors by host companies that hold IP and especially non-IP intangibles creates dangers for hosts due to opportunities for poaching from the contractors.

We are witnessing a transformation in the VC industry. The rise of intangibles has shattered traditional ownership models and created a new playing field for investors and startups. This change also presents new opportunities for higher profitability and growth. Startups can harness synergies by strategically combining various intangibles to create a unique value proposition. There is also a growing concern about poaching. As VCs become more selective in their investments, startups must defend against potential predators who may try to appropriate their valuable intangible assets.

Key Takeaways

Entrepreneurs must see spillovers as an opportunity rather than a threat. By embracing them, startups can use spillovers as the fuel to drive their success. However, poaching is relevant in various settings, including manufacturing and services, especially in various outsourced activities. We make out several typical business cases of poaching to clarify this concept.

Case 1 represents the situation of dual sourcing, a common practice in high-tech manufacturing industries. They use dual sourcing arrangements, where a host licenses technology to contractors to enable them to produce competing products in return for royalties. An example of such a broken partnership is the case of Intel Corporation, in which the contractor, AMD, became the most dangerous rival for Intel (see Chapter 1.3, "Investing in Intangibles: Pros and Cons" for more details).

Case 2 concerns technology-based services when a host company uses a third-party provider to manage its customers' accounts. A contractor providing a host with account administration can access the host's customer data. This contractor can use this data or resell it to third-party marketing firms or the host's competitors.

Case 3 depicts information technology consulting when a hosting company can hire a systems development consultant to build a computer system. After constructing the system, the consultant has considerable expertise in creating the host data system and has thoroughly tested the source code. The consultant is now in a solid position to market the system for itself "by copycatting it" or resell this information to the host's rivals.

Case 4 set out strategic consulting, when a hired contractor helps the host develop a computerized customer service system, including a database for customer information, various modeling tools, and marketplace monitor software. As a result, such contractors have all the necessary software and expertise to start their rivalrous business.

Entrepreneurs must consider opportunities to break ownership chains. The intangibles associated with tearing down traditional notions of ownership can positively impact businesses. Breaking free from conventional ownership chains creates new business opportunities.

Points to Ponder

Looking for synergetic effects in early-stage startups, investors and founders must consider issues of prospective appropriations of intangibles related to human capital, IP, organizational, and relationship capital. The three issues are significant:

Expected synergetic effects (SYNERGY)– showing how certain intangibles can contribute to the future venture's profitability and growth.

Opportunities for appropriation (OPPs)– demonstrating to what extent appropriation of certain intangibles is possible.

Risks of appropriation (RISKS) – denoting whether spillovers are worth the risk associated with their appropriation.

The infographic simplifies the decision-making process in complicated situations in which the four intangibles—Human Capital, IP, Organizational Capital, and Relationship Capital—are considered on the appropriation scale (LOW, MED, HIGH) for three issues. It is an approximate approach; nevertheless, it is a simple but practical tool for decision-making.

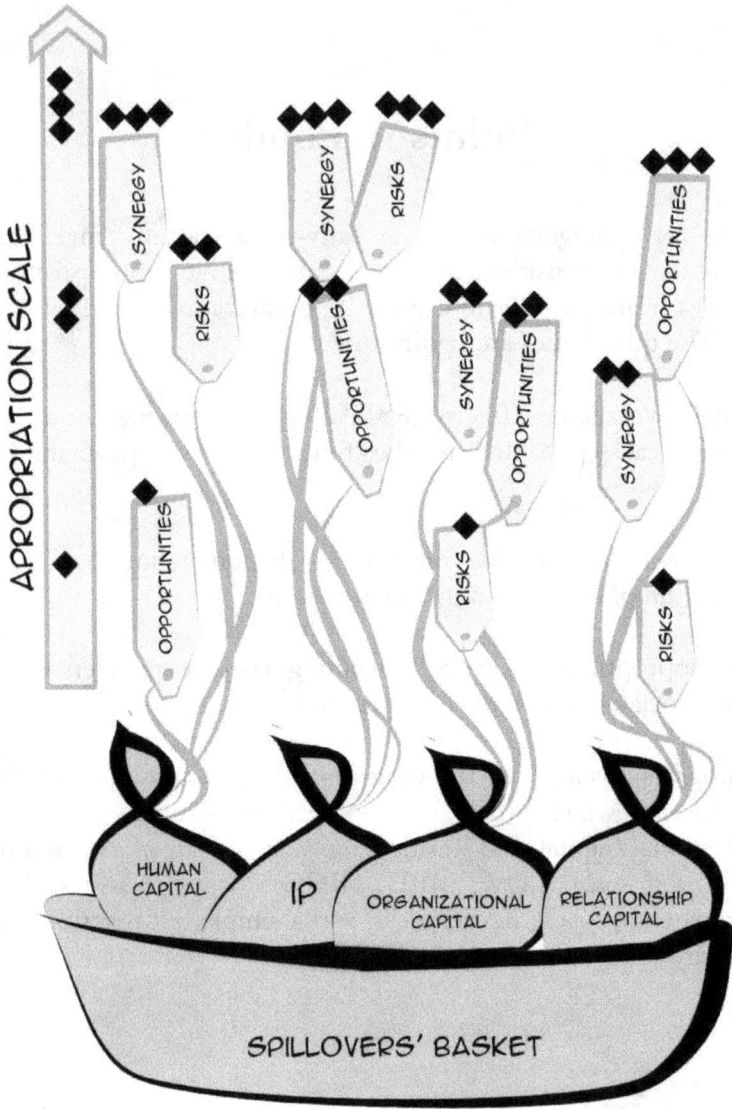

APPROPRIATION SCALE

SYNERGY

RISKS

SYNERGY

RISKS

OPPORTUNITIES

OPPORTUNITIES

SYNERGY

OPPORTUNITIES

OPPORTUNITIES

SYNERGY

OPPORTUNITIES

RISKS

RISKS

HUMAN CAPITAL

IP

ORGANIZATIONAL CAPITAL

RELATIONSHIP CAPITAL

SPILLOVERS' BASKET

APROPRIATION SCALE

◆ LOW

◆◆ MEDIUM

◆◆◆ HIGH

CONCLUSION

The PROFITomix's task was to clear up misunderstandings and illusions, explain the realities of today's VC world, and show the path to profit. How practical have the takeaways and points to ponder been? How entertaining and, at the same time, educational have the Digital Pizza episodes been?

PROFITomix promised to guide the two new and little-developed perspectives of the VC world: intangible assets and data-driven and AI-empowered approaches. Let's look at how the book has delivered on initial promises in its eight sections:

Section 1

Unlocking a hidden intangible potential and showing how to grow human capital through the identification and appropriation of intangible assets

Section 2

Understanding how AI and data intelligence create a solid information basis for profit and, thus, for funding

Section 3

Making sure that a startup and its team are fit for funding at the proper time

Section 4

Comprehending intangible-intensive business models, startup valuation, and just-in-time funding

Section 5

Showing how to overcome information asymmetry, create efficient exit scenarios and investor protective measures

Section 6

Demonstrating how to align investors' and founders' interests, building mutually beneficial partnerships

Section 7

Mastering experimental business models' validation, MVPs' planning, and creating trustworthy pitch decks

Section 8

Revealing how to use minimal resources to utilize synergies and appropriate spillovers for profit and growth

In today's ever-evolving VC world, staying ahead of the curve and embracing new concepts that can lead to profitable ventures is critical. PROFITomix gives readers a fresh perspective on starting and funding new ventures by challenging conventional 'gut feel' wisdom and introducing up-to-date methods and tools.

Key Takeaways

For startup founders: The methods of gathering and processing information with AI, experimental business model validation, and appropriating intangible assets for profit.

For investors: The value of data intelligence, intangible and tangible startup valuations, just-in-time funding, and well-protected exits.

For service providers: The AI-empowered Startup Dossier, the comprehensive Funding Roadmap, and validated learning.

Let's turn to the pizza metaphor to visualize how the VC industry stakeholders benefit from PROFITomix.

LAST YEAR, I HAD THE CHANCE TO SNATCH UP A 20% SLICE OF DIGITAL PIZZA. BUT DID I? NO!

I WAS TOO BUSY KNEADING THROUGH THEIR LEGAL ISSUES. AND WHAT I GET TODAY FOR THE SAME AMOUNT OF 2%.

FORTUNATELY, IT'S 2% INTO THE GREATEST GOURMET GROWTH THE TECH WORLD HAS EVER SEEN!

TODAY, EVEN FOOD HAS GONE BINARY. I'M JUST SOME DINOSAUR—THOUGH I PREFER "SEASONED ANGEL."

THAT'S A DEAL FLYING AWAY— QUITE LITERALLY.

WHILE I ASKED THEM ABOUT A BUSINESS PLAN, THEY CHOSE TO FLY SOLO. AND I'M WATCHING THAT DRONE FIZZLE OUT OF THE SKY LIKE MY DREAMS!

It is the end of the PROFITomix Story about Digital Pizza's journey. Still, it is only the beginning of implementing what PROFITomix offers: practical advice, scientifically proven solutions, and real-world examples. All actionable steps guide readers toward building and funding highly profitable and scalable ventures.

Good luck!

REFERENCES

Section 1

1. Lev, B., & Gu, F. (2016). *The End of Accounting and the Path Forward for Investors and Managers.* Wiley. https://www.amazon.com.au/Accounting-Path-Forward-Investors-Managers/dp/1119191092

2. Haskel, J., & Westlake, S. (2018). *Capitalism without Capital: The Rise of the Intangible Economy.* Princeton University Press. https://www.amazon.com.au/Capitalism-without-Capital-Intangible-Economy/dp/0691175039

3. Intangible Asset. (n.d). In *Cambridge Dictionary.* https://dictionary.cambridge.org/dictionary/english/intangible-asset

4. OECD (2021). *Bridging the gap in the financing of intangibles to support productivity.* Background paper. OECD Publishing. https://www.oecd.org/global-forum-productivity/events/Bridging-the-gap-in-the-financing-of-intangibles-to-support-productivity-background-paper.pdf

5. IAS 38. (2021). *Intangible Assets.* Issued IFRS Standards (Part A). https://www.ifrs.org/content/dam/ifrs/publications/pdf-standards/english/2021/issued/part-a/ias-38-intangible-assets.pdf

6. Marx, K. (1989). *Capital Volume One: A Critique of Political Policy.* KNOPF US. https://www.amazon.com.au/dp/039472657X

7. Brand Finance. (2019). *Global Intangible Finance Tracker (GIFT™)* — an annual review of the world's intangible value. https://brandfinance.com/wp-content/uploads/1/gift_2.pdf

8. Crouzet, N., Janice, C., & Eberly J. C. The Economics of Intangible Capital. (2022). *Journal of Economic Perspectives, V. 36, No 3,* 29–52. https://www.kellogg.northwestern.edu/faculty/crouzet/html/papers/EconIntan_published.pdf

9. McLain, C. (2023, April 4). *Why the NHS should embrace virtual wards.* Giant Ventures. https://www.giant.vc/insights/why-the-nhs-should-embrace-virtual-wards

10. Hazan E., Smit S., Woetzel J., Cvetanovski B., Krishnan M., Gregg B., Perrey, J., & Hjartar K. (2021). *Getting tangible about intangibles: The future of growth and productivity?* McKinsey Global Institute. https://www.mckinsey.com/capabilities/growth-marketing-and-sales/our-insights/getting-tangible-about-intangibles-the-future-of-growth-and-productivity

11. Lawrence, C. (1998). *An overview of ideas and principles on equity valuation that emerge from Warren Buffet's [i.e., Buffett's] letters to the shareholders of Berkshire Hathaway Inc.* Graduate Student Theses, Dissertations, & Professional Papers, University of Montana (8600). https://scholarworks.umt.edu/etd/8600

12. GLOBALINTO. (n.d.) *Public Policy and Intangibles: A Conceptualisation and Critical Appraisal.* Issued GLOBALINTO (D2.6). https://globalinto.eu/public-policy-and-intangibles-a-conceptualisation-and-critical-appraisal-d2-6/

13. Bouvier, P. (2023, February 15). *A Marxist Interpretation of Venture Investing. Finyear.* https://www.finyear.com/A-Marxist-Interpretation-of-Venture-Investing_a35970.html

14. Clemons, E. K., & Hitt, L. M. (2004). Poaching and the Misappropriation of Information: Transaction Risks of Information Exchange. *Journal of Management Information Systems, 21 (2),* 87-107. https://core.ac.uk/download/pdf/219377559.pdf

15. Canals, C. (2014). *Intangibles: The New Investment in the Knowledge Era.* CAIXA Bank Research. https://www.caixabankresearch.com/en/economics-markets/activity-growth/intangibles-new-investment-knowledge-era

Section 2

1. Retterath, A. (2022, September 15). *Data-driven VC #1: Why VC is broken and where to start fixing it.* Data-driven VC. https://www.datadrivenvc.io/p/data-driven-vc-1-why-vc-is-broken

2. Gompers, P., Gornall, W., Kaplan, S. N., & Strebulaev I.A. (2021, Marth-April). *How Venture Capitalists Make Decisions.* Harvard Business Review. https://hbr.org/2021/03/how-venture-capitalists-make-decisions

3. Data-intelligence (2012, August 9). In *Technopedia.* https://www.techopedia.com/definition/28799/data-intelligence

4. OECD (2014). *Data-driven Innovation for Growth and Well-being.* Report. OECD Publishing.

https://www.oecd.org/sti/inno/data-driven-innovation-interim-synthesis.pdf

5. Deloitte. (2023) *A new frontier in artificial intelligence: Implications of Generative AI for businesses.* Deloitte AI Institute.
https://www2.deloitte.com/content/dam/Deloitte/ie/Documents/Consulting/ie-generative-artificial-intelligence.pdf

6. Chanda, P. (2023, November 22). *How to Use Bloomberg GPT? Complete Tutorial.* AMB Crypto. https://ambcrypto.com/blog/how-to-use-bloomberg-gpt/

7. Allison, N., Grimberg, J. & Rhodes A. (2023, July 5). *Generative AI: hype, or truly transformative?* Goldman Sachs Report.
https://www.goldmansachs.com/intelligence/pages/top-of-mind/generative-ai-hype-or-truly-transformative/report.pdf

8. Ailinani, R., & Pratahkal, S. (2023, June 12). *Generating Value: Exploring Investment Opportunities in the Generative AI Landscape.* Dallas Venture Capital.
https://dallasvc.com/generating-value-exploring-investment-opportunities-in-the-generative-ai-landscape/

9. Retterath, A. (2020, December 1). *The Future of VC: Augmenting Humans with AI.* Medium. https://medium.com/birds-view/the-future-of-vc-augmenting-humans-with-ai-30f1d79a09c3

10. CBINSIGHTS. (2018, December 12). *Introducing Profile Dossiers — Beautiful Reports on Startups, Competitors, And Partners.* CBINSIGHTS Research Briefs.
https://www.cbinsights.com/research/team-blog/company-reports/

Section 3

1. Are Business Plans Useless or Useful? (2023, June 30). *Cesare Ferrari.*
https://cesareferrari.net/are-business-plans-useless-or-useful/

2. Fitness (n.d.). In *Cambridge Dictionary.*
https://dictionary.cambridge.org/dictionary/english/fitness

3. CBINSIGHTS. (2021, August 3). *The Top 12 Reasons Startups Fail.* CBINSIGHTS Research Report. https://www.cbinsights.com/research/startup-failure-reasons-top/

4. Gross, B. (2015, March). *The Single Biggest Reason Why Start-ups Succeed.* TED conference.

https://www.ted.com/talks/bill_gross_the_single_biggest_reason_why_start_ups_suc
ceed/transcript?hasSummary=true

5. Deloitte. (2023). *The Generative AI Dossier*. Deloitte AI Institute.
https://www2.deloitte.com/content/dam/Deloitte/us/Documents/consulting/us-ai-
institute-gen-ai-use-cases.pdf

6. Carbonara, M. (2023, August 21). *5 Ways Startups Can Use Generative AI To Build A
Competitive Advantage*. Forbes.
https://www.forbes.com/sites/forbesfinancecouncil/2023/08/21/5-ways-startups-
can-use-generative-ai-to-build-a-competitive-advantage

7. Ailinani, R. (2023, June 12). *Generating Value: Exploring Investment Opportunities in the
Generative AI Landscape*. Dallas Venture Capital. https://dallasvc.com/generating-value-
exploring-investment-opportunities-in-the-generative-ai-landscape/

8. Howarth, J. (2023, November 3). *Startup Success and Failure Rate Statistics (2024)*.
Exploding Topics. https://explodingtopics.com/blog/startup-failure-stats

9. Brattström, A. (2019, November). *Working with Startups? These are the Three Things You
Ought to Know about Startup Teams*. Research Gate.
https://www.researchgate.net/publication/337644505_Working_with_Startups_These
_are_the_Three_Things_You_Ought_to_Know_about_Startup_Teams

10. Sabato, N. (2023, August 7). *Why is it so hard to get VCs to invest in my Generative AI
startup?* Tech. https://www.calcalistech.com/ctechnews/article/hkjtk4ri3

11. KPMG. (2023). *Generative AI: From Buzz to Business Value: An Exclusive KPMG
Survey Shows How Top Leaders are Approaching this Transformative Technology*. KPMG.
https://kpmg.com/kpmg-us/content/dam/kpmg/pdf/2023/generative-ai-survey.pdf

12. Tzu, S. (n.d.). *Sun Tzu on the Art of War*. Allandale Online Publishing.
https://sites.ualberta.ca/~enoch/Readings/The_Art_Of_War.pdf

13. Scott, E. L., & Stern, S. (2018, May-June). *Strategy for Start-ups*. Harward Business
Review. https://hbr.org/2018/05/strategy-for-start-ups

14. Tarasov, K. (2022, November 29). *How AMD became a chip giant and leapfrogged Intel
after years of playing catch-up*. CNBC. https://www.cnbc.com/2022/11/22/how-amd-
became-a-chip-giant-leapfrogged-intel-after-playing-catch-up.html

Section 4

1. Nissen, H. J., Damerow, P. & Englund, R. K. (1993). *Archaic Bookkeeping.* Academia.edu. https://www.academia.edu/88331225/Archaic_Bookkeeping

2. Sorescu, A. (2017, June). *Data-Driven Business Model Innovation.* Research Gate. https://www.researchgate.net/publication/318131131_Data-Driven_Business_Model_Innovation_BUSINESS_MODEL_INNOVATION

3. Sena, V. & Nocker, M. (2021). *AI and business models: the good, the bad and the ugly.* University of Sheffield. https://eprints.whiterose.ac.uk/182363/3/

4. Kulkov, I. (2021, October 15). *Next-generation business models for artificial intelligence start-ups in the healthcare industry.* International Journal of Entrepreneurial Behavior & Research. https://www.emerald.com/insight/content/doi/10.1108/IJEBR-04-2021-0304/full/html

5. Schirmer, J., Eber, R. & Bourdon, I. (2020, January). *32 ways to innovate business models through data: Emerging data-driven solution business model patterns from a study of 471 late stage data-driven startups.* Université de Montpellier. https://hal.umontpellier.fr/hal-03006435

6. Atkins B. (2023, June 22). *Generative AI: The Next Frontier for Business Innovation.* Forbes. https://www.forbes.com/sites/betsyatkins/2023/06/22/generative-ai-the-next-frontier-for-business-innovation/

7. Nisar, Q. A., Shakeel, H. K., Ahmad, S., Niazi, K. & Ashraf, S. (2014, August 8). *Application of Just-In-Time Principles to Financial Services;* International Journal of Scientific & Engineering Research (Volume 5, Issue 8). https://www.ijser.org/onlineResearchPaperViewer.aspx?Application-of-Just-In-Time-Principals-to-Financial-Services.pdf

8. Fernandez, M. (2023, Marth 1). *Just-in-Time Funding: What it is and Why it's Vital to your SaaS Growth Strategy.* Capchase. https://www.capchase.com/blog/just-in-time-financing

9. BVS. (2016, November 9). *A Brief History of Valuation Companies.* Business Valuation Specialists. https://www.businessvaluations.net/blog/history-of-valuation-companies

10. *When the spinning stops.* (2006, January 26). The Economist. https://www.economist.com/special-report/2006/01/26/when-the-spinning-stops

11. Anastasio, L. E. (2020, May). *Valuation of Intangible Assets.* MPI. https://mpival.com/content/uploads/2020/06/MPI-Valuation-of-Intangible-Assets.pdf

Section 5

1 McCracken, H. (2015, June 10). *How the Bloomberg Terminal Made History—And Stays Ever Relevant.* Fast Company. https://www.fastcompany.com/3051883/the-bloomberg-terminal

2. Schuurs, R. J. & Brennan, K. (2023, June 20). *What is the Future of Venture?* Antler. https://www.antler.co/blog/what-is-the-future-of-venture

3. Teten, D. (2019, November 15). *Decide Which Type of Investor to Target for Raising Capital.* Tech Crunch. https://techcrunch.com/2019/11/14/decide-which-type-of-investor-to-target-for-raising-capital/

4. Tour, A. & Portincaso, M. (2021). *The Deep Tech Investment Paradox: a Call to Redesign the Investor Model.* BCG Report. https://hello-tomorrow.org/wp-content/uploads/2021/05/Deep-Tech-Investment-Paradox-BCG.pdf

5. Sauvage, N., Zeisberger, C. & Varadan, M. (2022, August 2). *Corporate VC Is Booming, but Is It What Your Start-Up Needs?* INSEAD. https://knowledge.insead.edu/entrepreneurship/corporate-vc-booming-it-what-your-start-needs

6. Novoa, J. (n.d.). *The basics of startup syndicate funding.* Startupxplore. https://startupxplore.com/en/blog/basics-startup-syndicate-funding/

7. Rodriguez, S. (2018, October 31). *One of Silicon Valley's most outspoken investors slams the 'bizarre Ponzi balloon' of the start-up economy.* CNBC. https://www.cnbc.com/2018/10/31/palihapitiya-venture-capital-created-a-bizarre-ponzi-balloon.html

8. Understanding the Lemons Problem and How to Solve It. (2021, November 29). In *Investopedia.* https://www.investopedia.com/terms/l/lemons-problem.asp

9. Samengo-Turner, W., Coady, E., Little, J. & Brooks, S. (2021, March 31). *Minority investments: How to use corporate venturing for strategic gain.* https://www.allenovery.com/en-gb/global/news-and-insights/publications/minority-investments-how-to-use-corporate-venturing-for-strategic-gain

10. Who Was Herbert A. Simon? Bounded Rationality and AI Theorist. (2022, September 20). In *Investopedia.* https://www.investopedia.com/terms/h/herbert-a-simon.asp

11. Glücksman, S. (2020). *Entrepreneurial experiences from venture capital funding: exploring two-sided information asymmetry.* Routledge.
https://research.chalmers.se/publication/519627/file/519627_Fulltext.pdf

12. Du, P., Shu, H. & Xia, Z. (2020, July 14). *The Control Strategies for Information Asymmetry Problems Among Investing Institutions, Investors, and Entrepreneurs in Venture Capital.* Frontiers. https://www.frontiersin.org/articles/10.3389/fpsyg.2020.01579/full

13. O'Reilly, T. (2021, March 11). *The End of Silicon Valley as We Know It? Four ways the party may be coming to an end.* O'Reilly. https://www.oreilly.com/radar/the-end-of-silicon-valley-as-we-know-it/

Section 6

1. Probert, D., R., Farrukh, C., & Phaal, R. (2003, September). *Technology Roadmapping-developing a practical approach for linking resources to strategic goals.* ResearchGate.
https://www.researchgate.net/publication/239406213_Technology_Roadmapping-developing_a_practical_approach_for_linking_resources_to_strategic_goals

2. Genpact. (2023, August 30). *How to integrate gen AI into your business processes.* LinkedIn.
https://www.linkedin.com/pulse/how-integrate-gen-ai-your-business-processes-genpact/

3. Boukherouaa, E., B., AlAjmi, K., Deodoro, J., Farias, A. & Ravikumar, R. (2021, October 22). *Powering the Digital Economy: Opportunities and Risks of Artificial Intelligence in Finance.* IMF eLibrary.
https://www.elibrary.imf.org/view/journals/087/2021/024/article-A001-en.xml

4. Knight, F.H. (1921). *Risk, Uncertainty, and Profit.* Houghton Mifflin Company.
https://fraser.stlouisfed.org/files/docs/publications/books/risk/riskuncertaintyprofit.pdf

5. White, L. (2023, November 28). *Startup Valuation: How To Value Your Company.* Fullstack. https://www.fullstack.com.au/startup-valuation-how-to-value-your-company/

6. Berkus, D. (2016, November 4). *After 20 Years: Updating the Berkus Method of Valuation.* BERKONOMICS. https://berkonomics.com/?p=2752

7. Payne, W. H. (2006). *The Definitive Guide to Raising Money from Angels.* Bill Payne.

8. PQRI. *Risk Ranking and Filtering*. Risk Management Working Group. https://pqri.org/wp-content/uploads/2015/08/pdf/Risk_Rank_Filter_Training_Guide.pdf

9. Rose, D. S. (2016). *The Startup Checklist: 25 Steps to a Scalable, High-Growth Business*. Wiley.

10. Corpion, K. (2023, January 25). *Startup founders: Don't cross the line between optimism and fraud*. VentureBeat. https://venturebeat.com/enterprise-analytics/startup-founders-dont-cross-the-line-between-optimism-and-fraud/

11. Silverneedle Ventures. (2023, September 26). *Unlocking Startup Success: Leveraging AI for Profitability, Burn Rate, and Valuation Analysis*. LinkedIn. https://www.linkedin.com/pulse/unlocking-startup-success-leveraging-ai-profitability/

12. John Nash: American mathematician (2023, December 12). In *Britannica*. https://www.britannica.com/biography/John-Nash

13. Sherman, A. S. (2001, May 23). *Key Term Sheet Clauses*. VentureChoice. https://www.venturechoice.com/articles/key_term_sheet_clauses.htm

14. Merler, S. (2018, July 18). *Economy of Intangibles*. Bruegel. https://www.bruegel.org/blog-post/economy-intangibles

15. *Aligning Interests in Tech Startup Investments*. (2023, December 17). FasterCapital. https://fastercapital.com/content/Aligning-Interests-in-Tech-Startup-Investments.html

16. Ebrahimian, M., Zhang, Y. (2023, December 26). *How Venture Capitalists and Startups Bet on Each Other: Evidence from an Experimental System*. SSRN. https://papers.ssrn.com/sol3/papers.cfm?abstract_id=3724424

Section 7

1. Knowledge at Wharton Staff. (2016, June 8). *Daniel Kahneman's Strategy for How Your Firm Can Think Smarter*. https://knowledge.wharton.upenn.edu/article/nobel-winner-daniel-kahnemans-strategy-firm-can-think-smarter

2. Contigiani, A. & Young-Hyman, T. (2021, December). *Experimentation, Planning, and Structure in Early-Stage Ventures: Evidence from Venture Pitches*. ResearchGate.

https://www.researchgate.net/publication/357031607_Experimentation_Planning_an
d_Structure_in_Early-Stage_Ventures_Evidence_from_Venture_Pitches

3. Eisenmann, T., Ries, E. & Dillard, S. (2013, June 10). Hypothesis-Driven
Entrepreneurship: The Lean Startup. Harvard Business School.
https://edisciplinas.usp.br/pluginfile.php/7633986/mod_resource/content/1/hde.pd
f

4. Göcke, L. & Weninger, R. (2020, November 14). *Business Model Development and
Validation in Digital Entrepreneurship*. SpringerLink.
https://link.springer.com/chapter/10.1007/978-3-030-53914-6_4

5. Ries, E. (2011, January 1). *The Lean Startup: How Today's Entrepreneurs Use Continuous
Innovation to Create Radically Successful Businesses*. Crown Business.
https://www.amazon.com/Lean-Startup-Entrepreneurs-Continuous-
Innovation/dp/0307887898

6. Bertfield, J., Hafele, B. (n.d.). *Navigating Through the Squiggles: A primer on how Lean
Startup can help your teams innovate with confidence AND build products customers love.* Lean
Startup Co. https://leanstartup.co/wp-content/uploads/2023/06/ebook-
NavigatingSquiggles-Final_61523.pdf

7. Briant, G. (2021). *Overview of Business Experimentation*. First Principles.
https://www.firstprinciples.ventures/insights/overview-of-business-experimentation

8. Ganguly, A. & Euchner, J. (2018, March). *Conducting Business Experiments: Validating
New Business Models*. ResearchGate.
https://www.researchgate.net/publication/323622952_Conducting_Business_Experi
ments

9. DimeADozen.AI. (2023). *Using AI for Business Validation: A Game-Changing Approach
for Startups and Business Owners: Introduction to AI Business Validators*. DimeADozen.AI.
https://www.dimeadozen.ai/blog/using-ai-for-business-validation

10. Murphy, S. (2017, April 24). *Frank Robinson's Minimum Viable Product Definition*.
SKMurphy. https://www.skmurphy.com/blog/2017/04/24/frank-robinsons-
minimum-viable-product-definition/

11. Lye, C. (2020, January 29). *A visual history of pitch decks*. SketchDeck.
https://sketchdeck.com/blog/pitchdeck-history/

12. Church, J. (2020, October 31). *Investable Entrepreneur: How to convince investors your
business is the one to back.* Rethink Press. https://www.amazon.com.au/Investable-
Entrepreneur-convince-investors-business/dp/1781334900

13. Reason Street. (2023). *AI-driven venture capital vs. regular venture capital.* Reason Street. https://reasonstreet.co/capital-library/ai-driven-venture-capital/

14. Gartner. (2021, March 10). *Gartner Says Tech Investors Will Prioritize Data Science and Artificial Intelligence Above "Gut Feel" for Investment Decisions By 2025.* Press release. https://www.gartner.com/en/newsroom/press-releases/2021-03-10-gartner-says-tech-investors-will-prioritize-data-science-and-artificial-intelligence-above-gut-feel-for-investment-decisions-by-20250

15. Drenik, G. (2023, November 29). *How This Startup Is Using AI To Make Sense Of Financial Data.* Forbes. https://www.forbes.com/sites/garydrenik/2023/11/29/how-this-startup-is-using-ai-to-make-sense-of-financial-data/

Section 8

1. Foust-Mason, J. (2022, August 14). *Disorderly Conduct: The Mathematical Connections of Chaos Theory.* Southern New Hampshire University. https://www.coursesidekick.com/mathematics/328802

2. Peters, T. (1991, August 2). *Thriving on Chaos: Handbook for a Management Revolution.* Harper Collins. https://www.harpercollins.com/products/thriving-on-chaos-tom-peters?variant=32118125461538

3. Dantas, O., Frenay, L., Pimentel, A., Mattosinho, P., Carrera, H. & Neves, F. (2023, March 8). *What startup founders expect from venture capital funds.* BCG Report. https://www.bcg.com/publications/2023/brazil-what-startup-founders-expect-from-venture-capital-funds

4. AIContentfy. *Understanding the Role of Investors in Startups.* (2023, November 6). AIContentfy. https://aicontentfy.com/en/blog/understanding-role-of-investors-in-startups

5. Levi-Weiss, G. (2021, January). *The Non-obvious Guide to Fundraising.* NFX. https://www.nfx.com/post/the-non-obvious-guide-to-fundraising

6. Thien, T. H. & Hung, H. X. (2023, January 11). *Intangible investments and cost of equity capital: An empirical research on Vietnamese firms.* Tailor & Francis Online. https://www.tandfonline.com/doi/full/10.1080/23322039.2022.2163075

7. Morris, M. H., Santos, S. & Neumeyer, X. (n.d.) *Tool #9 Getting Resources When You Have No Money: Bootstrapping and Resource Leveraging.* https://gppe.nd.edu/assets/384357/tool_9.pdf

8. Dlamini, S. & Barnard, B. (2020). *Entrepreneurship, Innovation, and Value Creation: Customer Benefits Entrepreneurs and Innovators Build into New Products*—Expert Journal of Marketing, Volume 8, Issue 1. https://marketing.expertjournals.com/ark:/16759/EJM_802barnard9-40.pdf

9. Daum P. (2013). *International Synergy Management: A Strategic Approach for Raising Efficiencies in the Cross-border Interaction Process.* Academic Papers. https://m.anchor-publishing.com/document/287417

10. Lynch, R. P. & Prozonic, N. (2013, July 4). *Quest for Synergy: How the Greeks Created the First Age of Innovation.* Academia.edu. https://www.academia.edu/42757246/Quest_for_Synergy_How_the_Greeks_Create d_the_First_Age_of_Innovation_Tracing_the_Roots_of_Synergy_and_Co_Creativity

11. FasterCapital. (2023, December 23). *Synergy: Unlocking New Opportunities through Strategic Joint Ventures.* FasterCapital. https://fastercapital.com/content/Synergy--Unlocking-New-Opportunities-through-Strategic-Joint-Ventures.html

12. Lax, D. A. & Sebenius J. K. (2006, August 24). *3-D Negotiation: Powerful Tools to Change the Game in Your Most Important Deals.* Harvard Business Review Press. https://www.amazon.com.au/3-d-Negotiation-Powerful-Change-Important-ebook/dp/B007OVSQVS

13. Park, J., Rahman, H. A., Suh, J. & Hussin, H. (2019, December 2). *A Study of Integrative Bargaining Model with Argumentation-Based Negotiation.* MDPI. https://www.mdpi.com/2071-1050/11/23/6832

14. Hall, T. J. & Archer, J. A. (2020, February 20). *The Slow Expansion of Conversion Claims to Cover Intangible Property.* New York Law Journal. https://nortonrosefulbright.com/-/media/files/nrf/nrfweb/knowledge-pdfs/the-slow-expansion-of-conversion-claims-to-cover-intangible-property.pdf

15. KPMG. (2020). *Protecting intangible assets: Preparing for a new reality.* KPMG Report. https://assets.kpmg.com/content/dam/kpmg/uk/pdf/2020/08/lloyds-intangibles-6-aug-2020-.pdf

16. Seelig, T. & Savoia, A. (2016). *Quick Reference: Basic Pretotyping Techniques.* Stanford. https://www.albertosavoia.com/uploads/1/4/0/9/14099067/pretotyping_quick_refe rence_for_stanford_ms_e_277.pdf

17. Bakhtiari, S. & Breunig, R. (2016, December 28). *The Role of Spillovers in Research and Development Expenditure in Australian Industries.* Australian National University. https://crawford.anu.edu.au/files/uploads/crawford01_cap_anu_edu_au/2017-07/rdspillover_v3.pdf